CARVING FISHERMEN AND THE TALL TALE

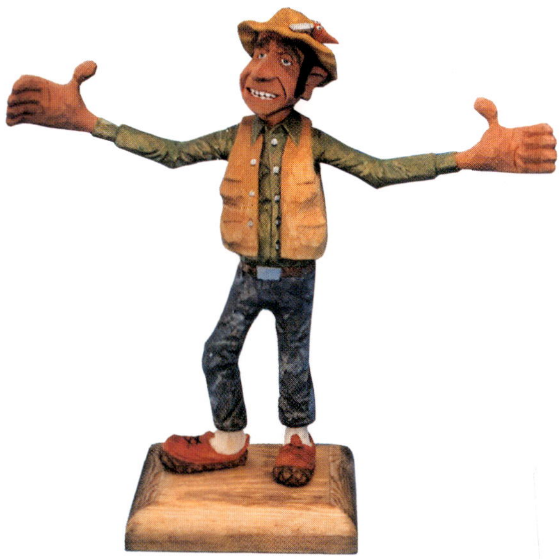

CLEVE TAYLOR

Text Written with and Photography by Jeffrey B. Snyder

Schiffer Publishing Ltd

77 Lower Valley Road, Atglen, PA 19310

Dedication

To Sandy, who is inspiration for life itself. Thanks.

Library of Congress Cataloging-in-Publication Data

Taylor, Cleve.
Carving fishermen and the tall tale / Cleve Taylor ;
text written with and photography by Jeffrey B. Snyder.
p. cm.
ISBN 0-88740-903-2 (pbk.)
1. Wood-carving--Patterns.
2. Wood-carved figurines.
3. Fishers in art.
I. Snyder, Jeffrey B.
II. Title.
TT199.7.T387 1996
731.4'62--dc20 95-41460
CIP

ISBN: 0-88740-903-2
Printed in China

Published by Schiffer Publishing Ltd.
77 Lower Valley Road
Atglen, PA 19310
Please write for a free catalog.
This book may be purchased from the publisher.
Please include $2.95 for shipping.
Try your bookstore first.

Contents

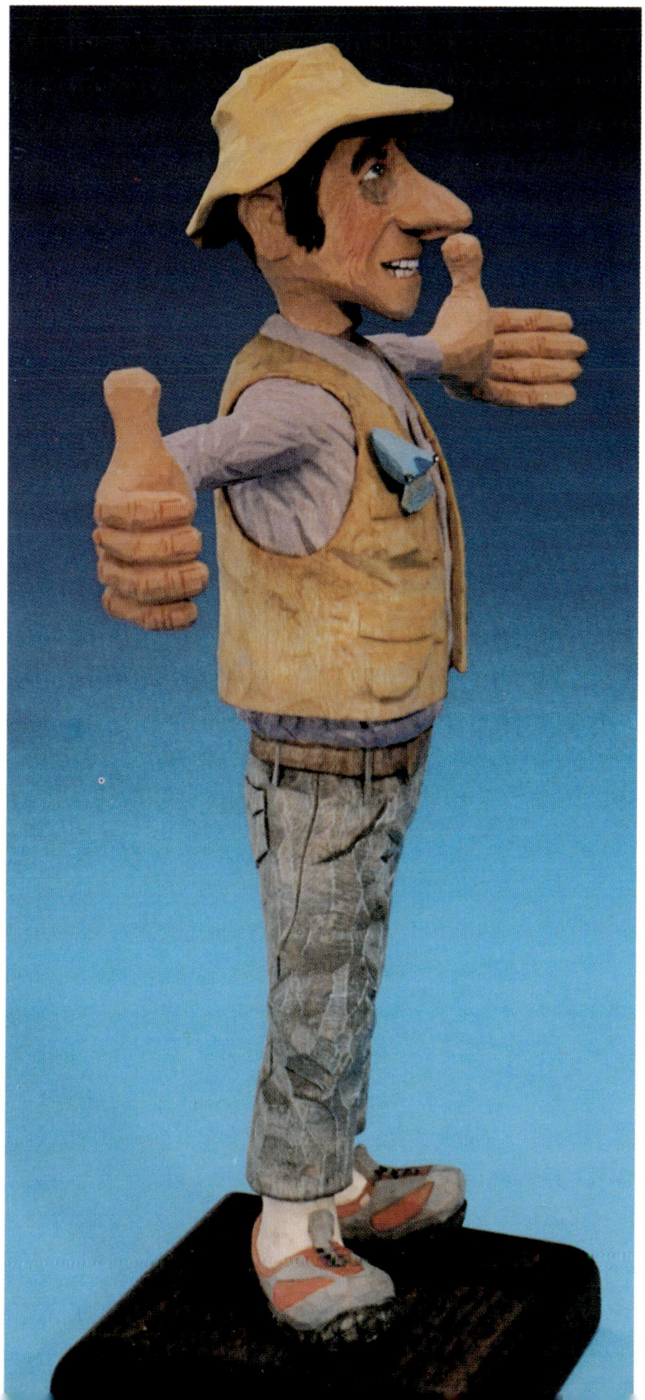

Introduction

The inspiration for this book came from a true to life southern gentleman and carver named Burt Jaeger. I met Burt and his wife Harriet at an art show in Sun Valley, Idaho several years ago. He and I have talked about going fishing together ever since. We have had the opportunity to sit on my back porch, smoke our pipes, tell a few yarns, and carve a little. But we've never been fishing together. Burt generally calls me in the Spring and Fall with tall tales of monster bluegills and crappie, and I phone him in the Summer and Winter with stories of trout and wild steelhead that got away.

I visited Burt and Harriet in their home in Clarksdale, Mississippi about two years ago while on a tour of the States on my Harley. But the Mississippi was flooded and we missed our chance to fish together. Chin up Burt, we'll make it yet.

A flexible Fisherman pattern is available for $20.00 plus $1.00 shipping from the author who resides, until at least the year 2005, at 11052 Sandhurst Drive, Boise, Idaho 83709.

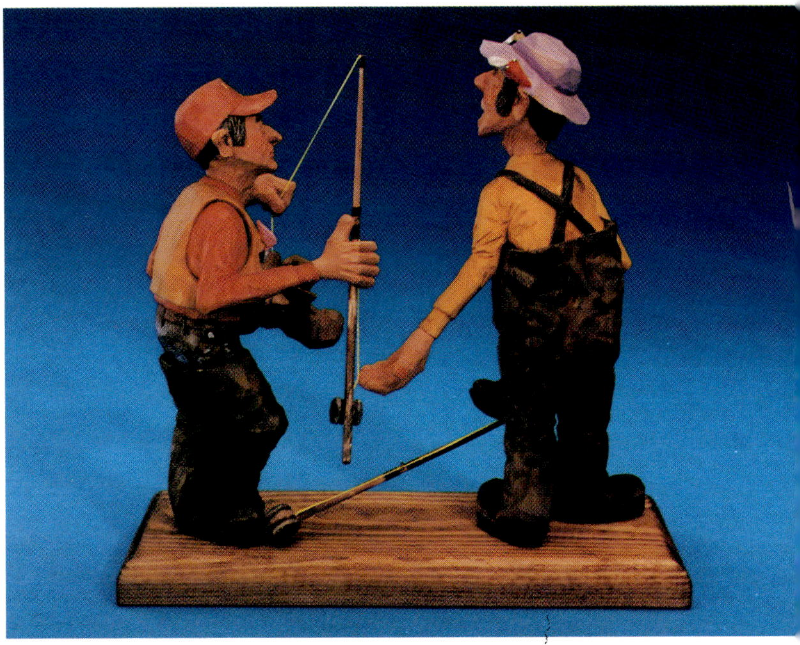

Tools

Here are the tools you will need for this project:

I use a Kevlar carving glove impervious to knife cuts, a series of bench knives, a Foredom or Dremel rotary power tool with a Kutzall burr, and a band saw. The gouges I use are a 1/4" #9 gouge, 1/2" #3 fishtail gouge, three different size V tools (1/4", 1/8", and a micro 2 mm or 1/16" V gouge), a 3/16" deep gouge, a 1/8" #5 gouge, and a 1/2" #7 gouge, 3/32" deep gouge (deep gouges are also called veiners).

I use Ceramcoat brand pre-mixed acrylics and several brush sizes including #1, #2, and #000.

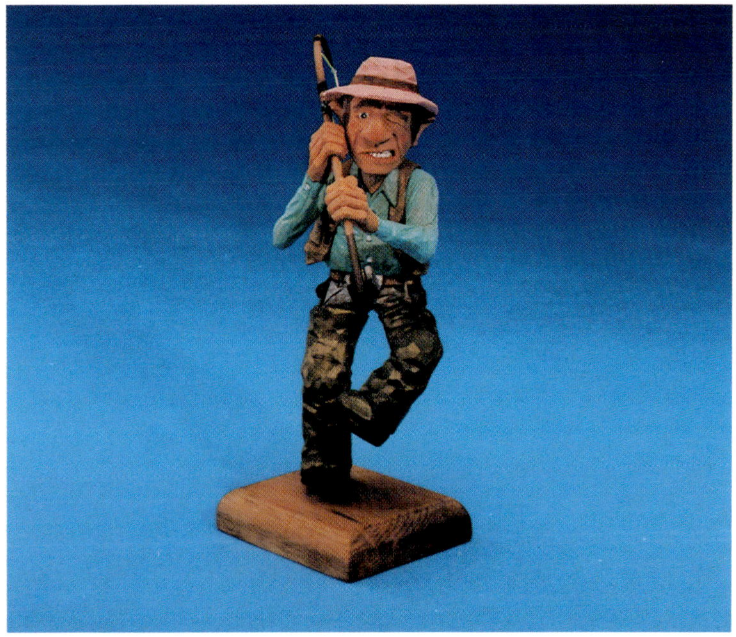

Carving the Fisherman

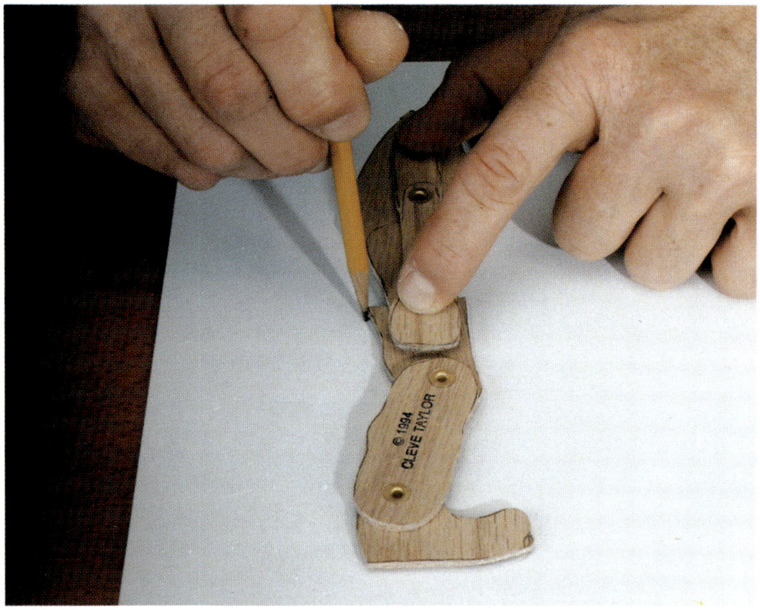

Let's begin this exercise by designing our pattern. Trace the perimeter of the jointed flexible pattern.

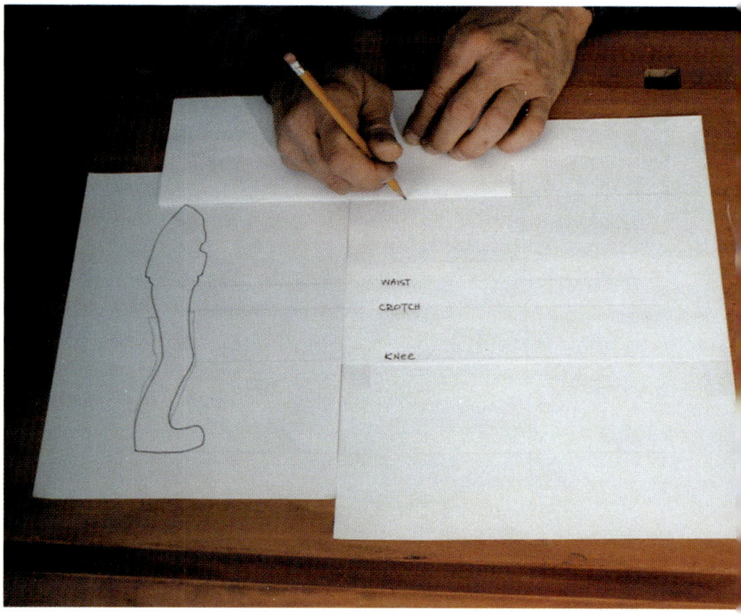

Transfer the height of the fisherman from the profile view to a larger sheet of paper. We'll also want to transfer major features from the profile view such as the knee, crotch and waistline.

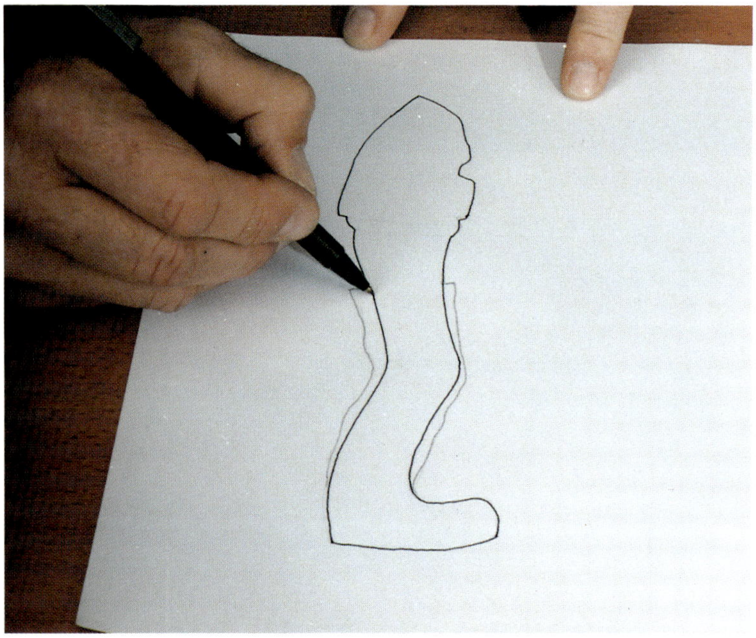

The flexible pattern has waders. We'll delete these by sketching the leg as shown.

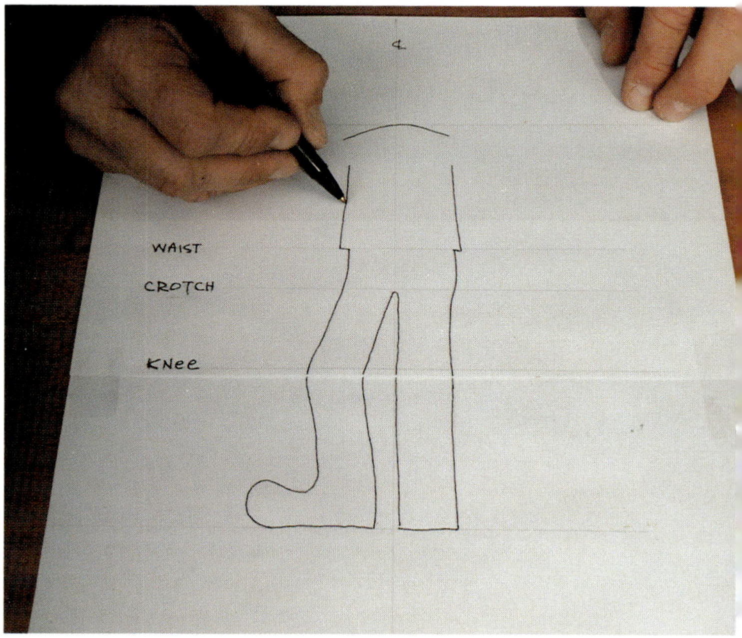

Sketch the front view of the legs and upper body.

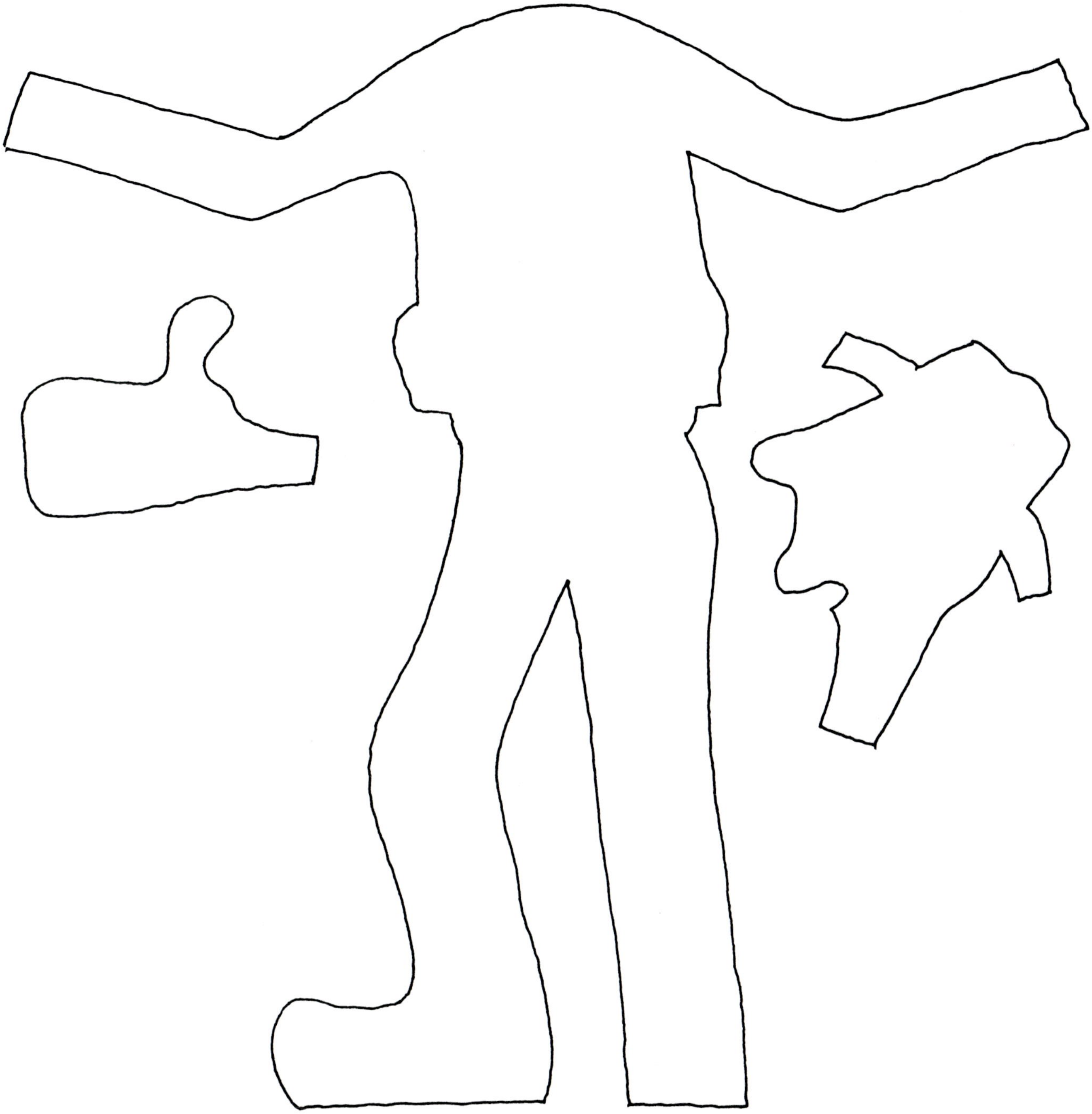

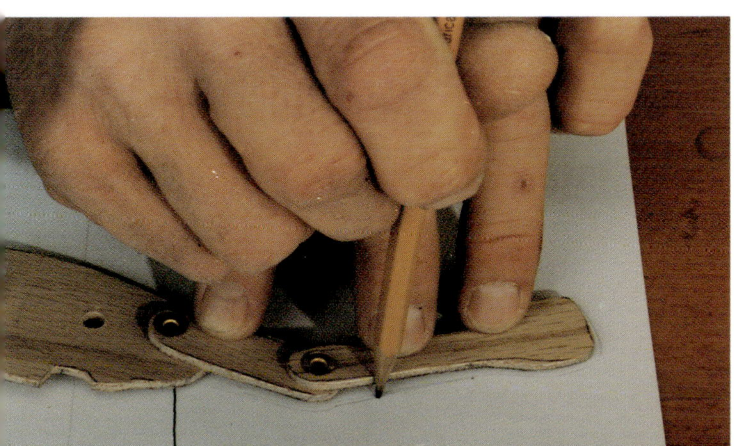

Using the jointed pattern, draw the arm and hand.

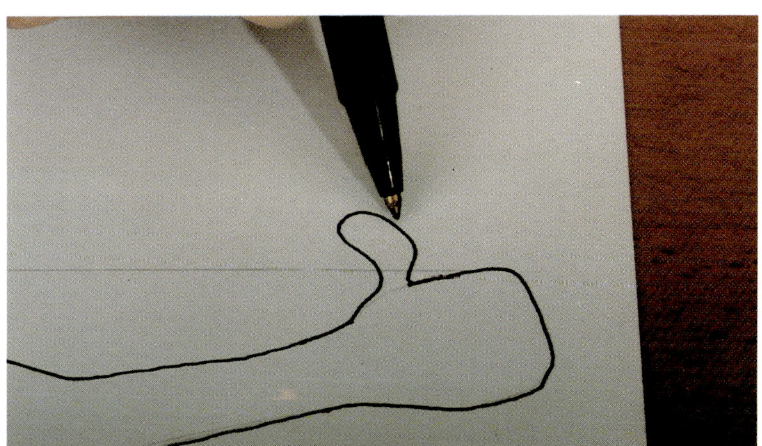

Add the thumb.

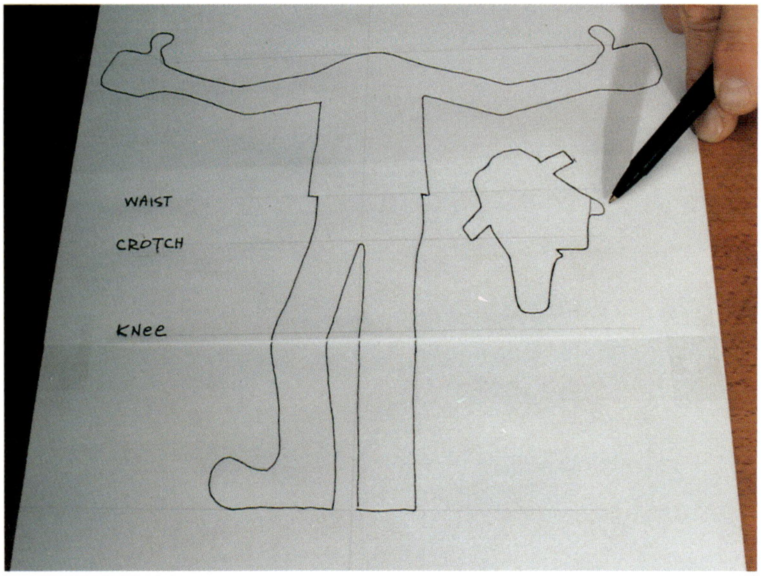

Construct the other arm and hand by reversing the flexible pattern. Since we're going to reduce this pattern, add a profile of the head. This old feller is going to be a prevaricator. As such, he should have a Pinocchio nose. Add a larger than normal nose to the head pattern.

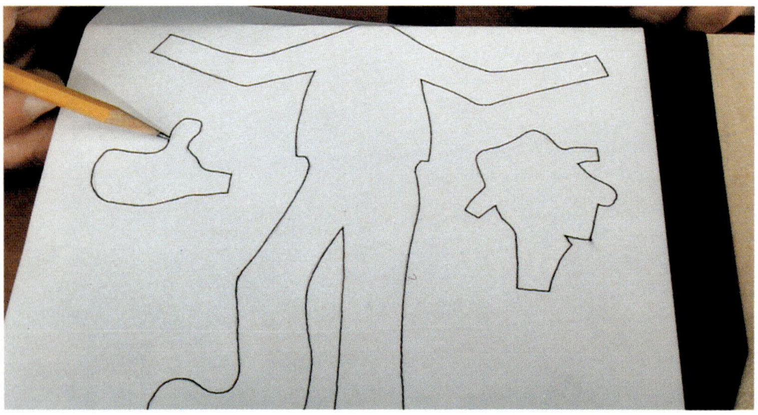

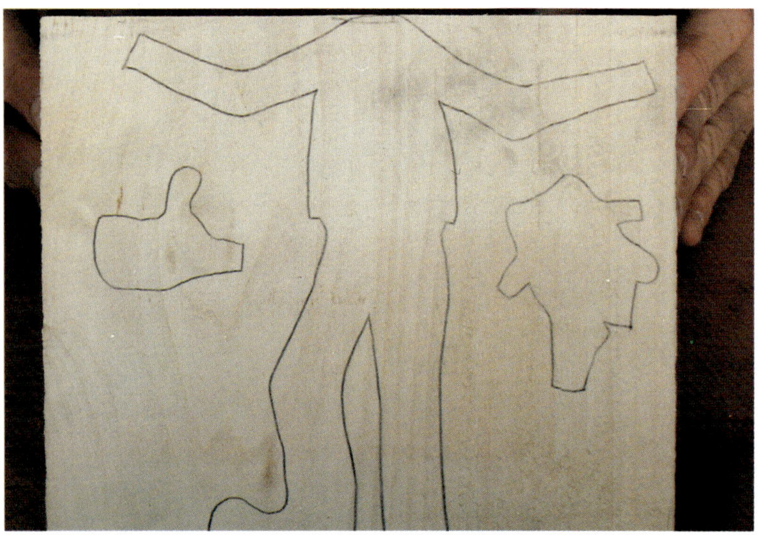

Use carbon paper to transfer the patterns to a piece of 2" thick basswood. Notice that I have removed the hands from the arms. I did this because the combination of thin arms and perpendicular grain direction would most likely lead to hands broken off in the band saw if they were left in place. We will insert the hands into the arms after we have completed the carving. Now we are ready to go to the band saw.

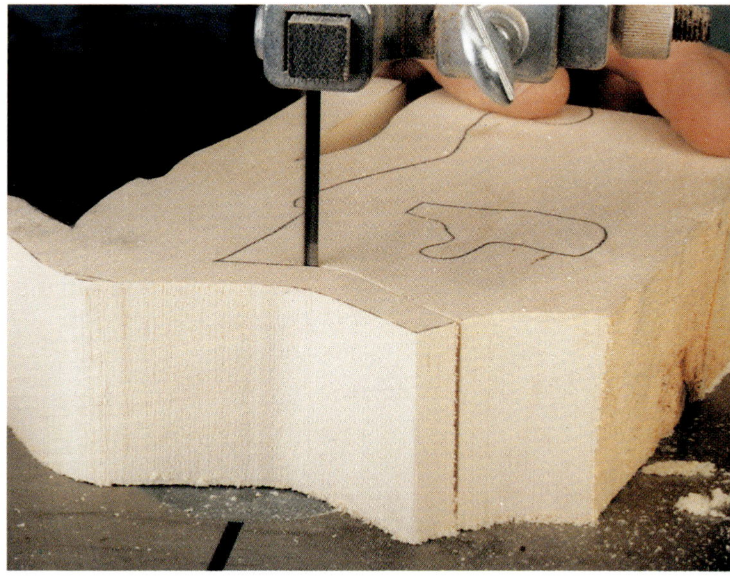

Cut out the pattern from the basswood block with the band saw.

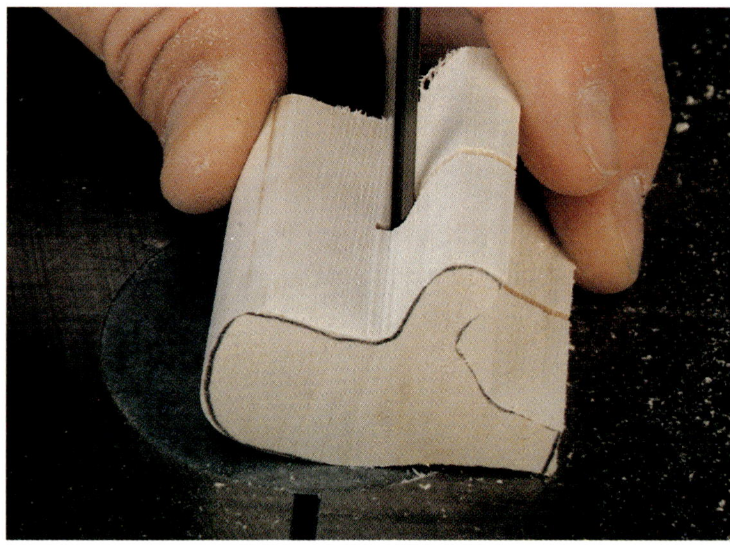

Cut the rough hand blank into two 1" thick pieces from the original two inch block. Watch your fingers!

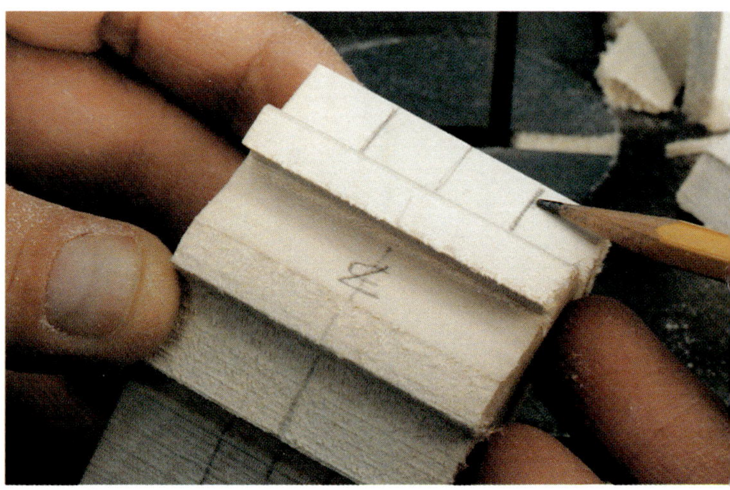

After cutting the profile of the head, mark the centerline and draw in the crown of the hat and the width of the head.

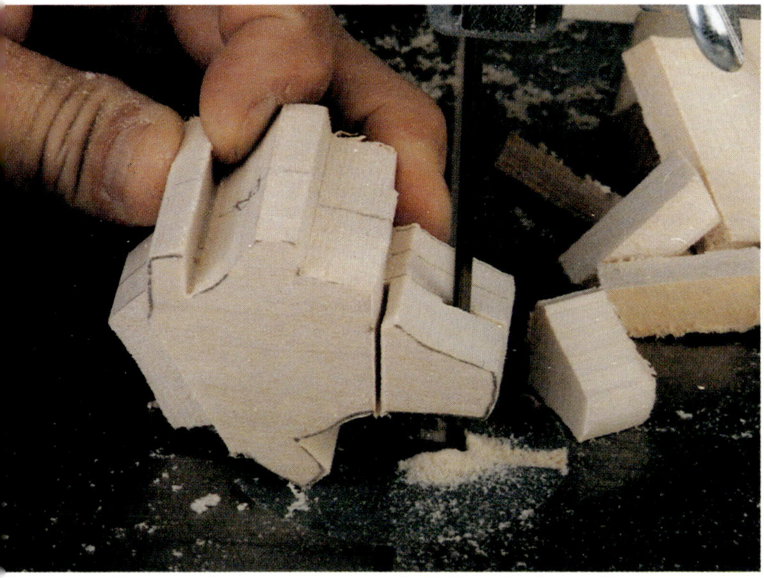

Cut away the excess wood from the sides of the hat and neck with the band saw.

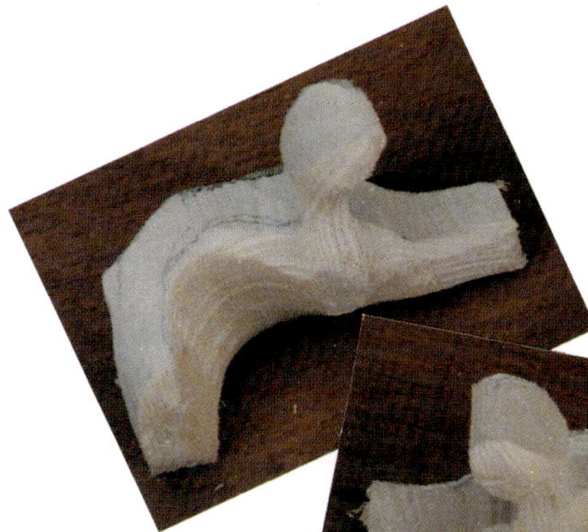
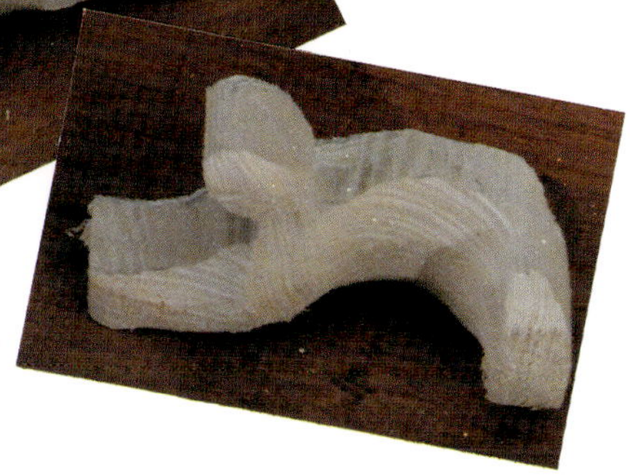

The roughed out hands.

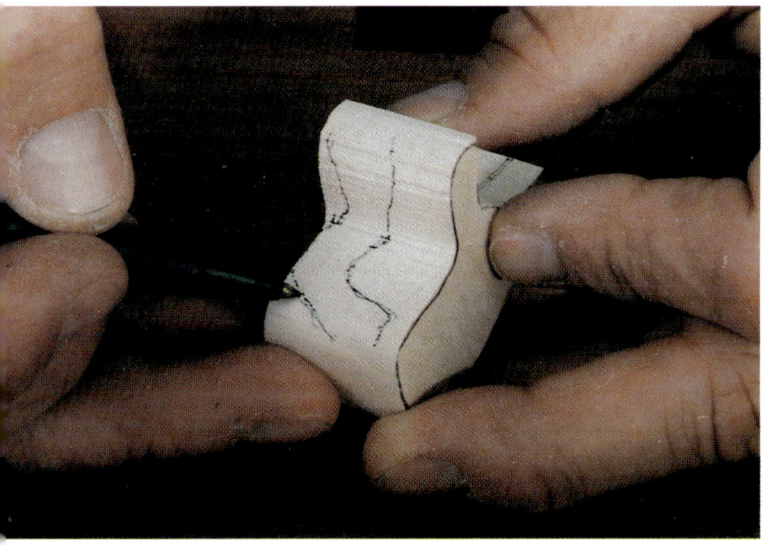

Sketch the top view of hands.

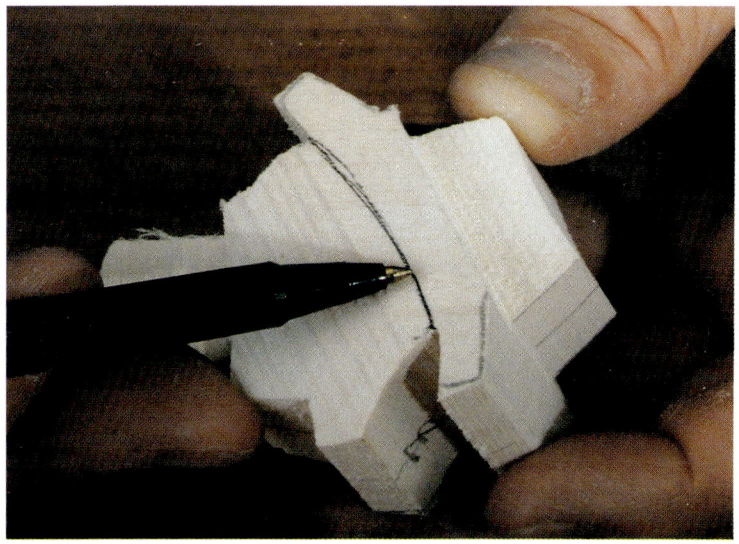

On the profile of the head sketch in the bottom of the hat brim ...

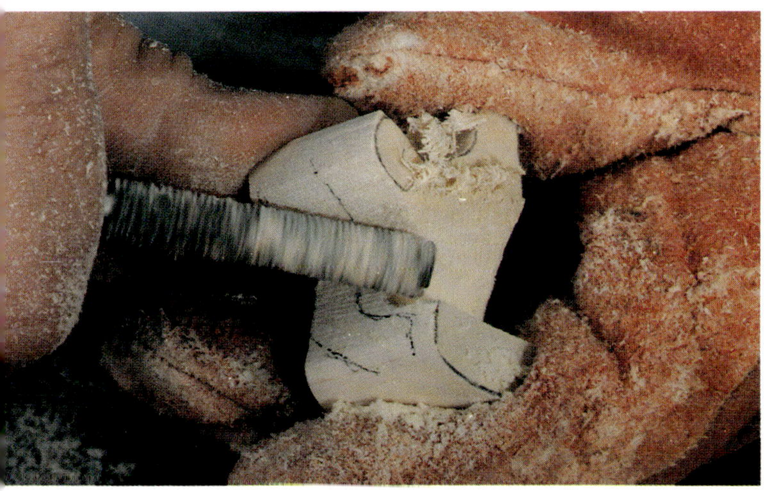

Remove unwanted wood with a Foredom with a 1/4" Kutzall bit.

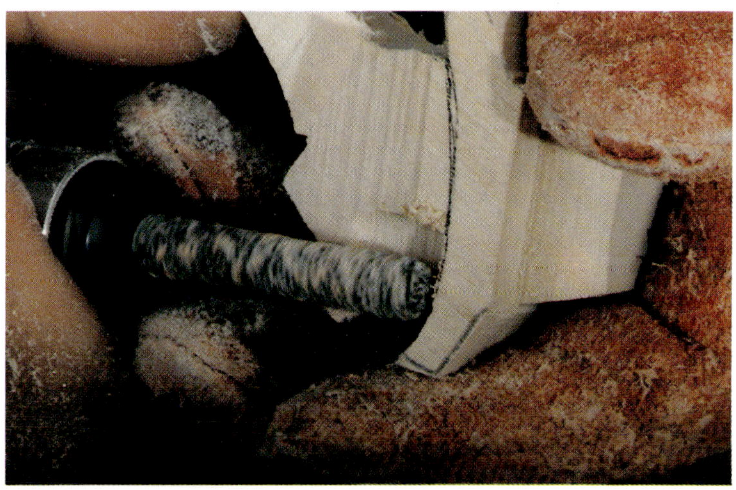

... and remove unwanted wood from below the hat brim with the Foredom.

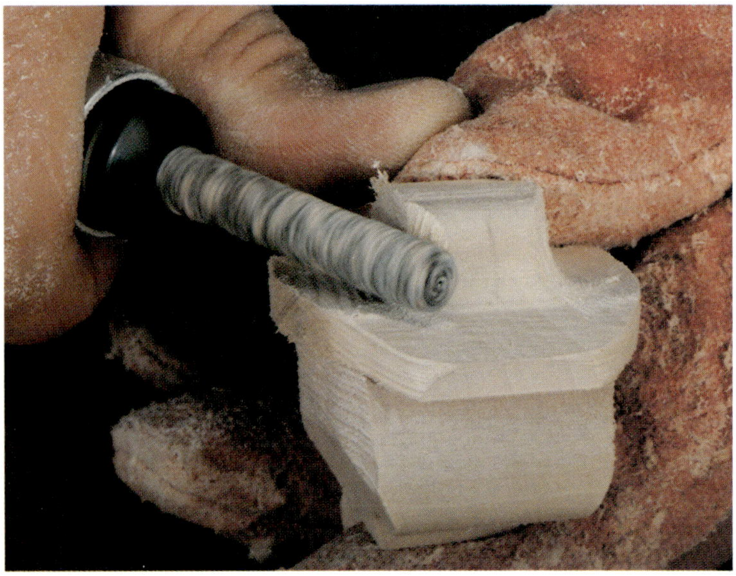

You can also round the corners of the hat with the Foredom.

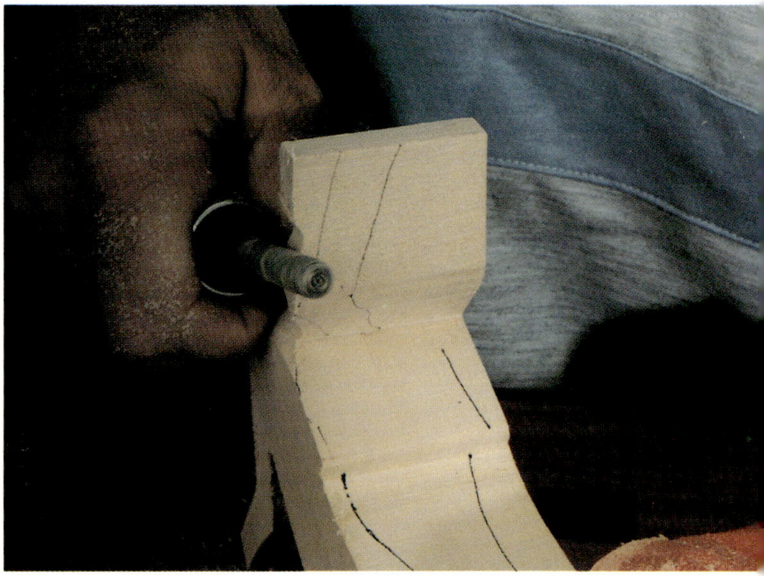

Remove the unwanted excess wood from the body with the Foredom and the 1/4" Kutzall bit.

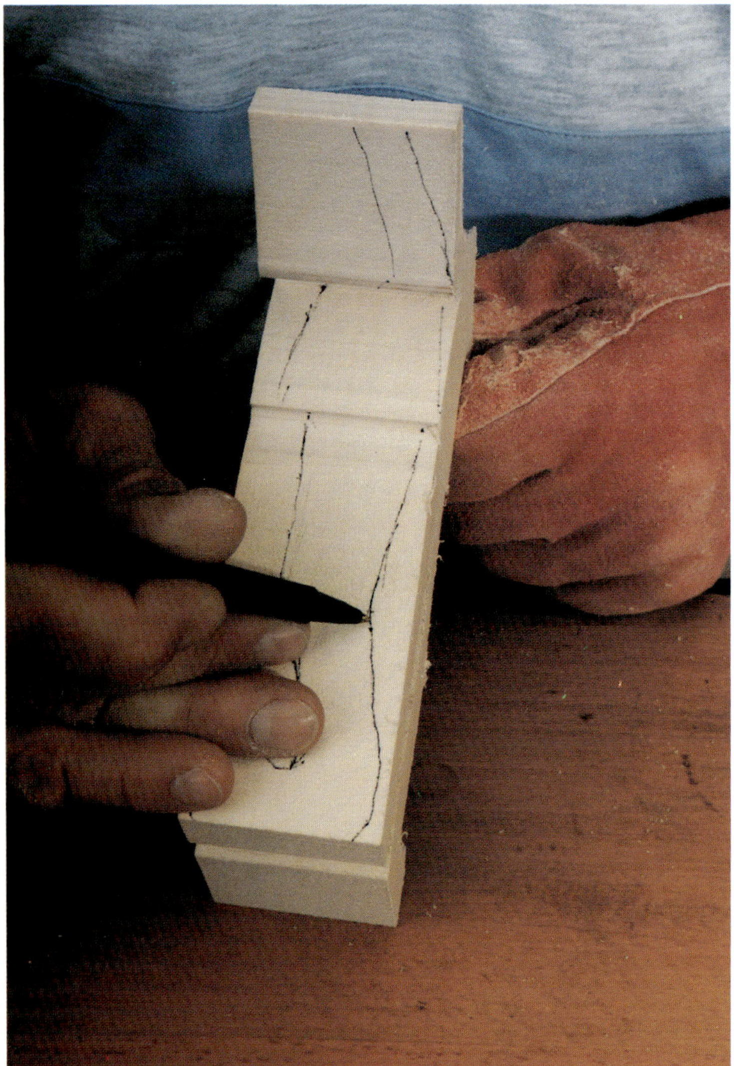

Sketch in the profile of the body on both the left and right sides.

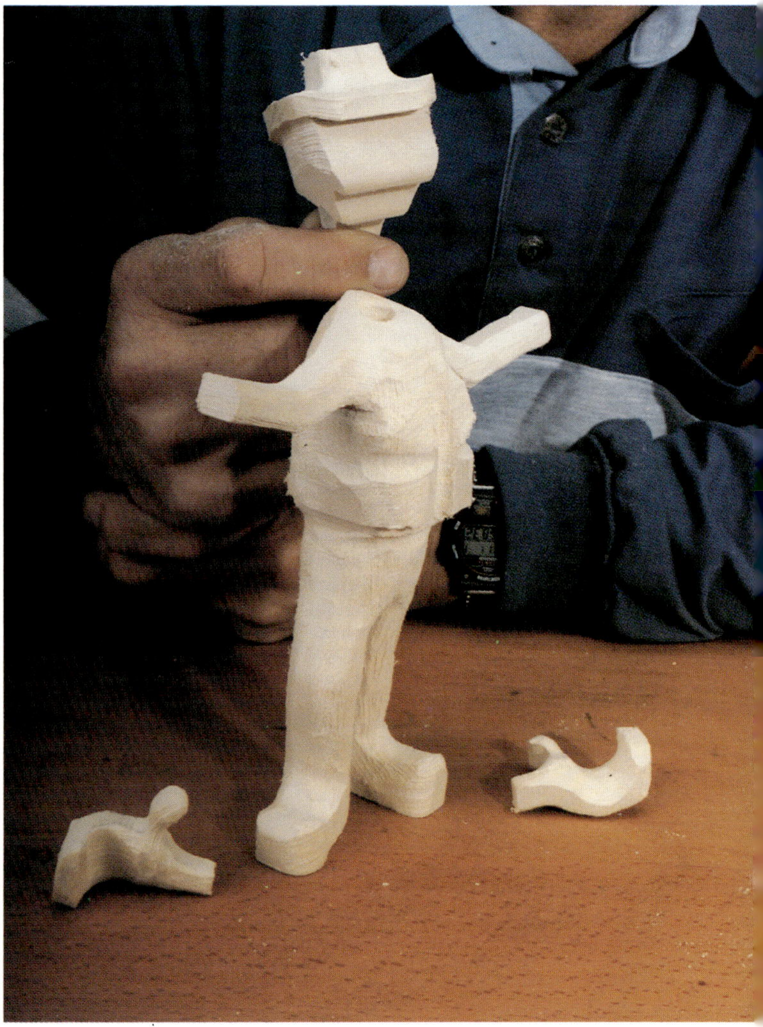

This is what the roughed out fisherman should look like upon completion of the Foredom steps. The last thing I do is drill a 1/2" hole for the neck to fit into. You can cock the head to one side or the other by drilling the hole skewed to the body's centerline.

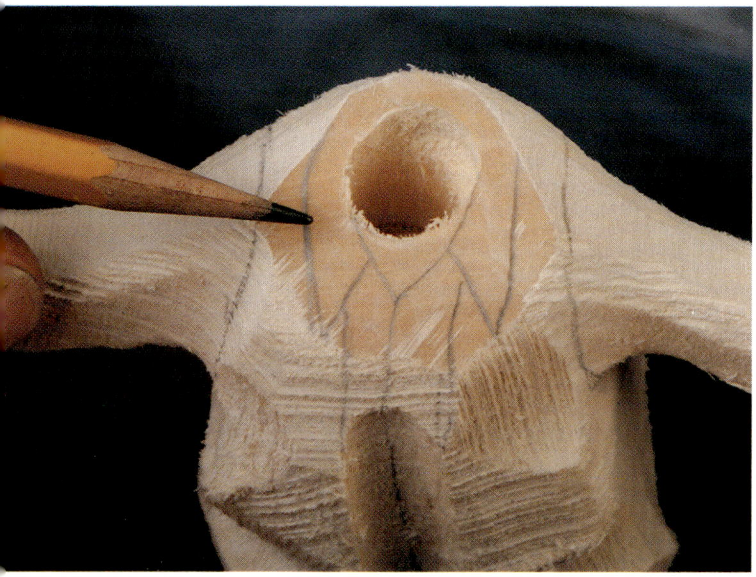

After removing burrs and saw marks around the neck area, sketch in the shirt collar.

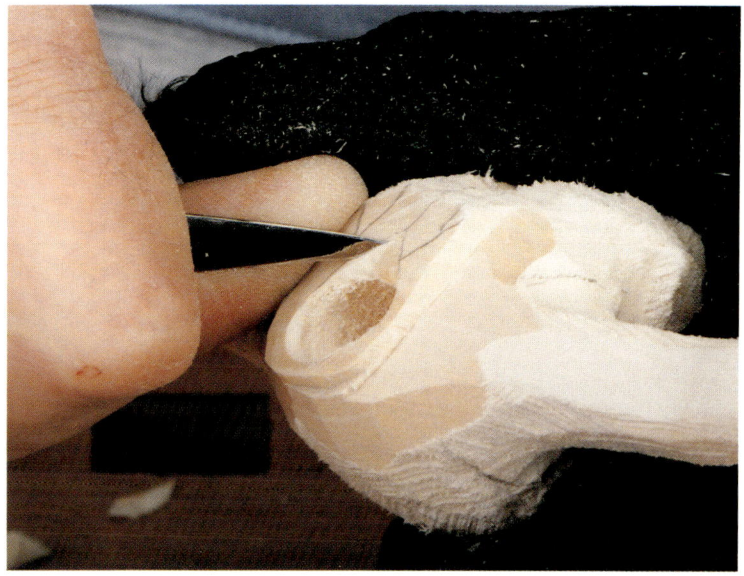

Using a detail knife, remove wood from the neck hole to the leading edge of the collar.

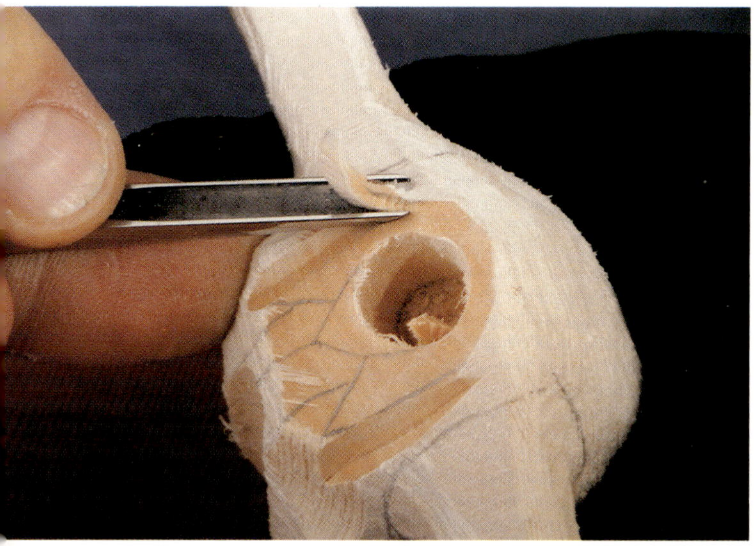

Using a 1/4" V tool, remove wood from the perimeter of the collar.

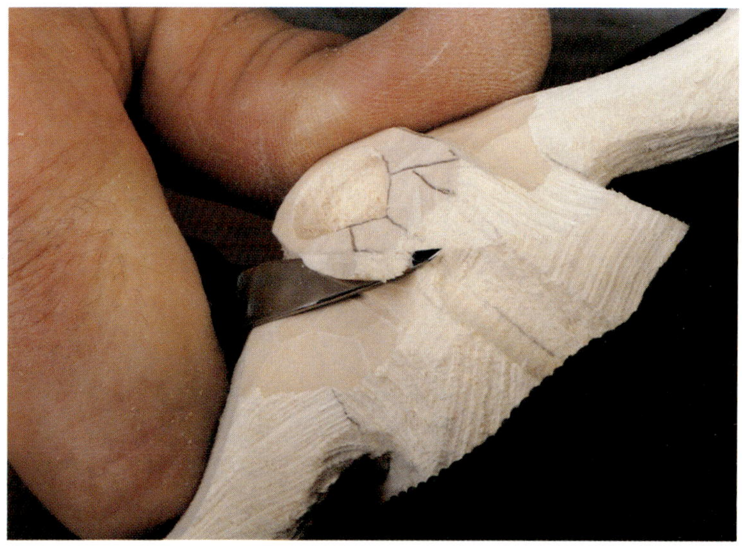

Create an inclined plane from the tips of the collar to the collar ridge around the neck hole.

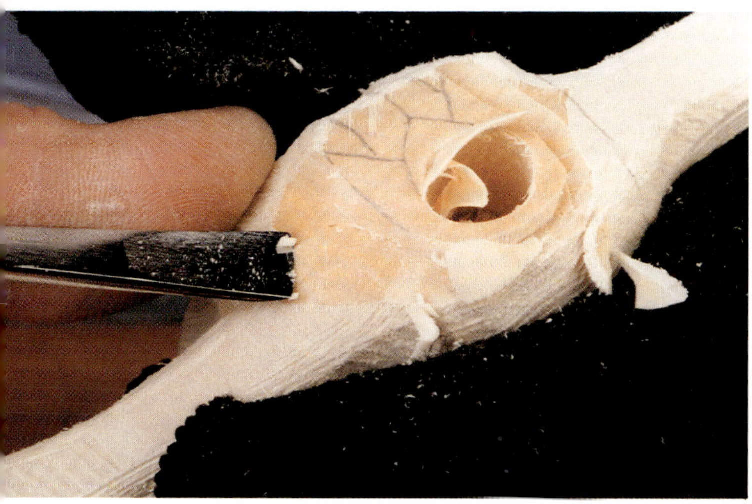

Using a 1/2" fishtail gouge, relieve the shoulders to the bottom of the shirt collar.

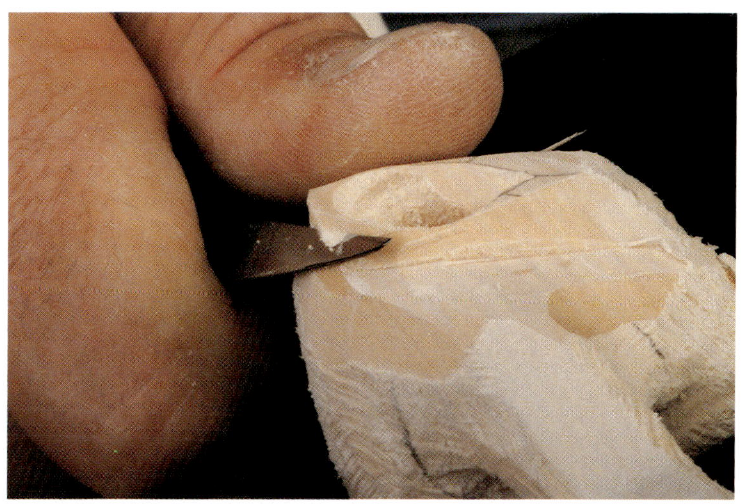

Continue this inclined slope from the bottom to the top of the collar around the perimeter of the neck.

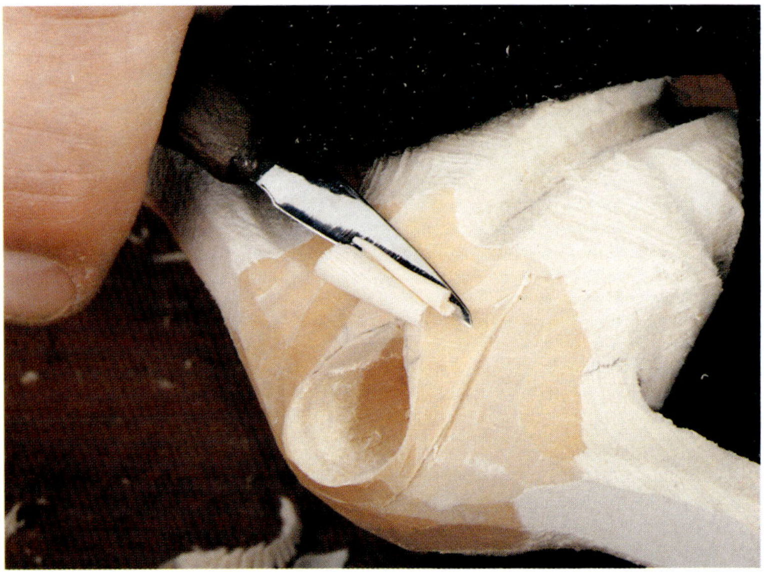

Remove wood from the front of the shirt to the intersection of the collar at the front of the neckline.

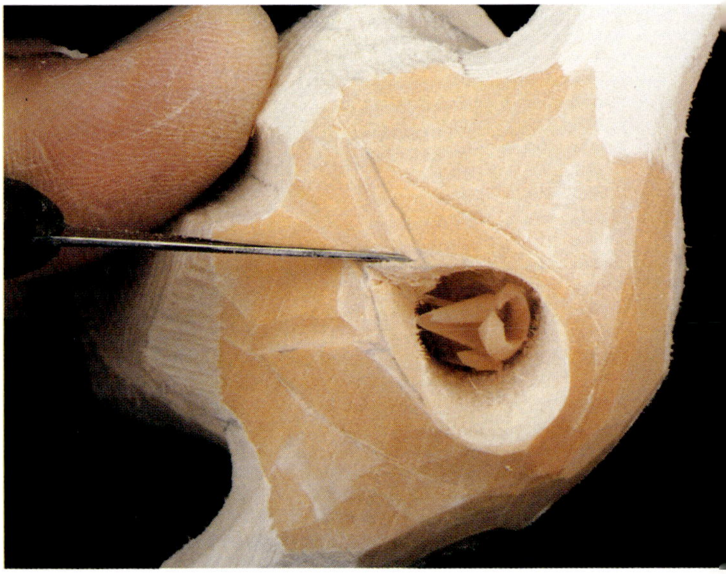

Using the detail knife, stick the blade straight in alongside the shirt front ...

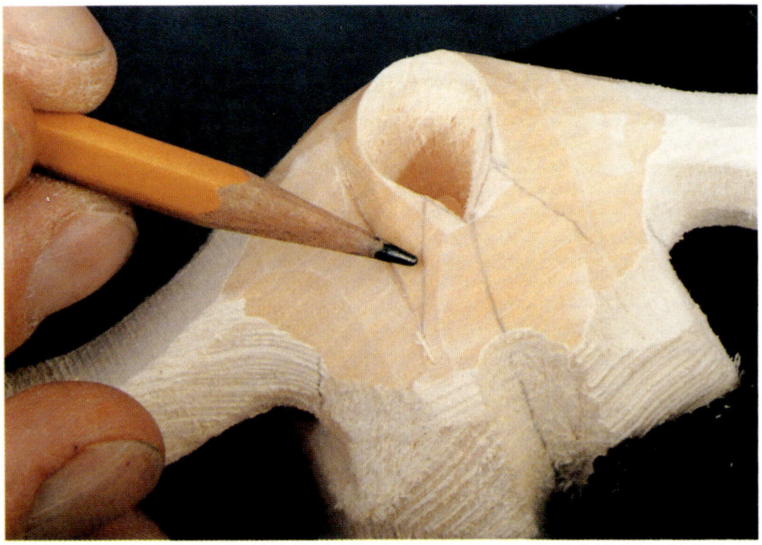

Resketch the front of the shirt collar.

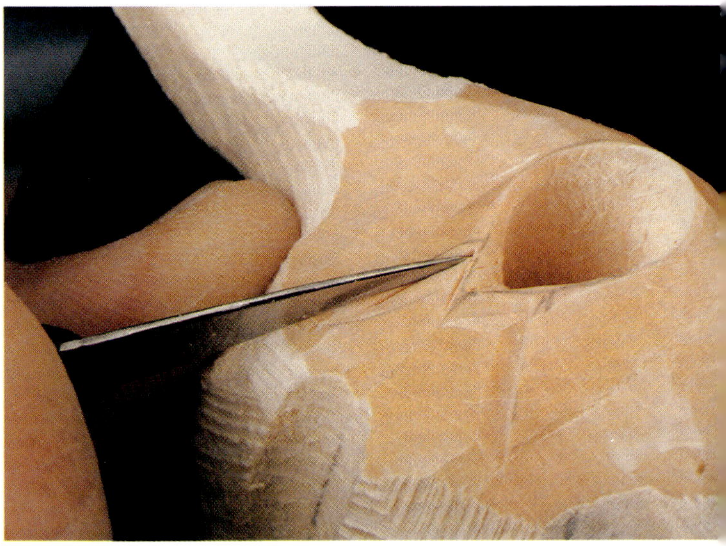

... and along the side of the collar.

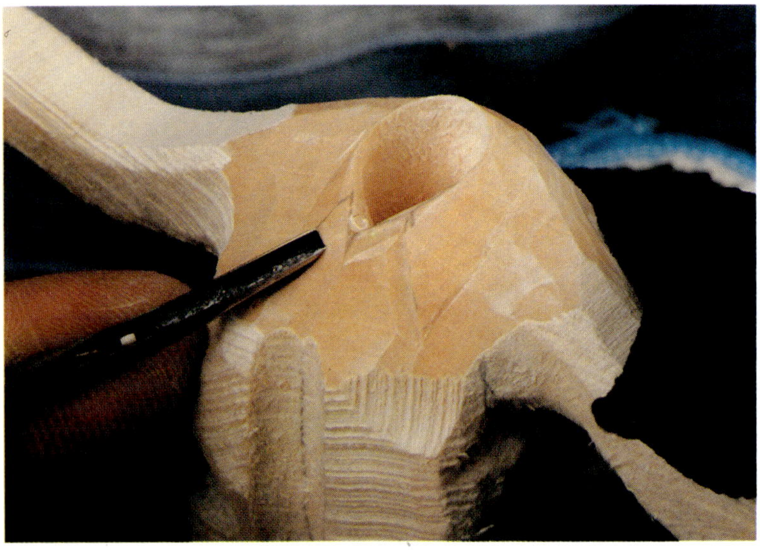

Use a 1/8" V tool to outline the front of the collar.

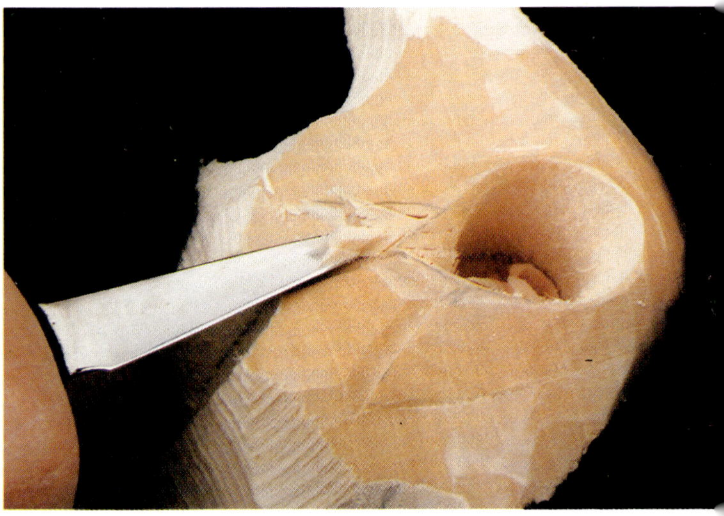

Use your knife tip to remove the small triangle of wood from underneath the shirt collar.

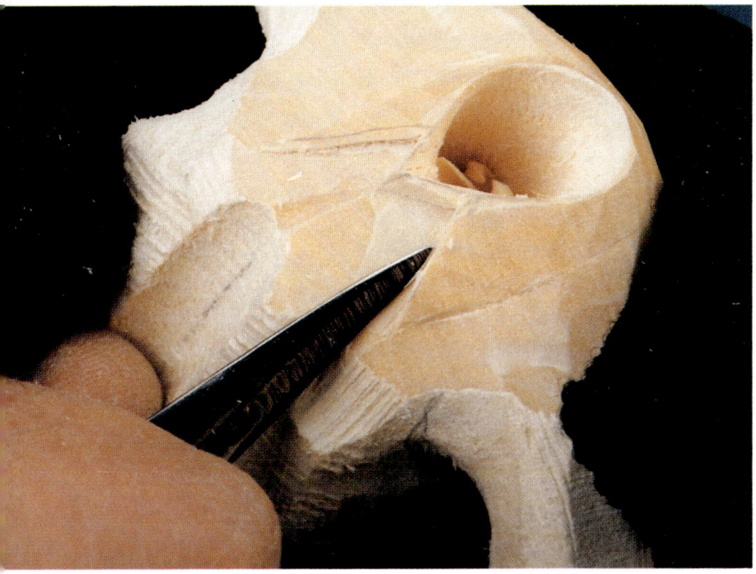

Repeat with the other collar.

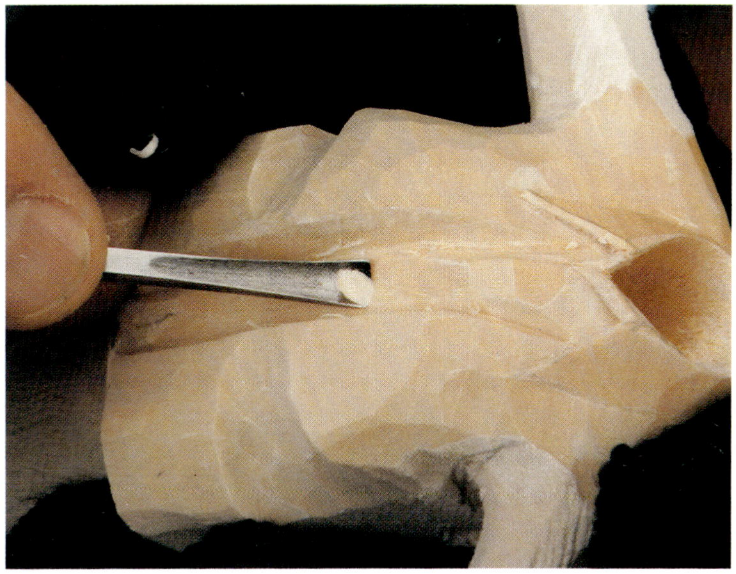

Use the 1/4" shallow gouge to clean saw marks on the front of the shirt in the vest opening.

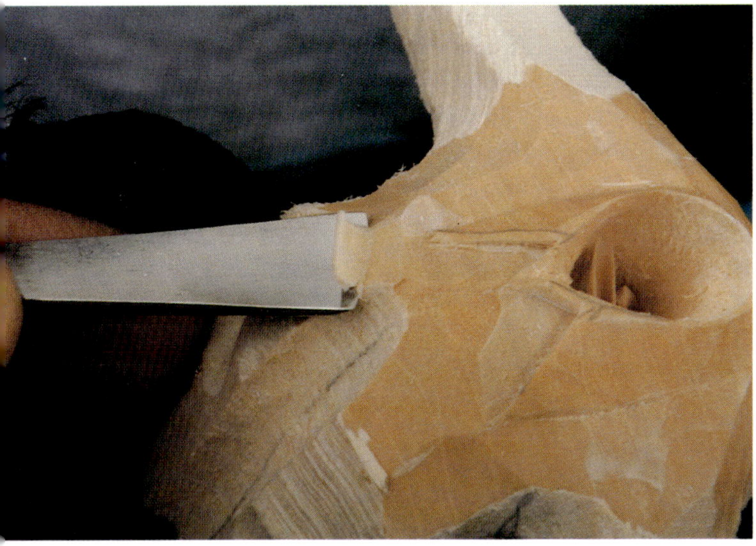

Use a 1/2" fishtail gouge to clean saw marks and burr marks from the front of the vest. Be sure to leave plenty of wood for the pockets in the vest.

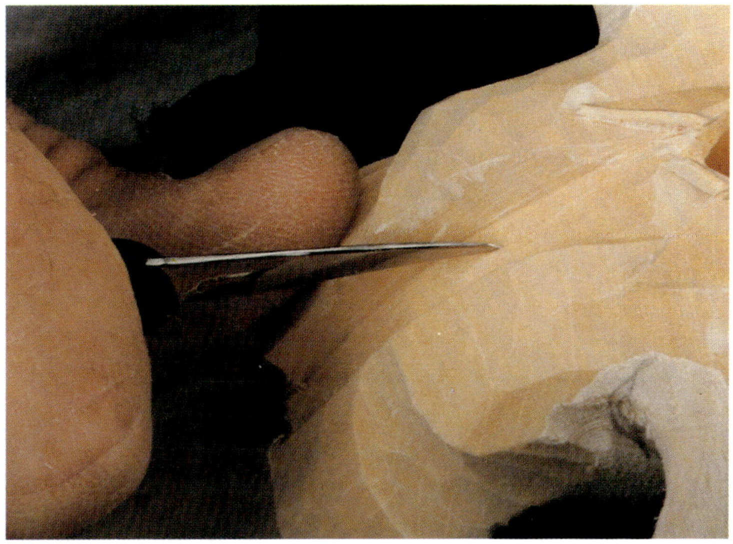

Using the tip of your detail knife, carve a line about 1/16" deep for the shirt placket.

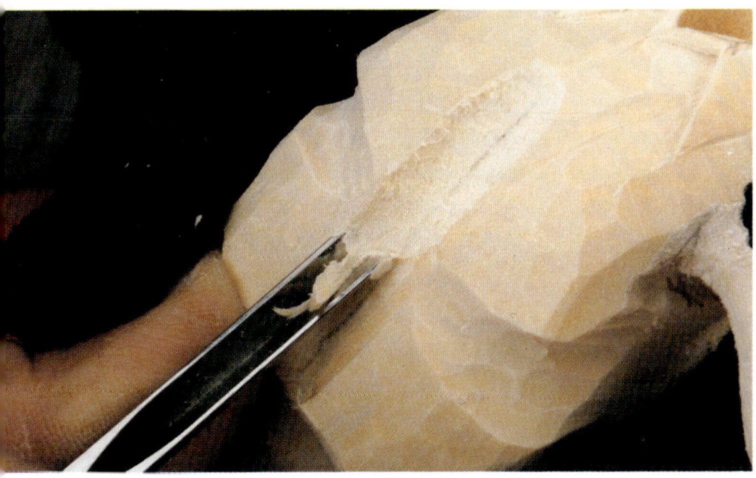

Use a large V tool to outline both sides of the vest front. Continue this cut up under the collar.

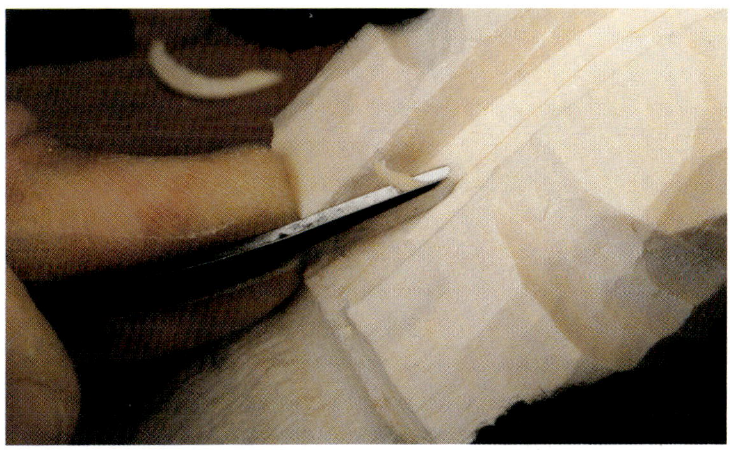

Use your 1/4" V tool — turned so that one side of the blade is laying flat on shirt front — to follow this freshly cut line to the collar, relieving wood from the right side of the shirt placket.

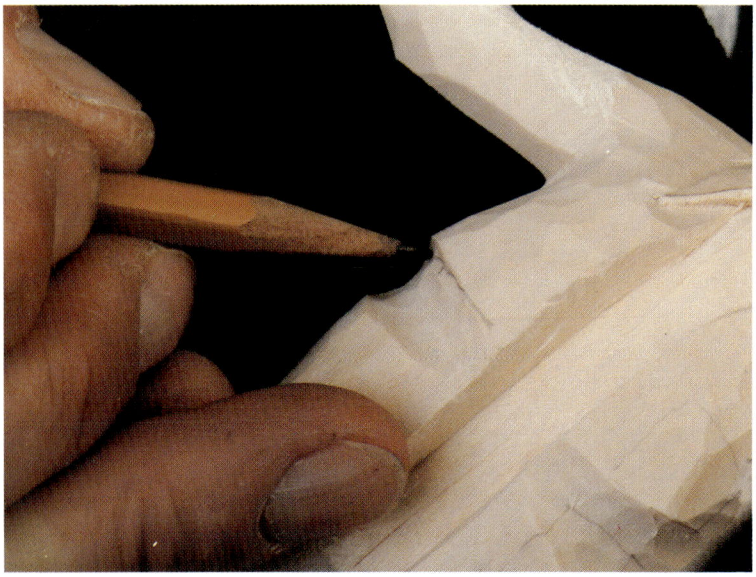

Sketch in the locations of pockets on the vest ...

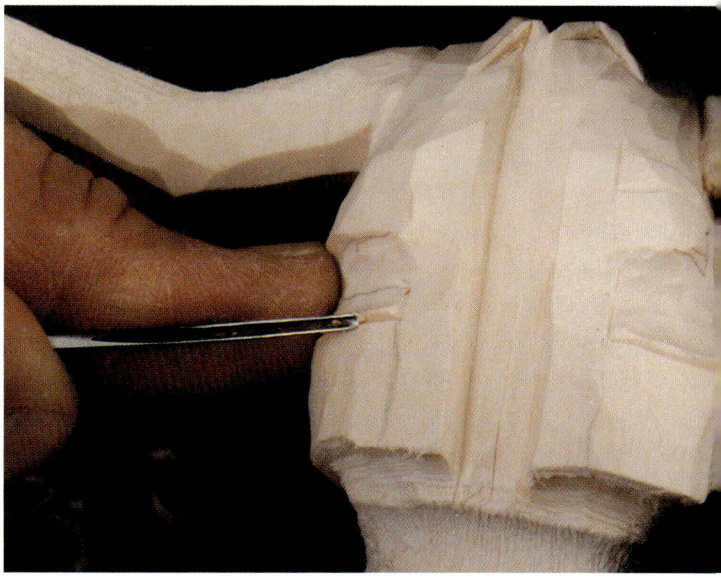

Using your small V tool, cut around the flaps over the pockets.

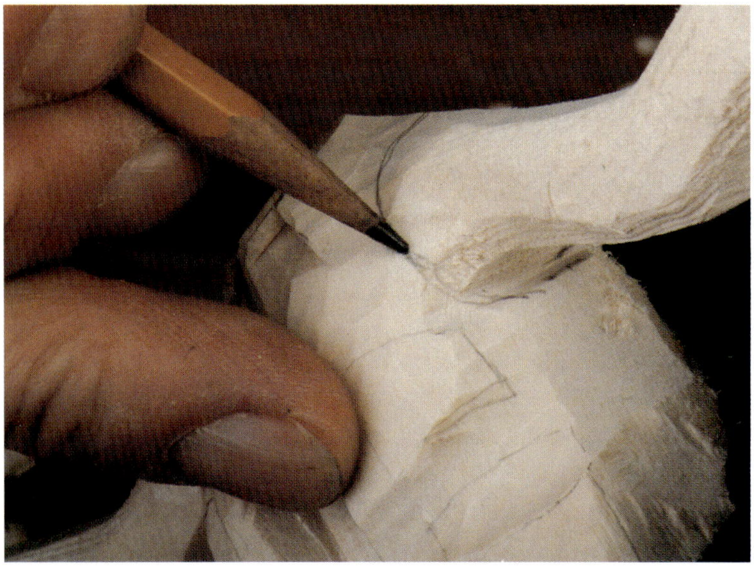

... and the locations of the vest's armholes as well.

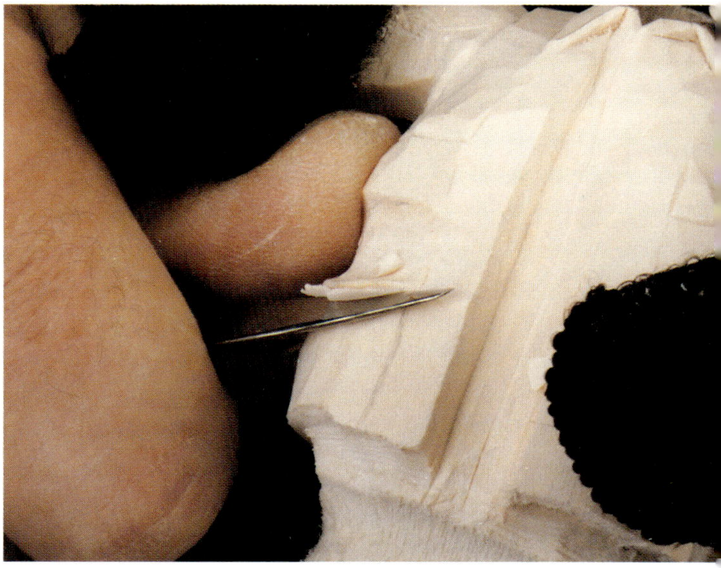

Relieve wood from under the pocket flap with your detail knife.

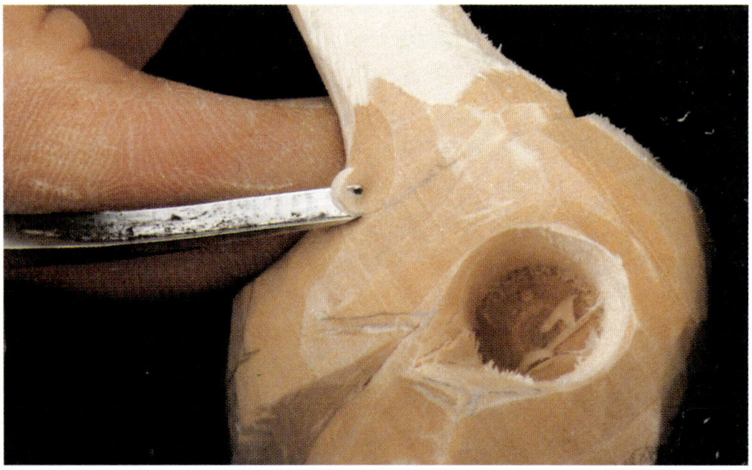

Use your 1/8" V tool and cut along the arm holes in the vest.

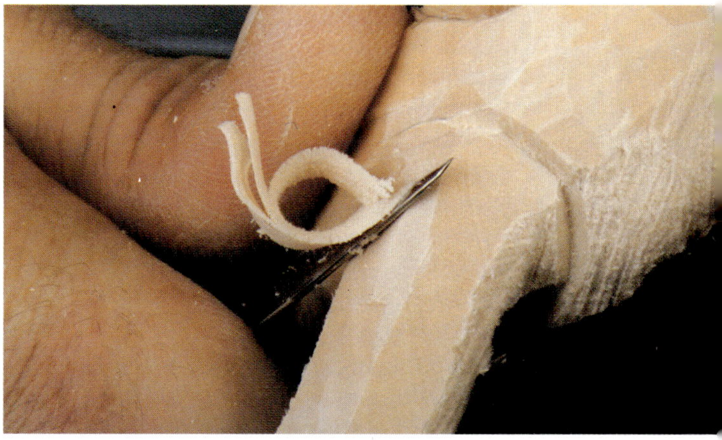

Use your detail knife to remove saw marks, burr marks, and to round out the arms into the armholes of the vest.

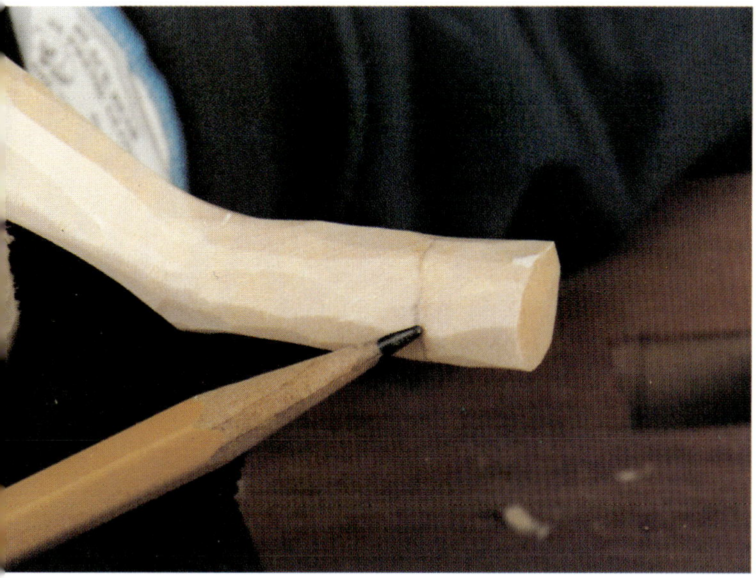

Sketch the top of the cuff line on the rounded arm.

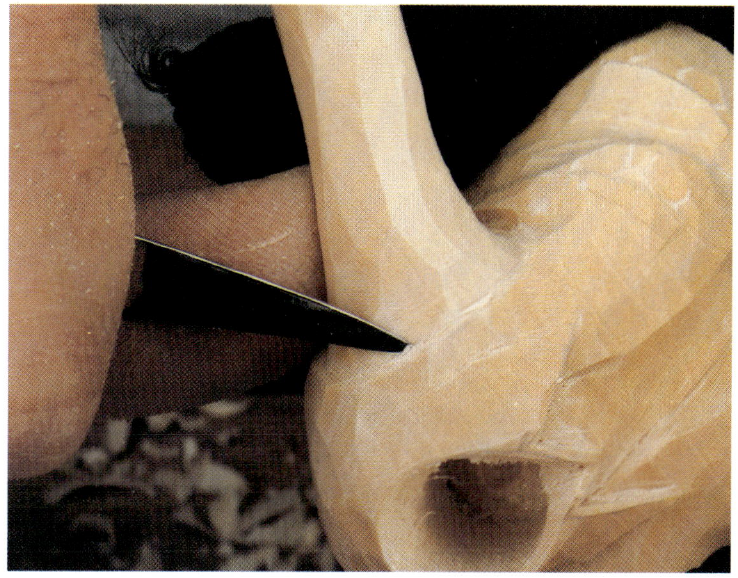

Let's relieve the arm holes in the vest. Using your detail knife, make a cut around the arm hole with the knife blade laying against the arm.

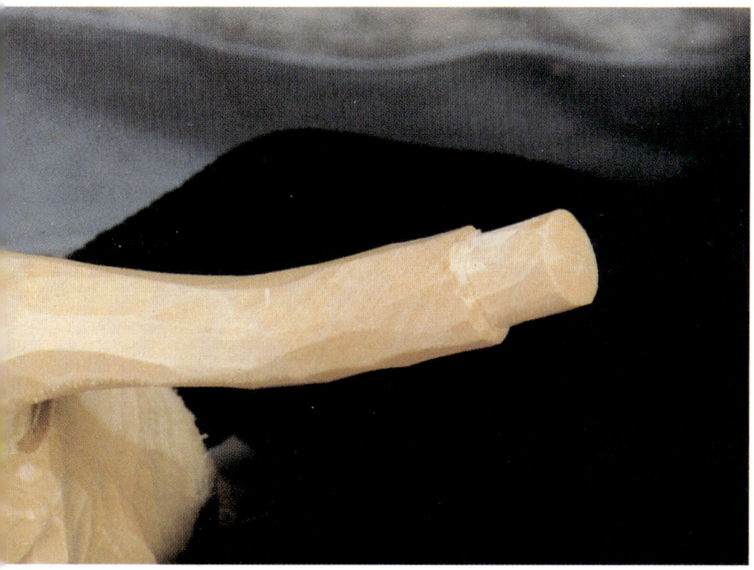

Follow this cuff line with a 1/8" V tool to a depth of about 1/8". Relieve wood to the end of the arm from the bottom of this cuff line, like so.

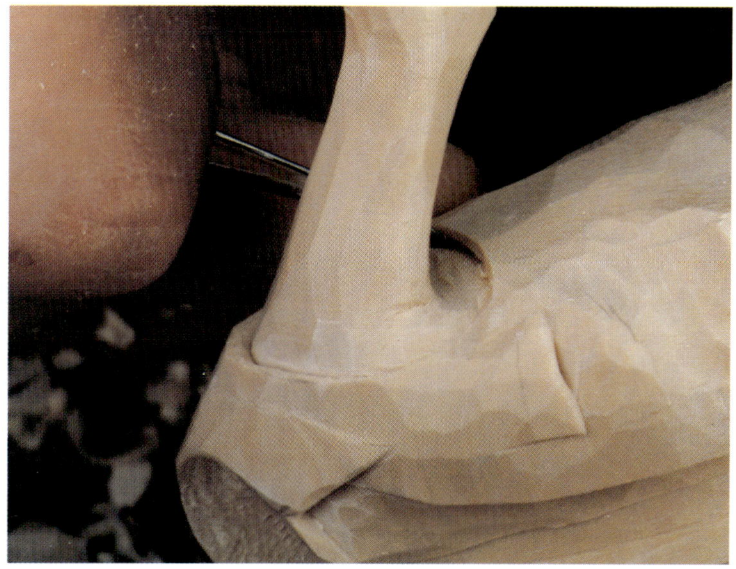

To relieve the arm hole, position your knife blade at a 45 degree angle to the first cut and cut away with the knife tip.

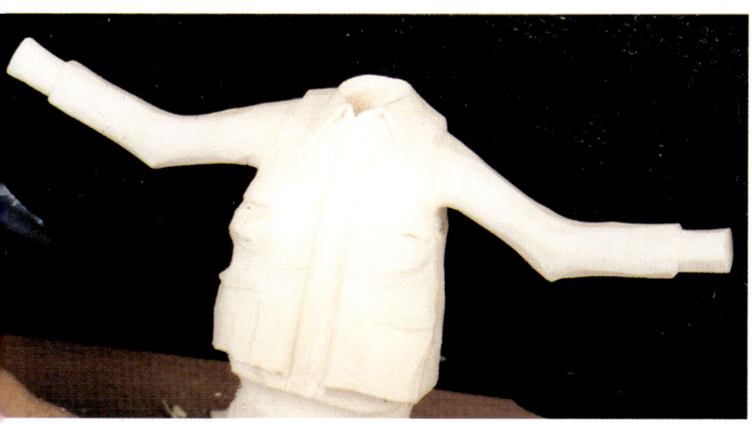

Be very careful when carving the arms to support them as you cut. The grain is very short along the length of the arms and they break easily. Here's how the arms should look so far.

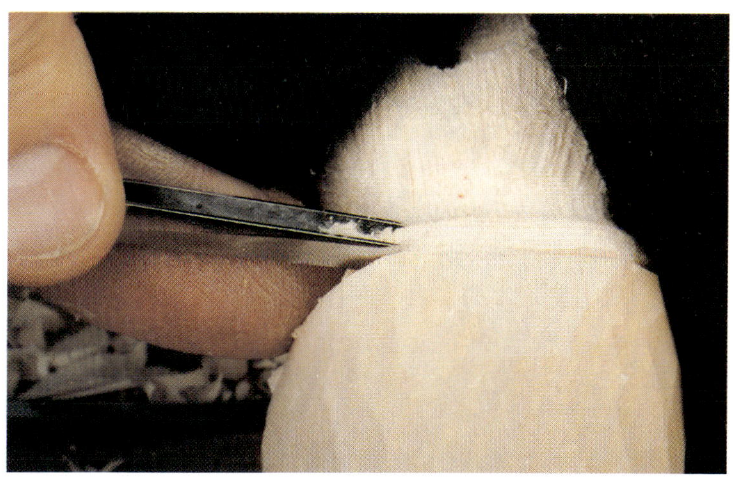

Use your 1/4" V tool to cut along the bottom of the vest ...

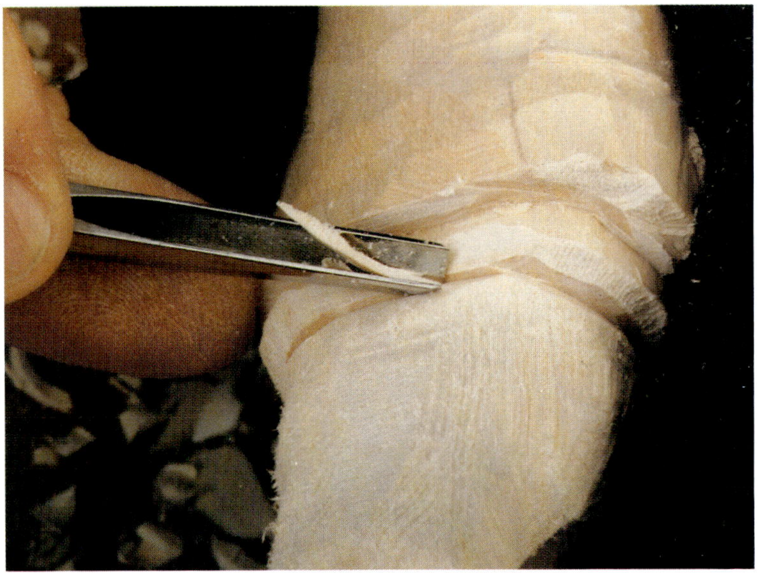

... and the waistline.

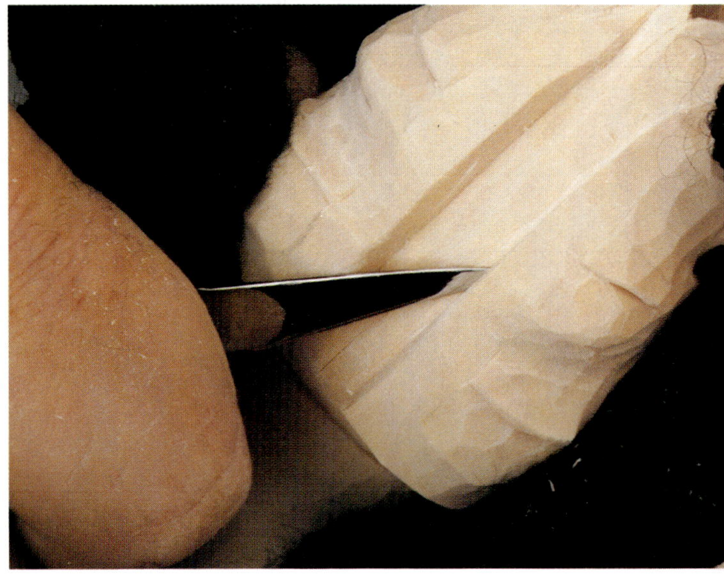

Relieve the front of the vest by first cutting into the vest with the edge of the knife flush with the shirt front ...

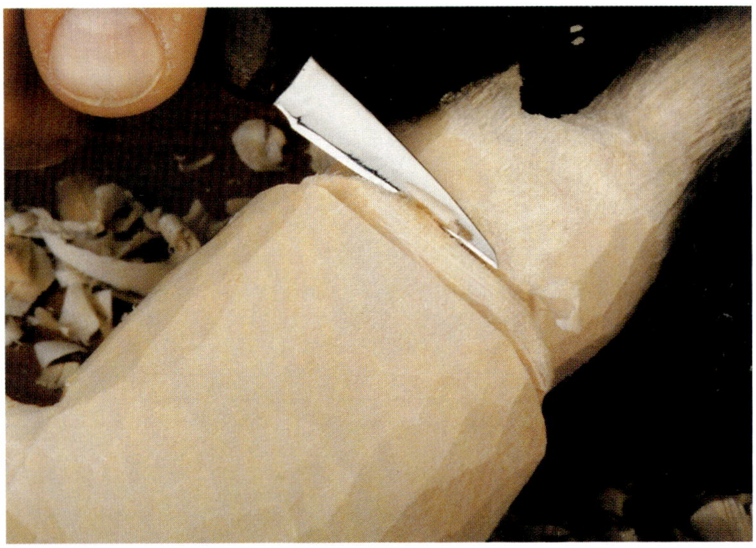

Remove saw and burr marks on the pants up to the waistline.

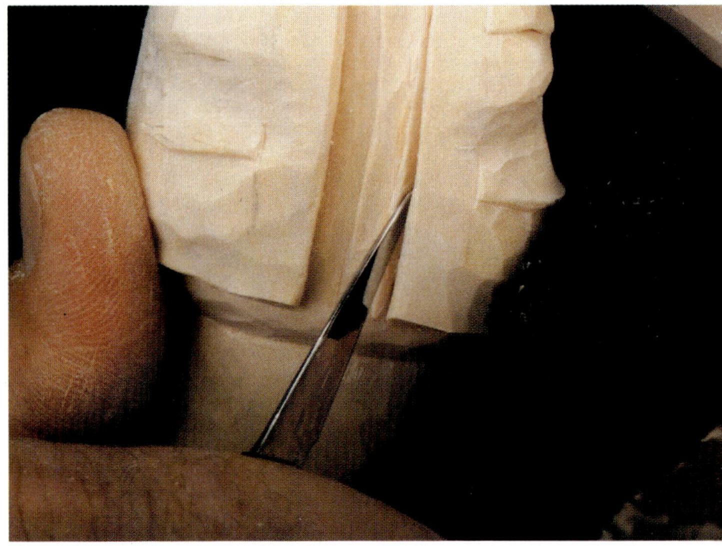

... and then, with knife at a 45 degree angle to first cut, remove wood from along the front of the vest.

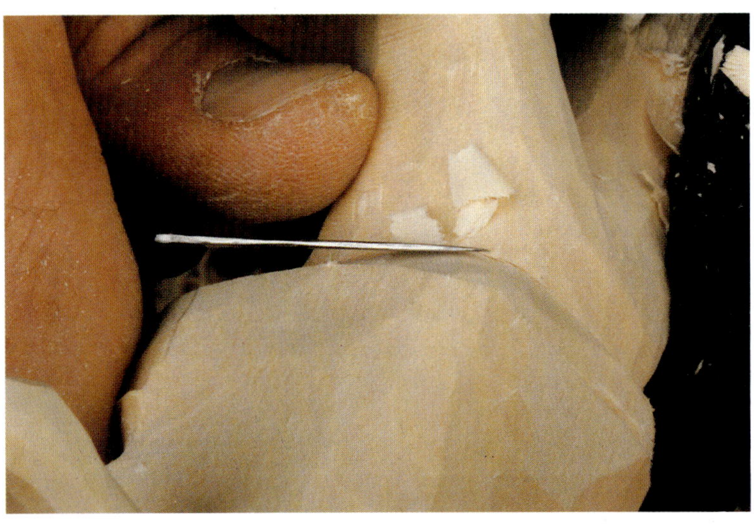

Blouse the bottom of the shirt from the vest down to the waistline.

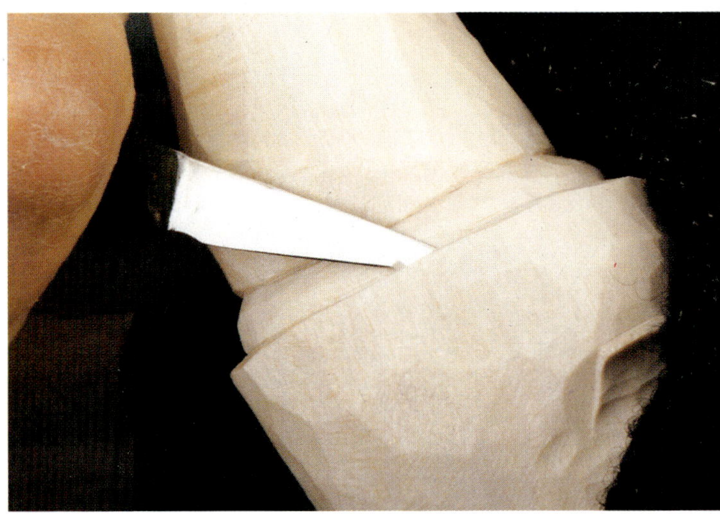

In a similar manner undercut the bottom of the vest.

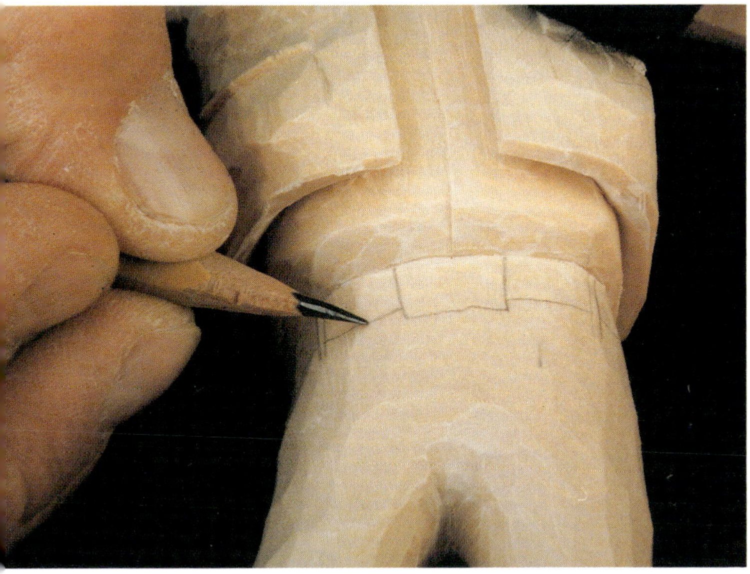

Draw in the belt buckle, the belt loops and the bottom of the belt at this time.

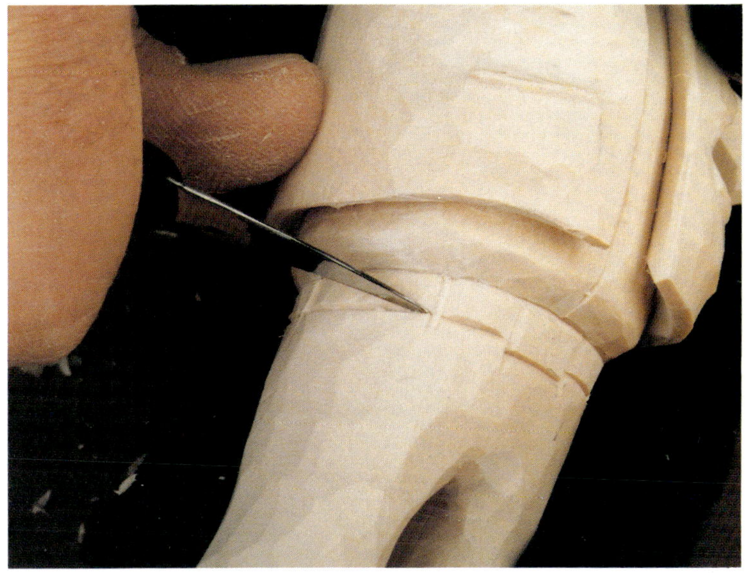

With your knife tip, press under the belt on each side of the belt loop ...

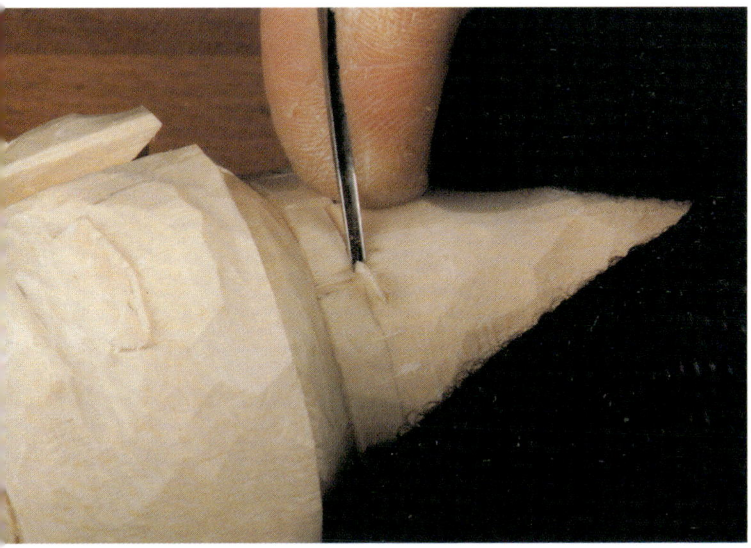

With the smallest V tool, follow the outline of the belt buckle and loops. Using the same V tool, cut in the bottom of the belt itself. Be very careful not to cut across the belt loop.

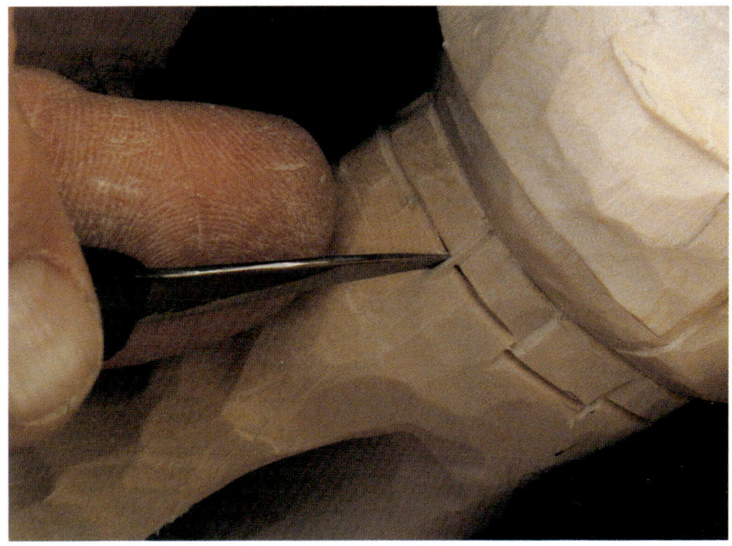

.... and along the length of the belt loop.

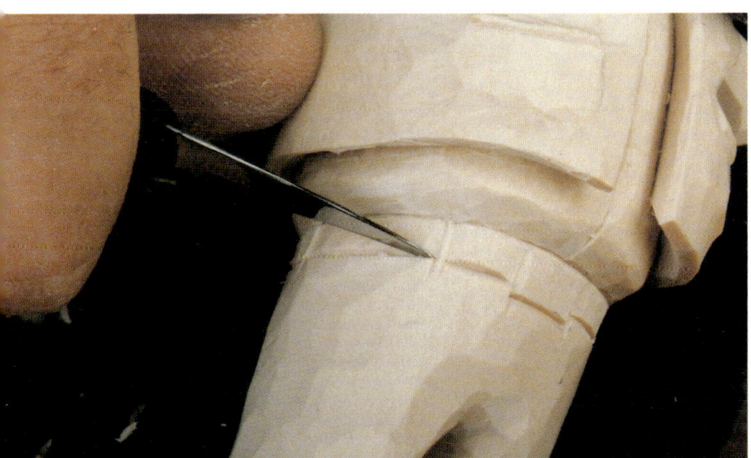

With your knife tip, gently relieve the belt on both sides of the belt buckle and each loop.

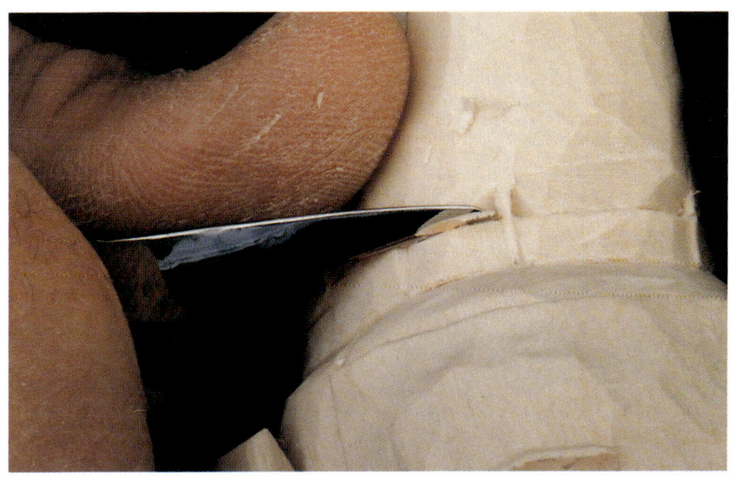

Use your knife tip to remove the triangle at the intersection of the belt loop and the bottom of the belt, leaving the pants under the belt.

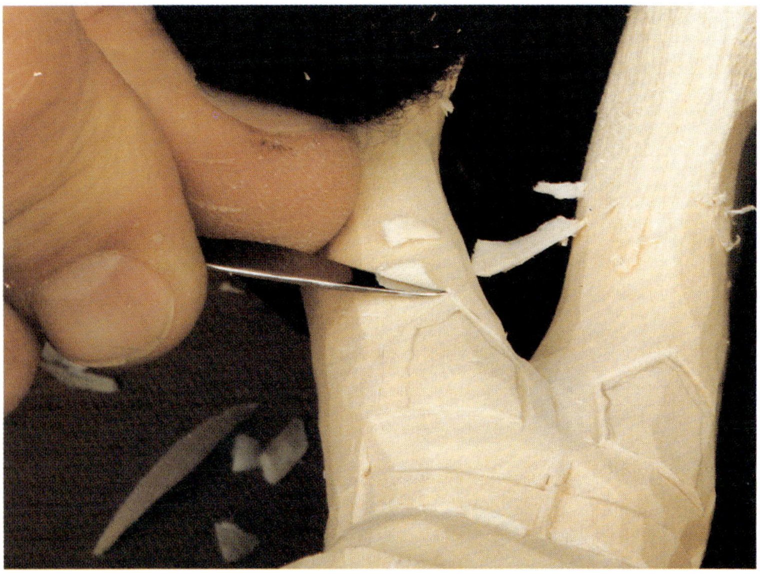

Draw in the rear pants pockets. Use your smallest V tool to cut in the lines of the pockets. Use your knife tip to relieve the wood around the pockets.

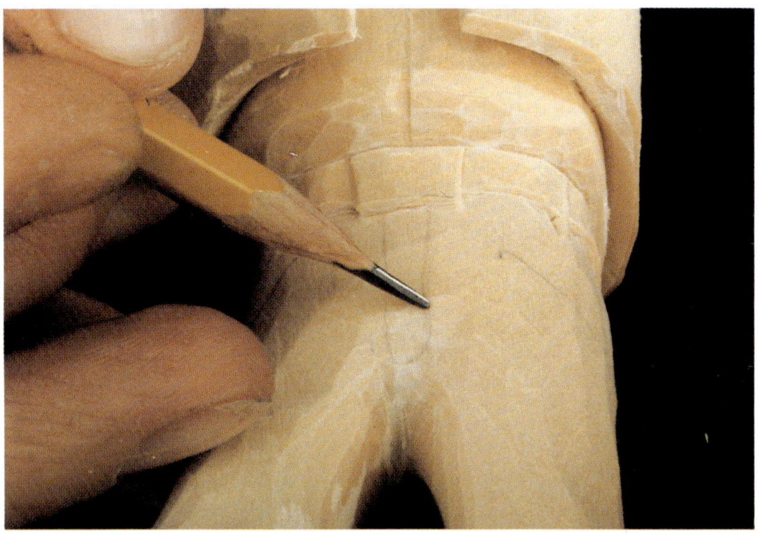

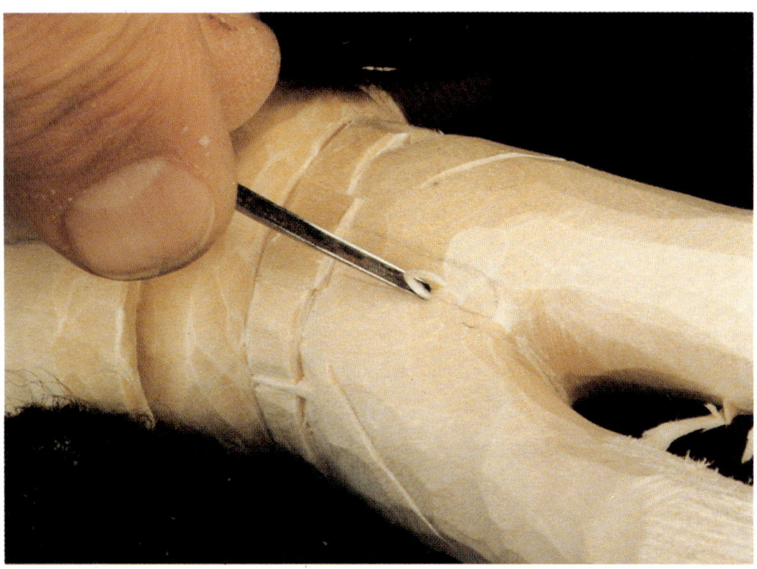

Sketch in the fly and the front pockets. Use the smallest V tool to cut around these lines.

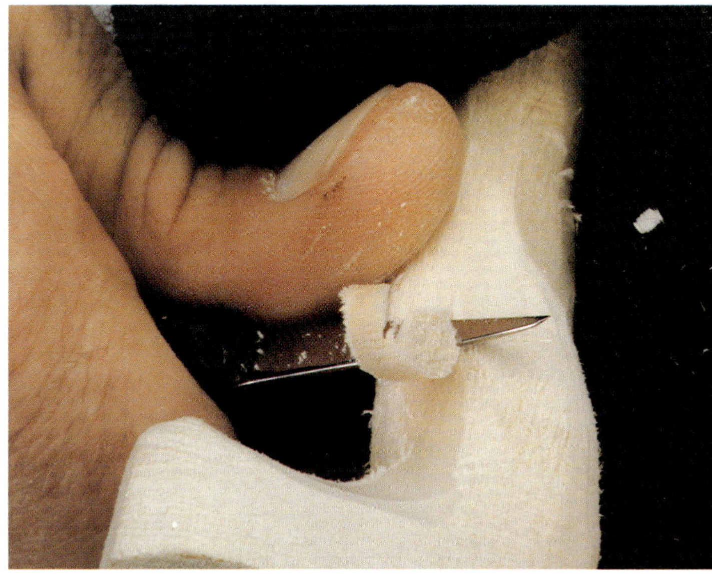

Use the detail knife to remove saw and burr marks, form the pant legs ...

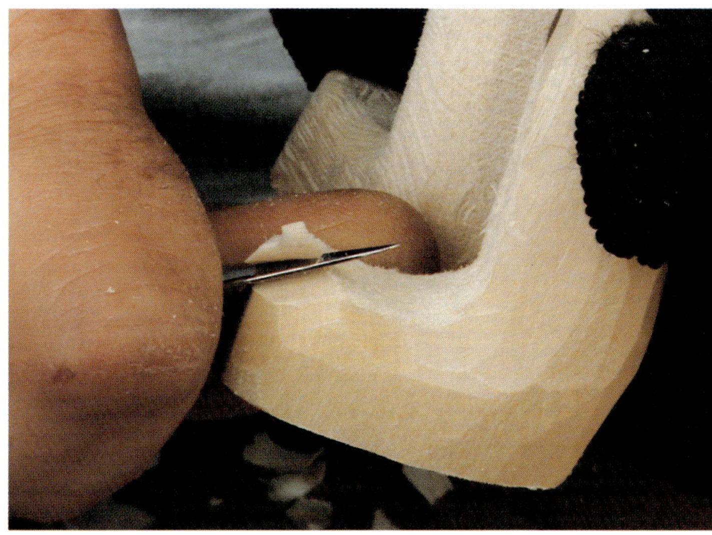

... and shape the feet.

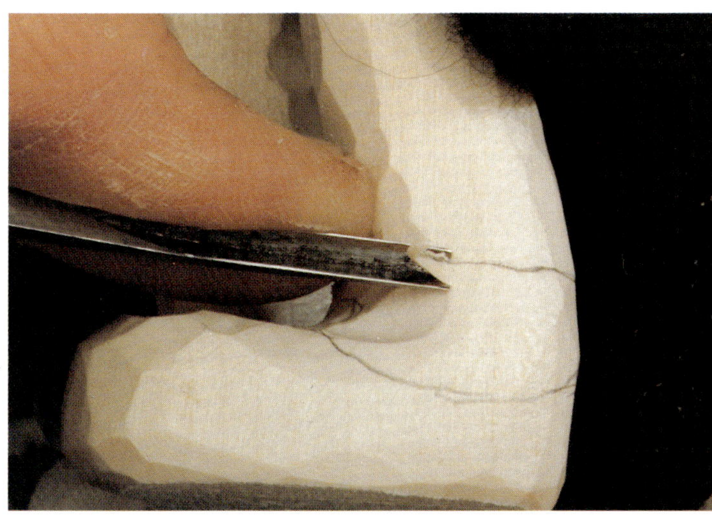

Sketch in the bottom of each pant leg and the shoe tops.

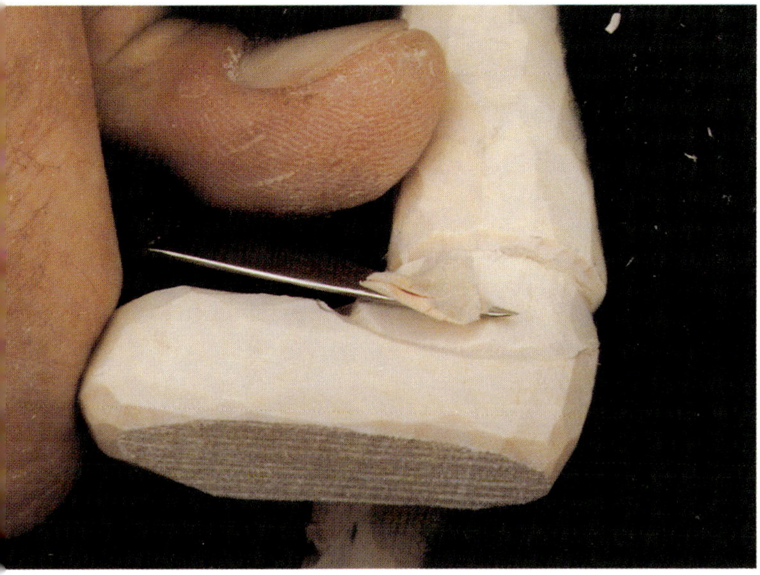

Use your 1/8" V tool to cut in the line around the bottom of each pant leg and to outline the shoe. Use your detail knife to relieve from the top of the shoe to the bottom of the pant leg, forming the ankle.

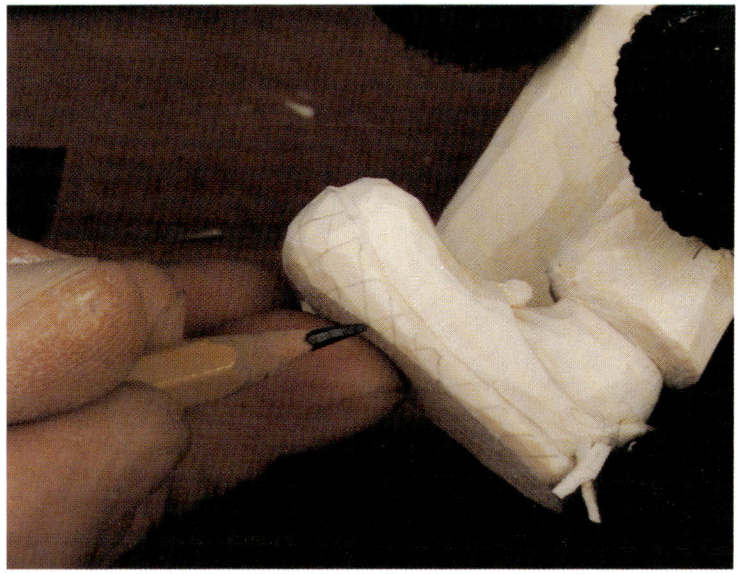

Draw some tread lines on the sole of the shoe.

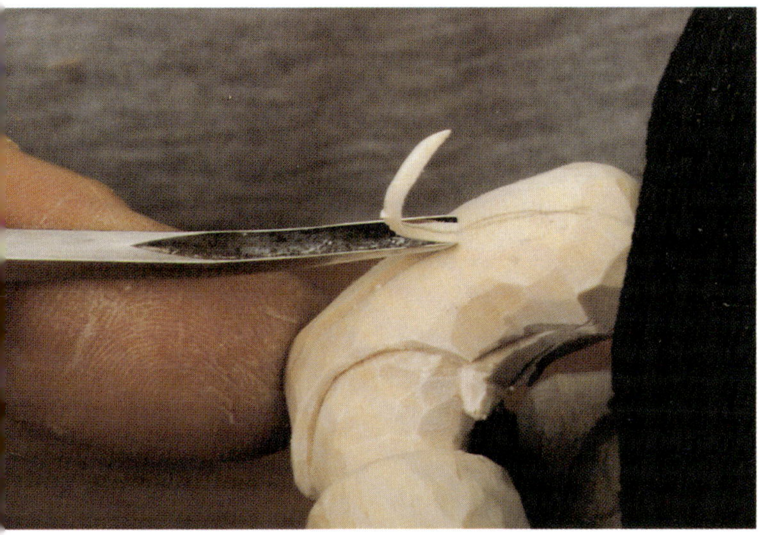

Sketch in the sole of the shoe and trace around this line with the V tool.

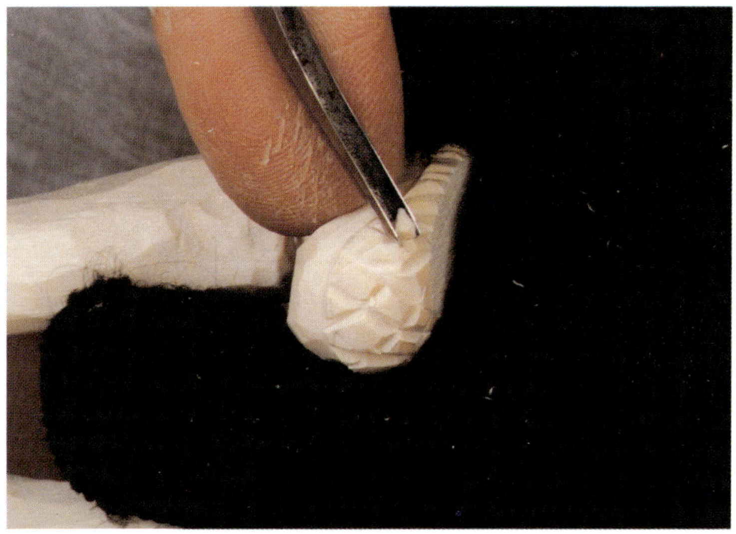

Follow these with a medium sized V tool.

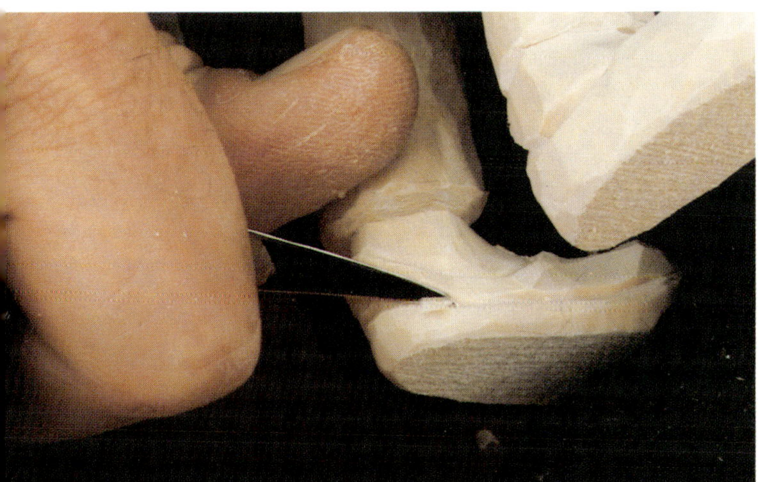

Relieve a little of the shoe above the sole line using gouges and knives, whatever suits you.

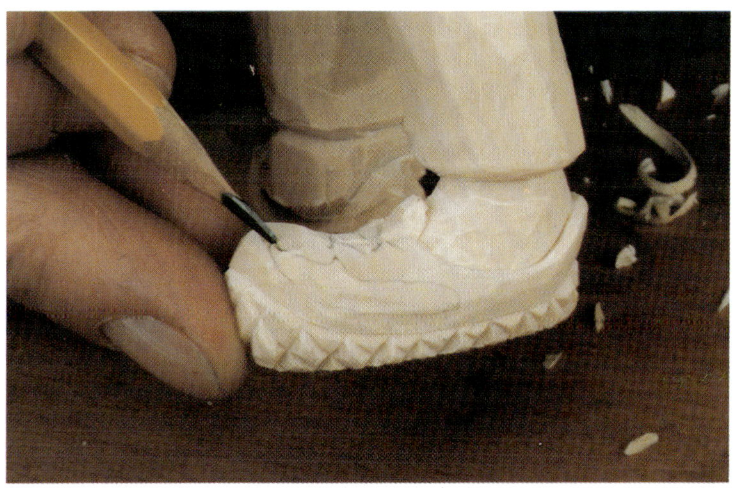

Since these are canvas shoes, we'll sketch in some kind of design. When we paint the shoe, we will have contrasting colors. Also sketch in some crossed lines indicating shoe laces.

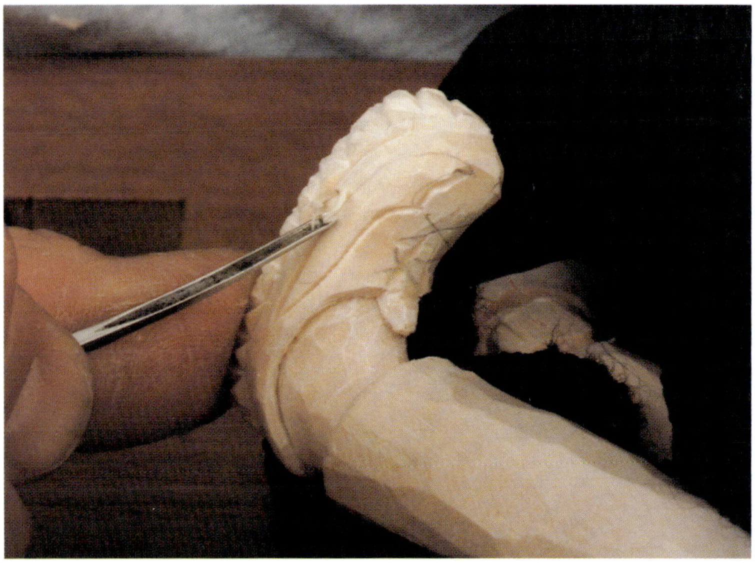

Use a small V tool to outline these details.

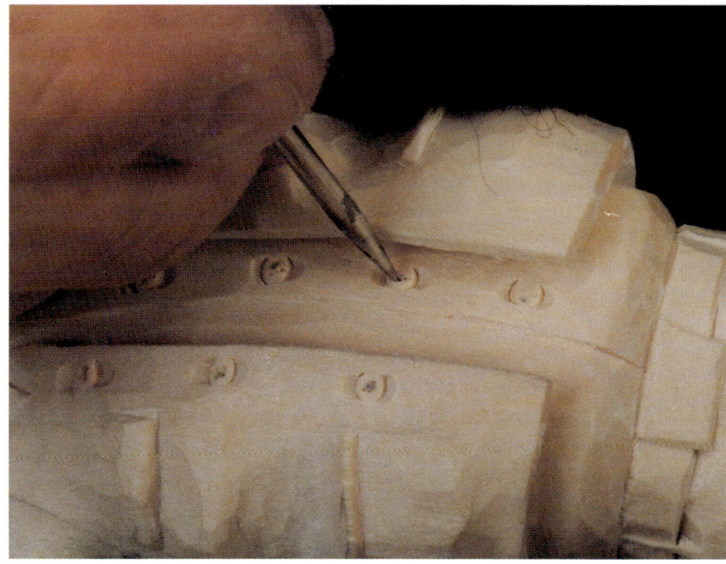

With a small awl depress several button holes into the buttons. In a similar manner, carve the buttons in the rest of the vest and the shirt.

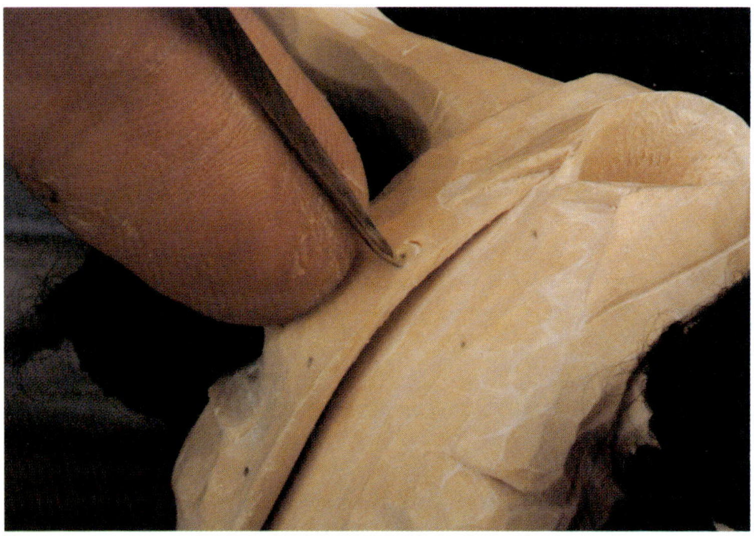

Mark the locations of buttons on the vest and shirt fronts. With your 1/8" shallow gouge, form a half moon above and below the center of each button by sticking the gouge in perpendicular to the surface of the vest.

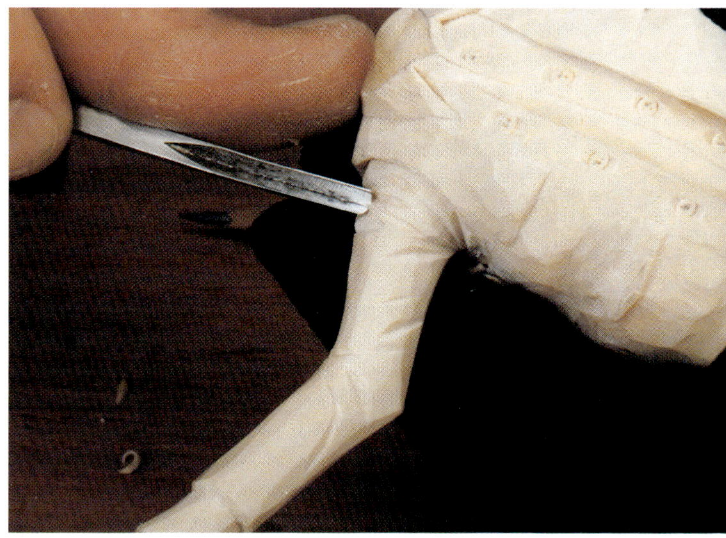

Let's add some folds to the shirt. With a 1/8" V tool, add some creases and folds along the shirt sleeves at the elbows, shoulders, and underneath each shoulder.

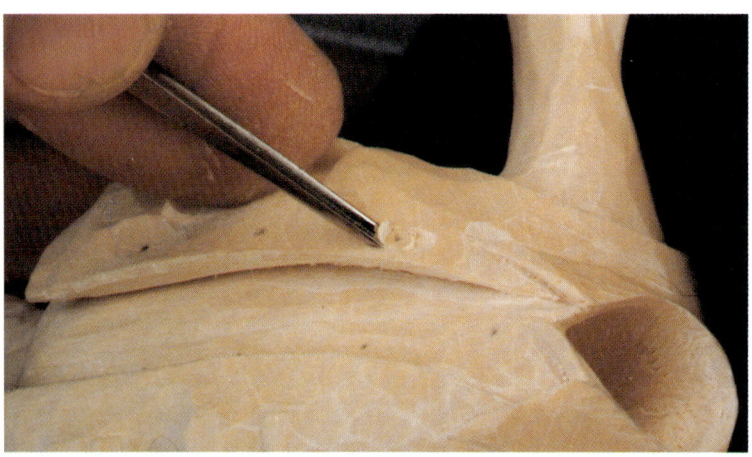

At an angle to this first gouge cut, relieve the under and upper side of the button with the same gouge.

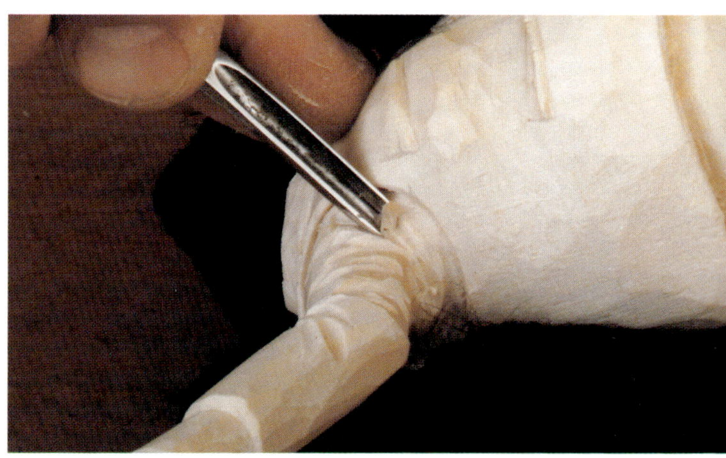

With a 3/16" gouge, deepen and widen the folds formed by the V tools.

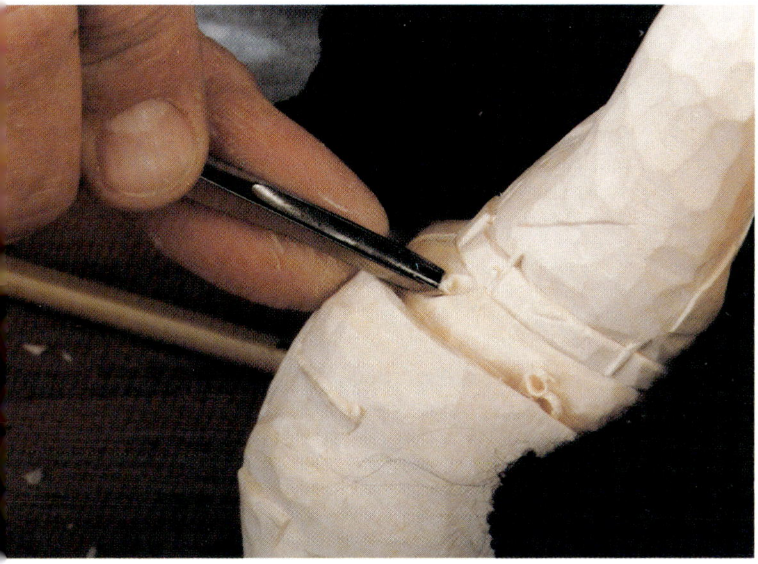

Add some folds where the shirt tucks into the pants.

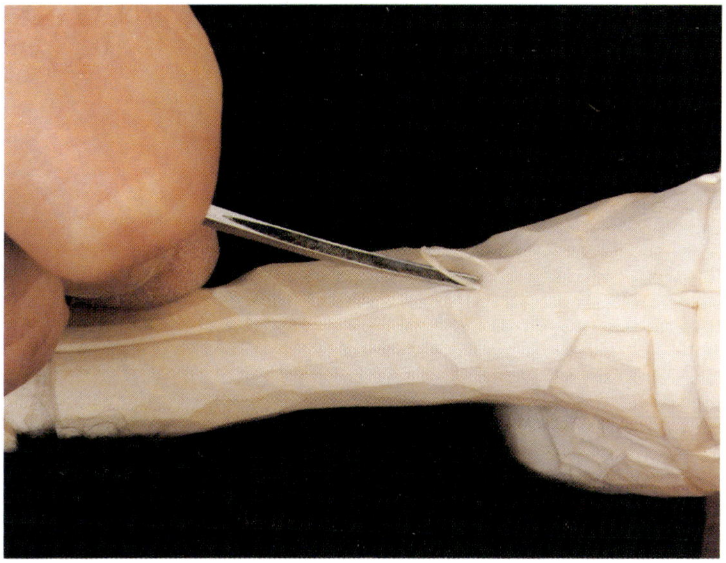

Use your V tool to form a seam up the side of the pant leg.

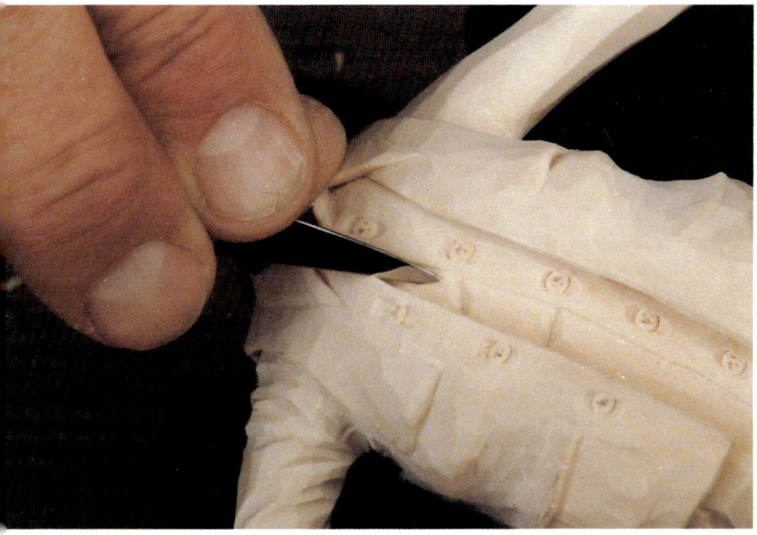

Add some folds to the front of the shirt as well.

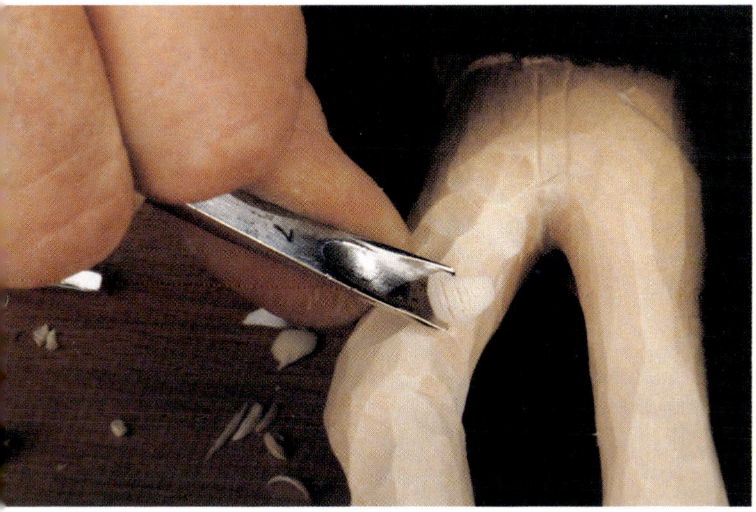

Use your knife and large gouges to form folds along each pant leg.

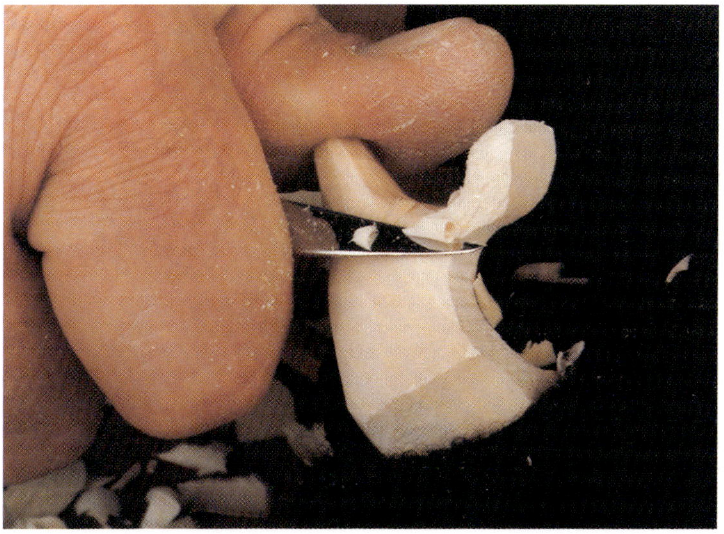

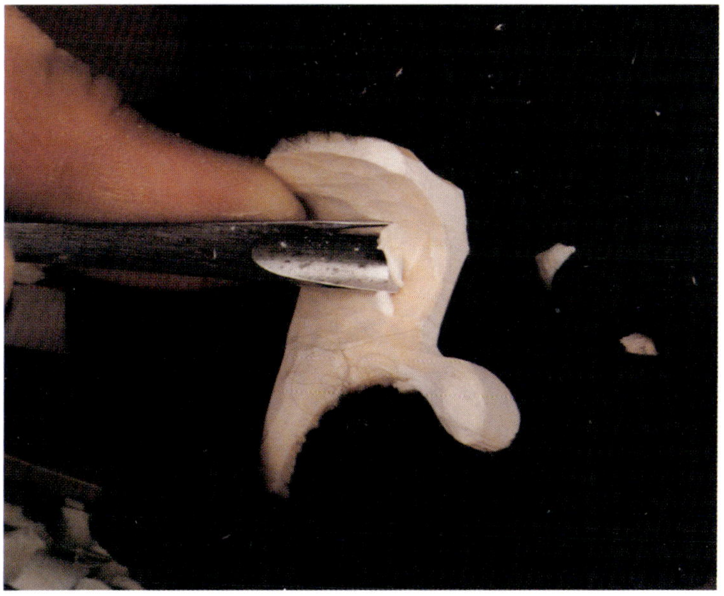

Using your knife blade and gouges, remove saw and burr marks from each hand while finishing the forming of the hands.

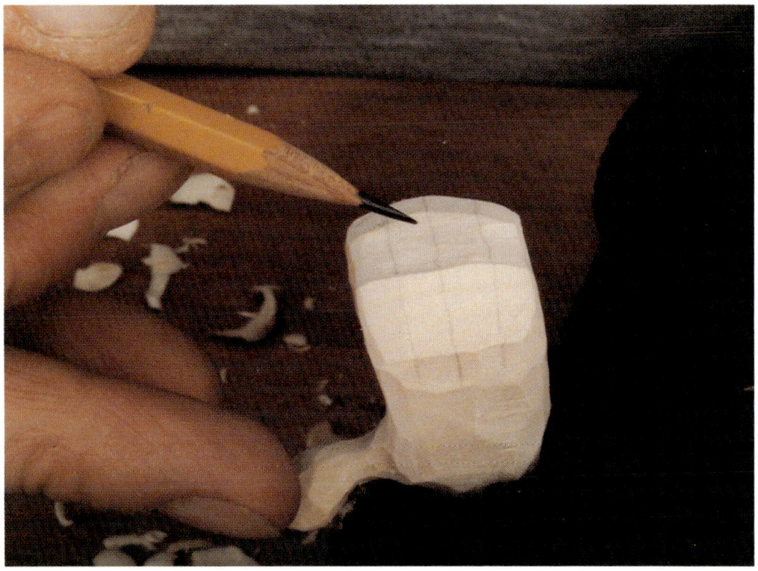

Draw in the fingers.

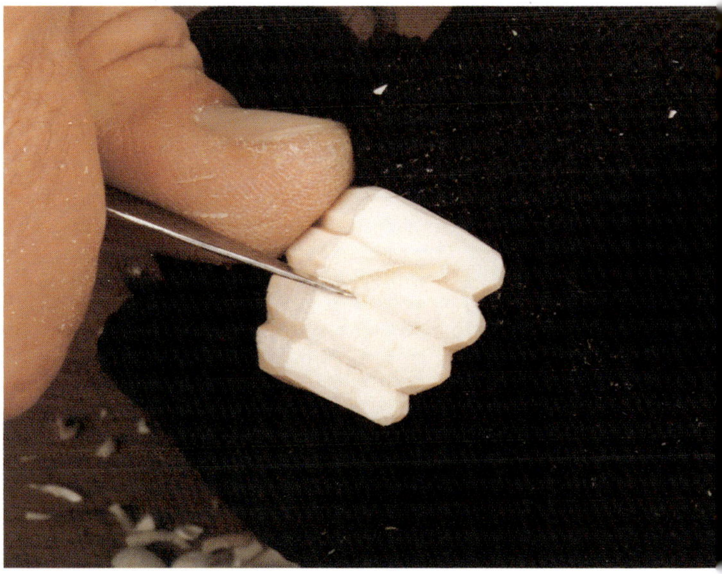

Round the fingers with your knife tip.

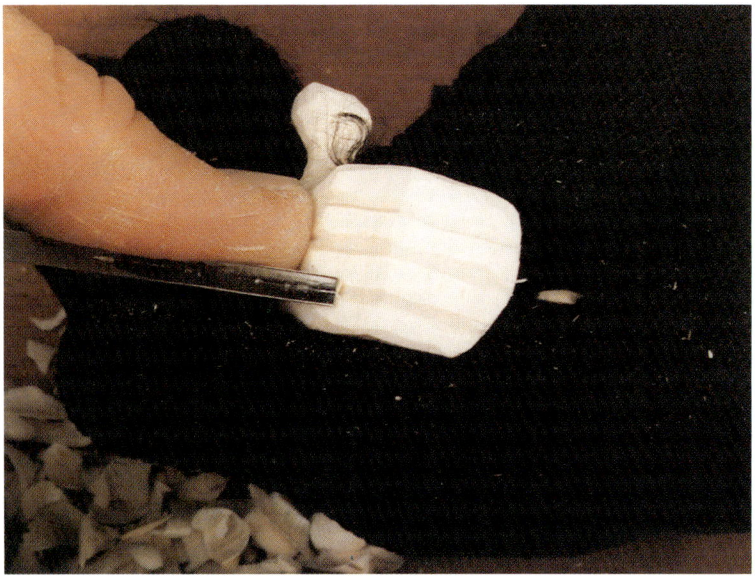

Follow the lines of the fingers with the 1/8" V tool.

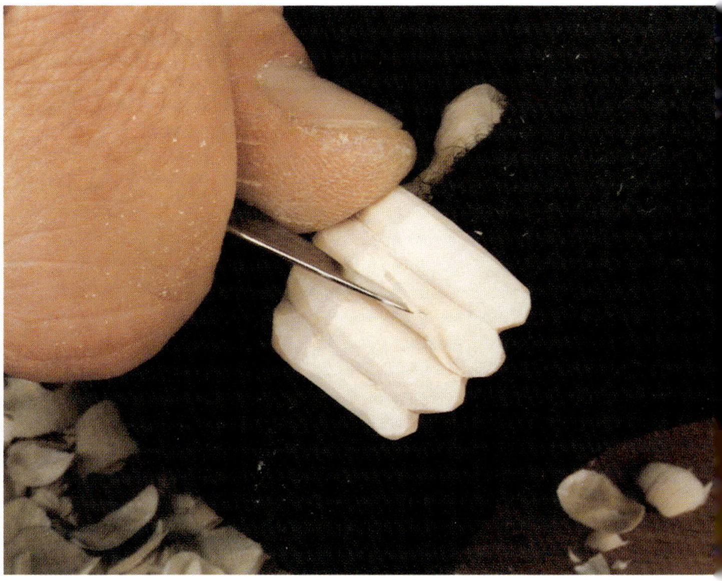

Accent the space between the fingers with a very deep cut on either side of the fingers.

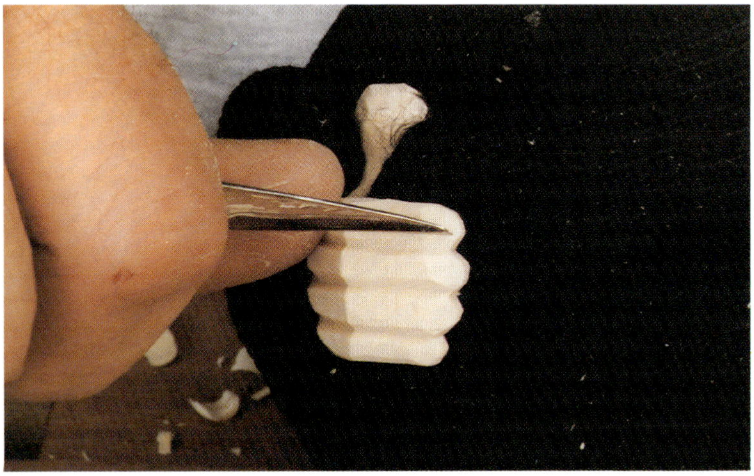

Shape the ends of the fingers with your knife.

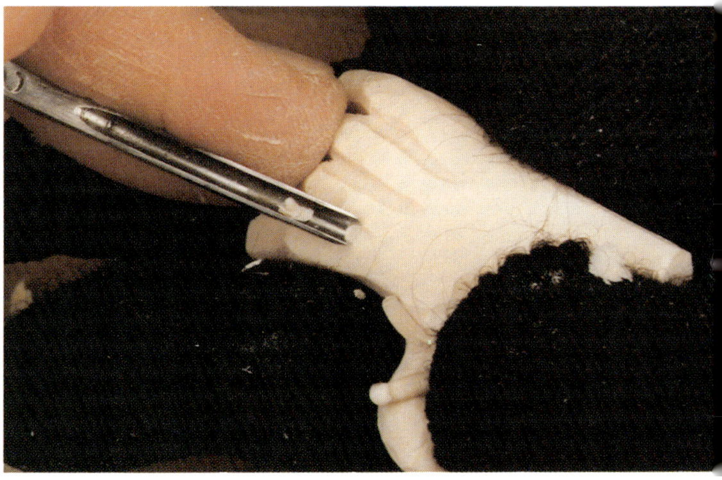

To simulate ligaments on the back side of hand, use a deep gouge.

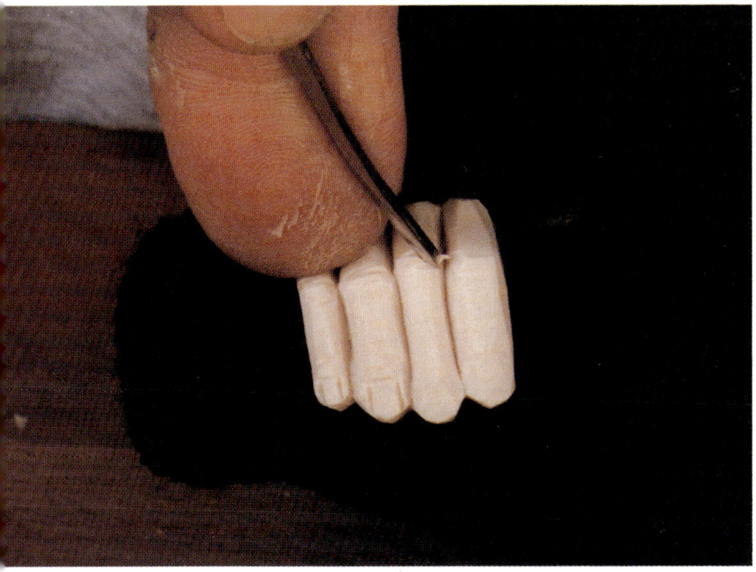

Use your small V tool to cut around the fingernails and along the knuckles of the fingers.

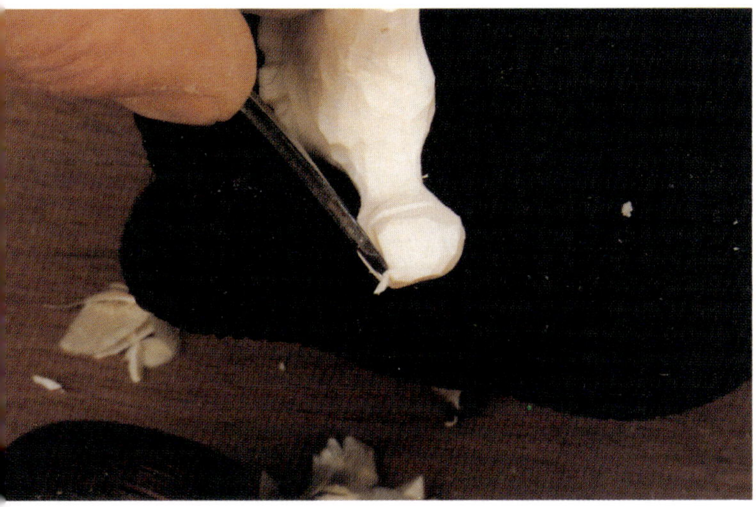

Don't forget to carve the nails.

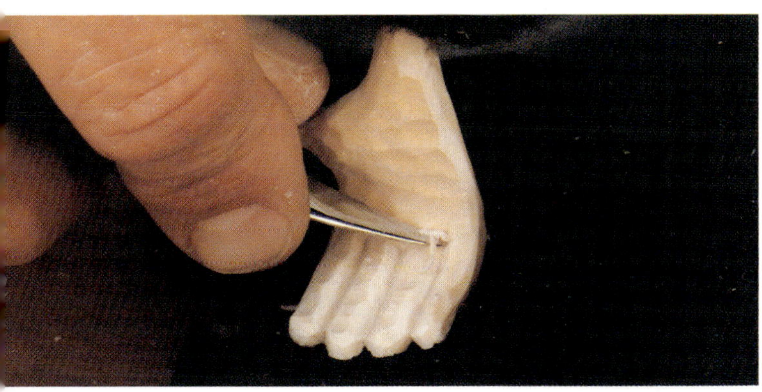

Since the fingers will be seen from the inside of the hand as well, you will need to carve them in using similar techniques to those you used on the outside of the hand. A V tool was used to separate the fingers and the knife tip was used to round the fingers along the edges of the cuts.

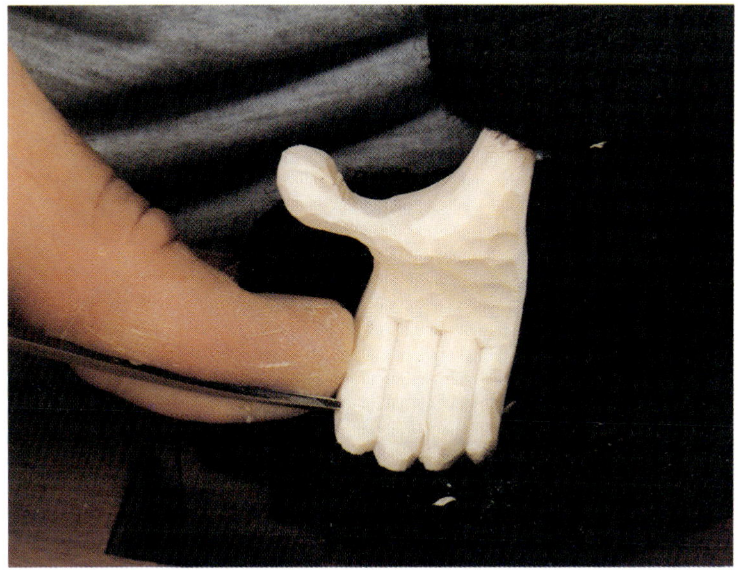

Use your smallest V tool on the inside of each hand to carve the folds opposite to the knuckles. For those of you concerned about the amount of life remaining for this liar after telling his tale to trusted friends, use this same V tool to indicate a short life line along the palm.

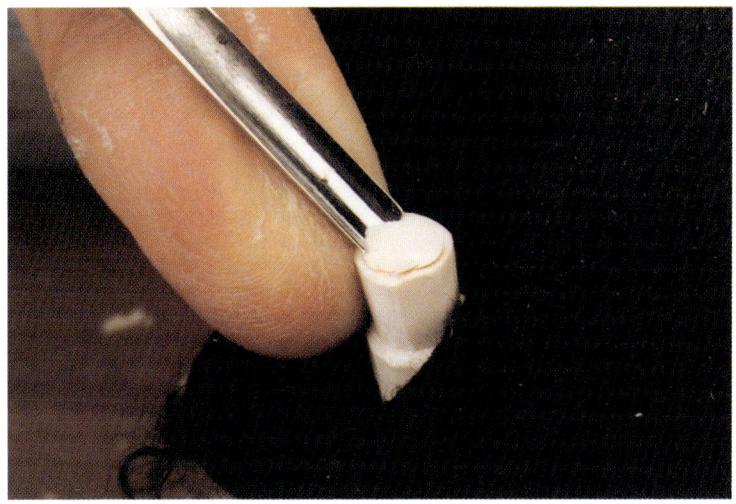

To prepare the cuff to receive the carved hand, use a shallow gouge to outline the diameter of the wrist at the cuff line.

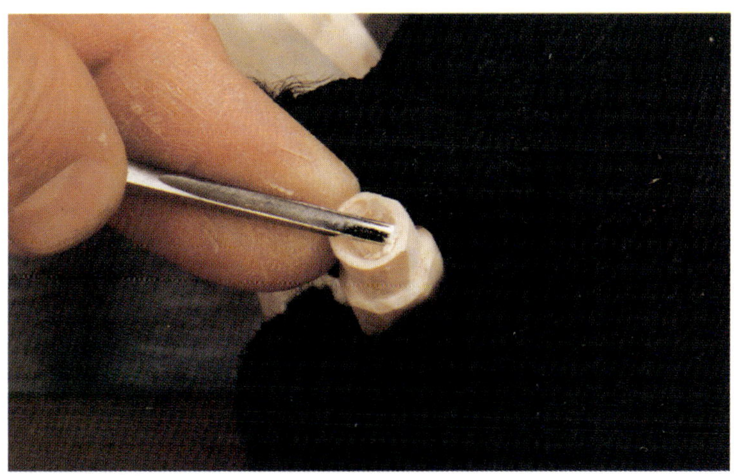

Continue digging into the cuff to a depth of about 1/8". Be extremely careful not to chip the cuff.

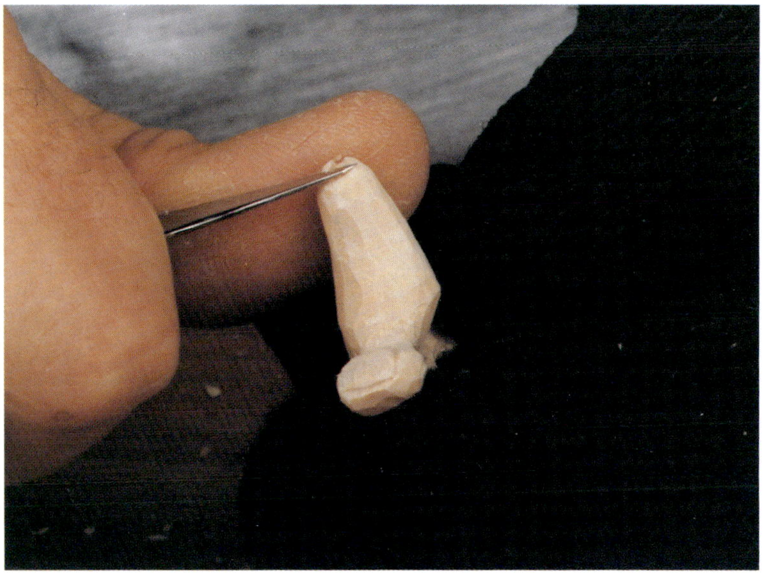

Shape the end of the wrist that fits into the cup into a dome shape.

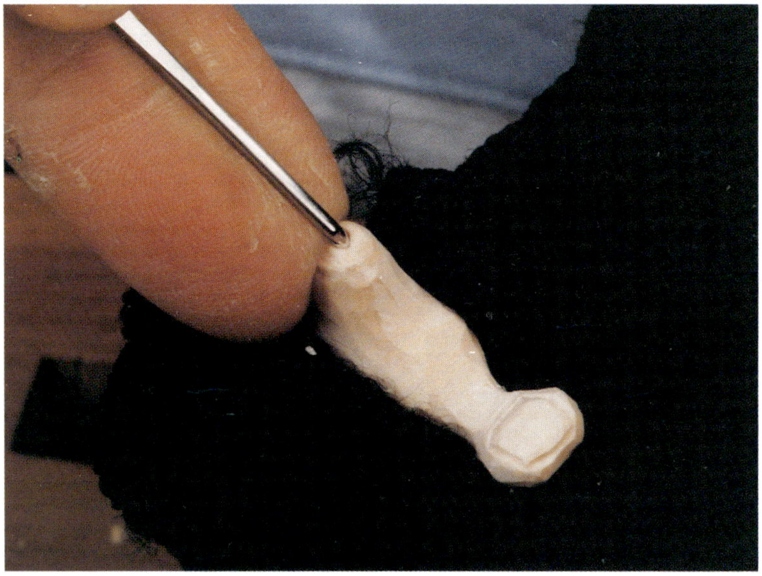

This next step is not absolutely necessary but I like to insert a dowel made from a small toothpick into both the cuff and the hand. This gives a little more support to an otherwise weak area. With a 1/16" shallow gouge, drill a hole into the wrist portion of the hand and into the cuff.

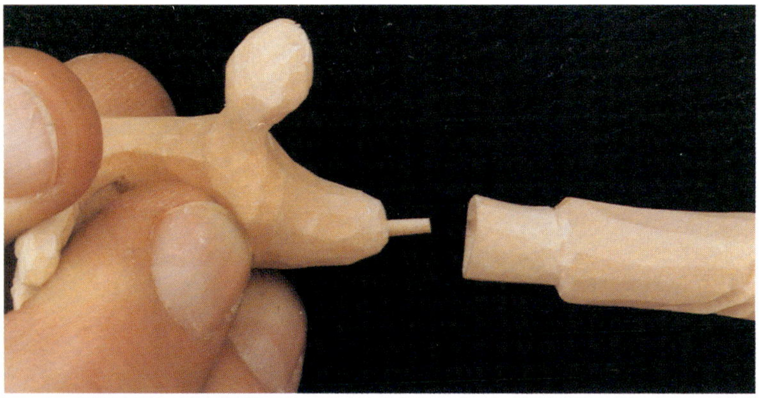

Insert a small portion of the toothpick dowel into the hole in the wrist, place a small amount of Elmer's glue into the dowel and then place both into the cuff.

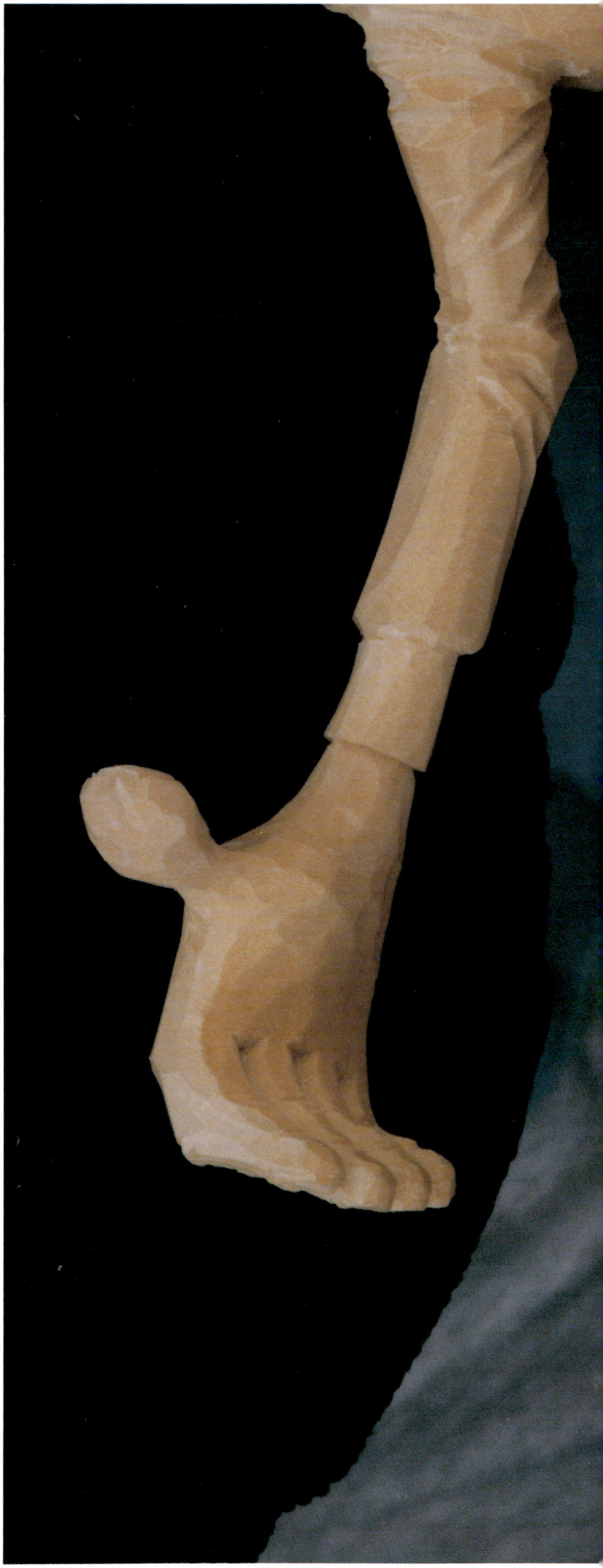

Insert the hand into the cuff.

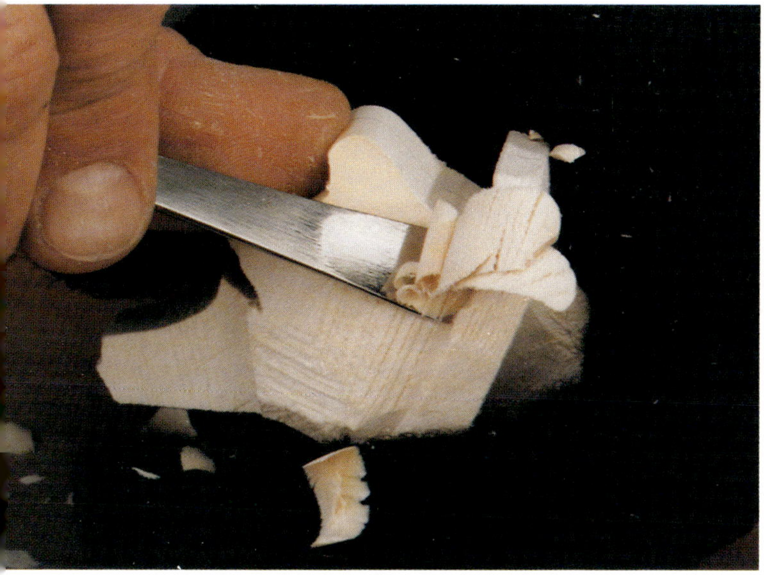

Use the 1/2" fishtail gouge to remove wood along the underside of the hat brim and along the side of the head. Begin shaping the head so that, when it is viewed from the neck up toward the hat brim, it will appear as an oval. In the front of the head, the gouge strokes should be made from the bottom of the head toward the top.

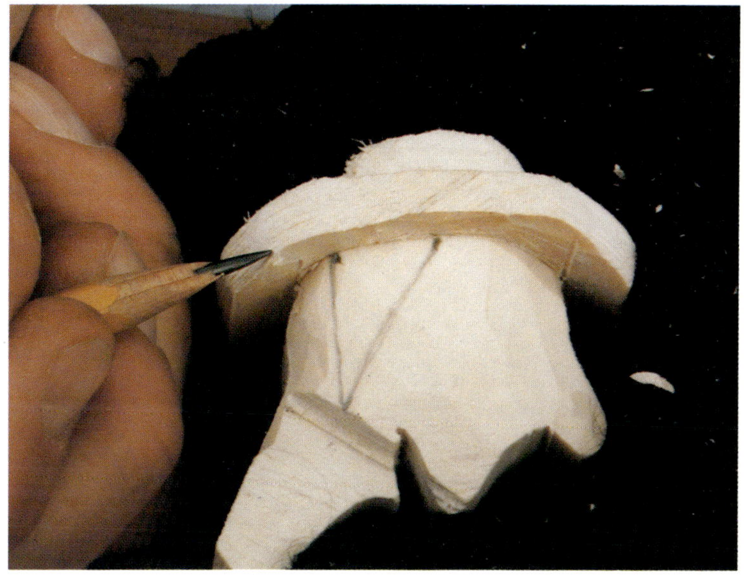

Place a third point along the bottom of the hat brim about 1/2" behind the first mark. Connect this point with the one at the bottom of the head, forming a triangle which will later be carved into an ear. Repeat this same process on the other side of the head.

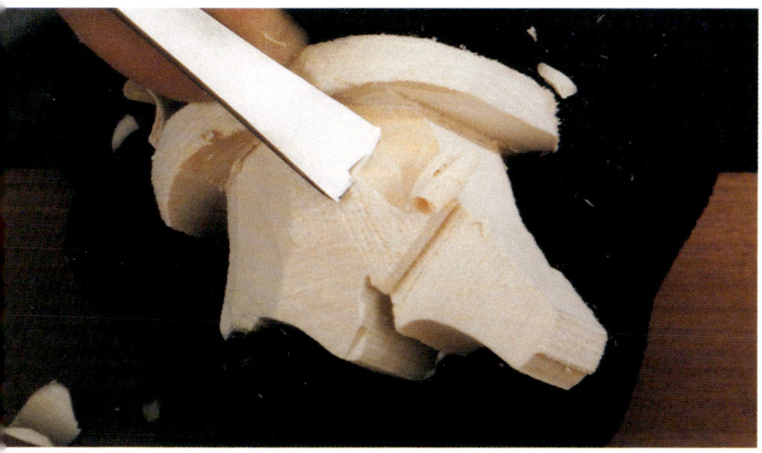

In the back of the head, the cuts made by the 1/2" fishtail gouge should be made from the hat brim toward the neck. This keeps your strokes following the orientation of the grain.

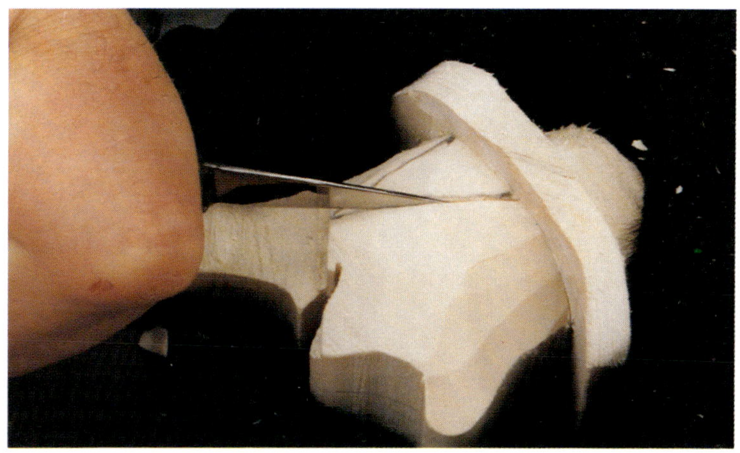

With your detail knife, score along both lines of the triangle ...

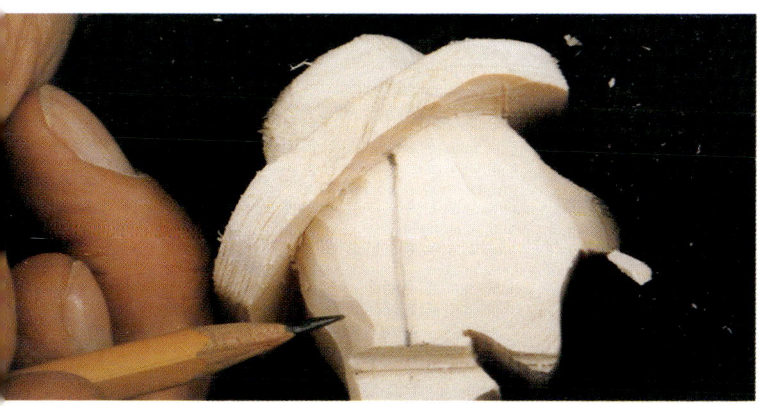

Place a mark along the underside of the hat brim that is half the distance from the front of the head to the back of the head. Place a mark along the neck at the bottom of the head that is half the width of the neck. Connect these two points with a line.

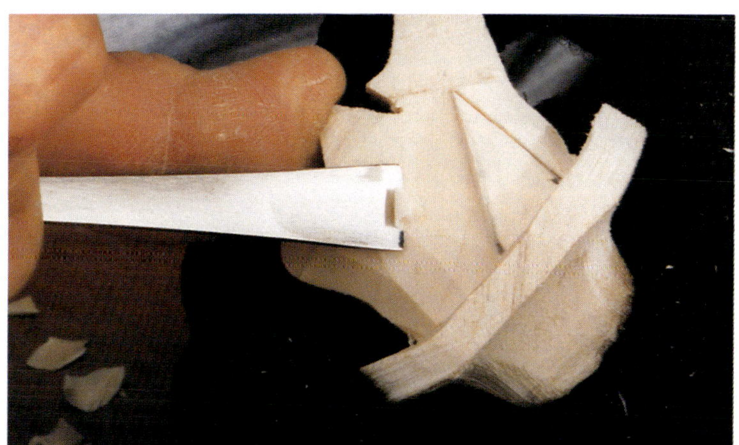

... and remove the wood in front of the ear mound with the fishtailed gouge.

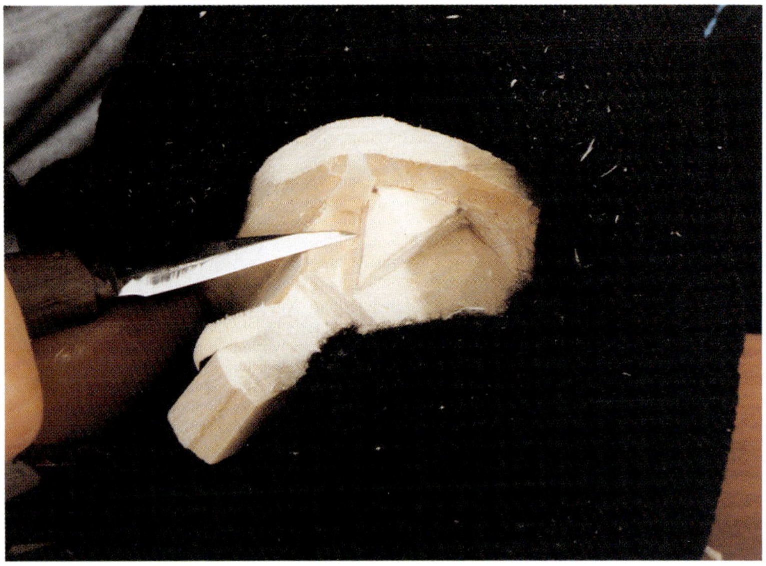

Remove the wood behind the ear mound with your knife. Remember to make your cuts from the hat brim toward the neck.

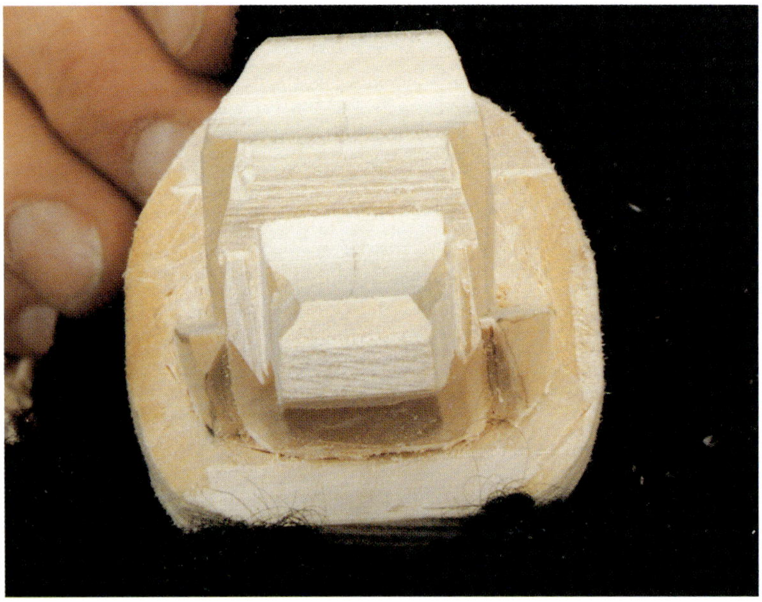

This shot shows the location of the ear mounds on both sides of the head when viewed from the neck toward the hat brim. Note also the oval shape of the head that we have obtained so far.

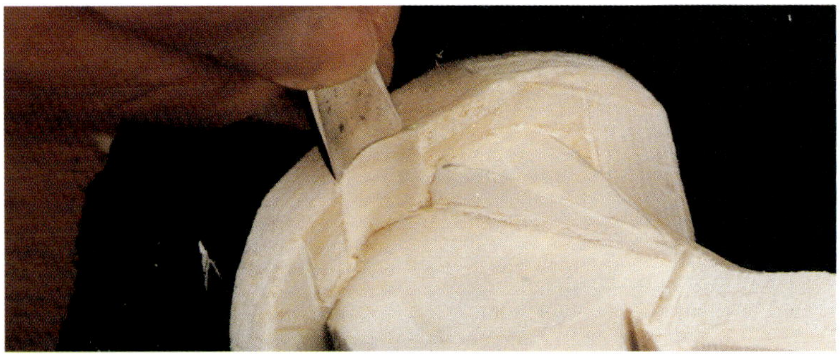

At this point we need to leave the head and outline the scalloped shape of the hat brim with a large #7 gouge. We will do this by cutting parallel to the bottom of the hat brim to a depth that does not cut into the head.

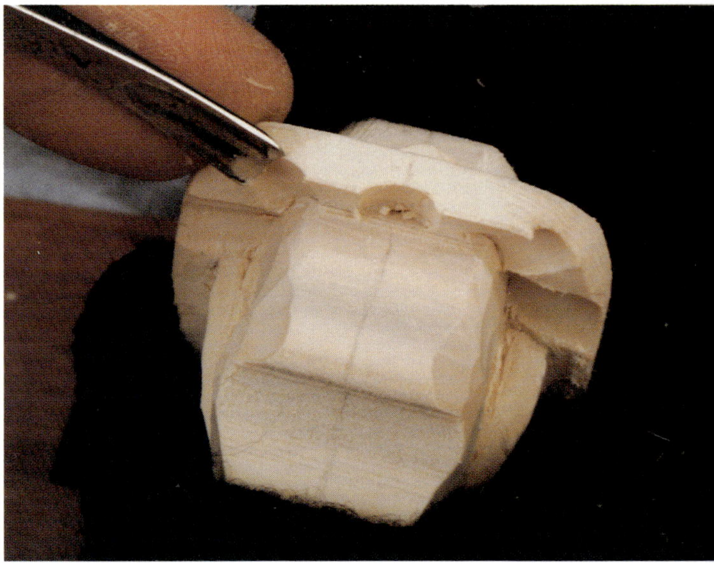

Working around the perimeter of the head, continue this scalloping of the hat brim.

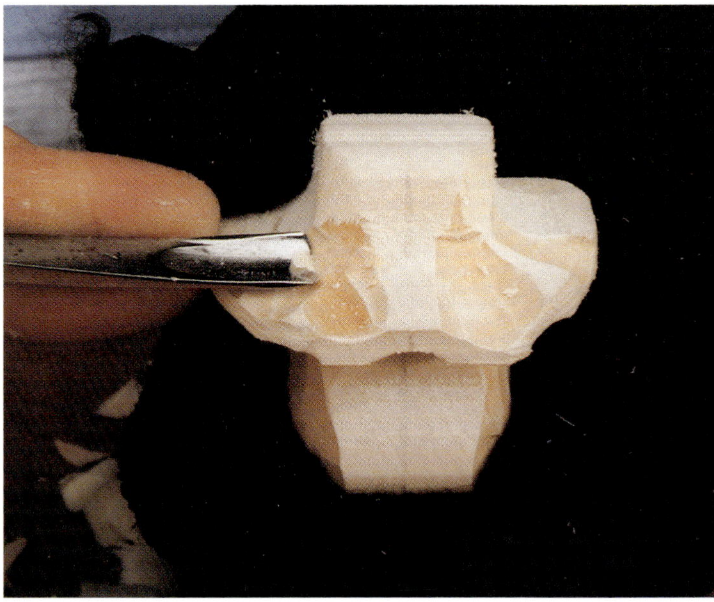

Once you have completed the scalloping along the bottom side of the hat brim, move to the top of the brim and alternate similar cuts with those under the hat brim to create the wavy fishing hat brim.

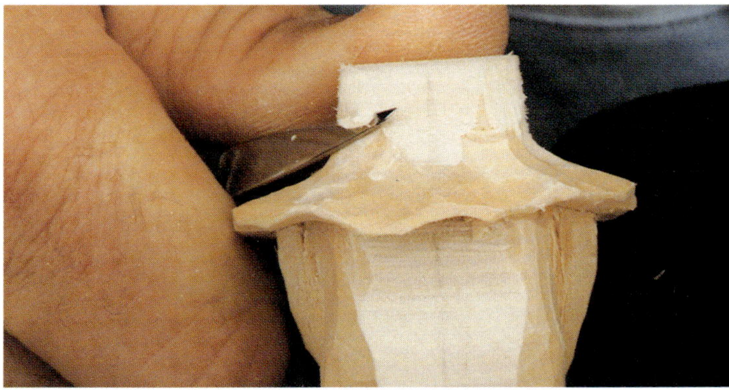

Here we've knocked off the sharp edges and further shaped the hat brim.

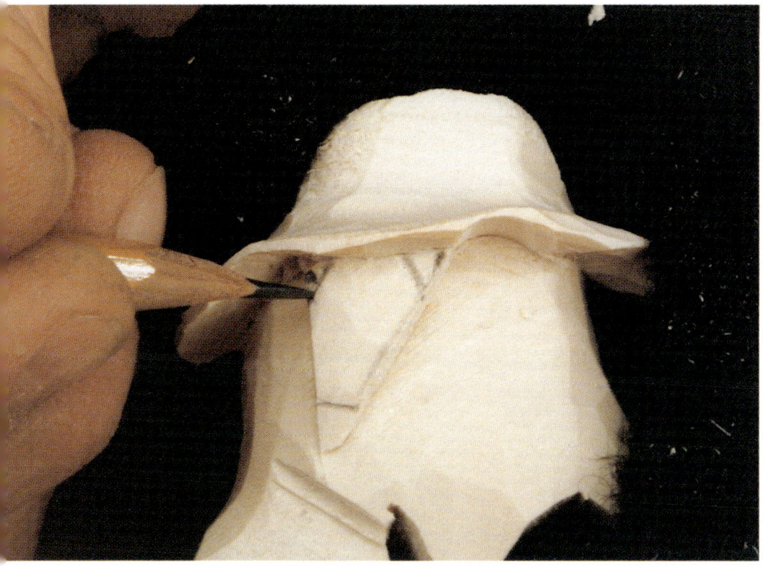

Now we can go back to the ears and detail them. Mark small triangles to be notched out as shown.

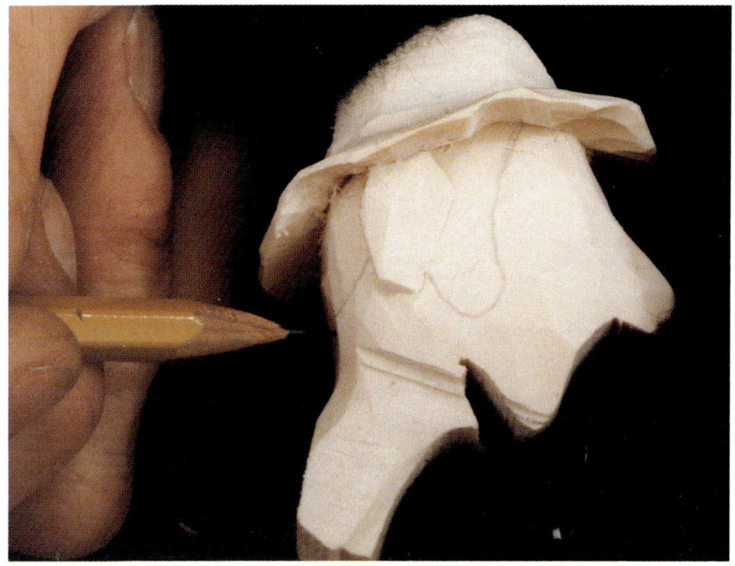

At this point we need to draw in the sideburns and the back of the hair line.

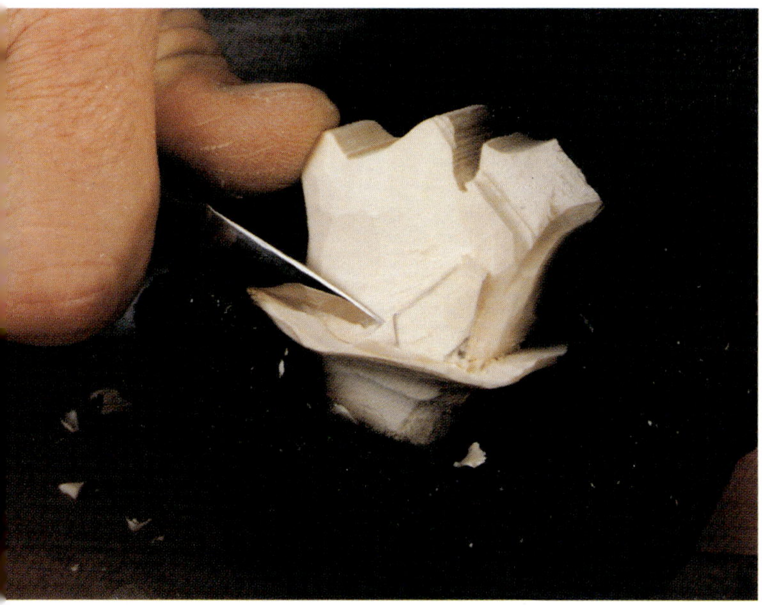

Notch out the triangles using your knife tip.

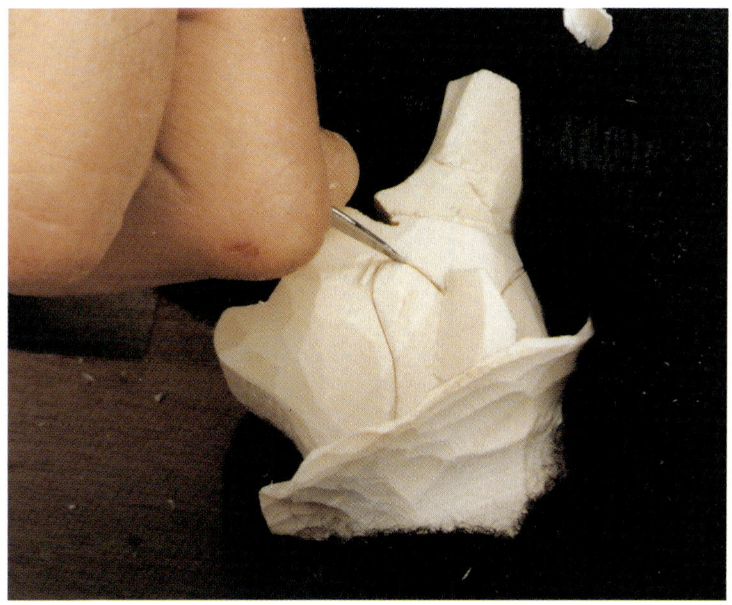

With your knife tip perpendicular to the side of the head, score around the hairline, the back of the head, and along the sideburns.

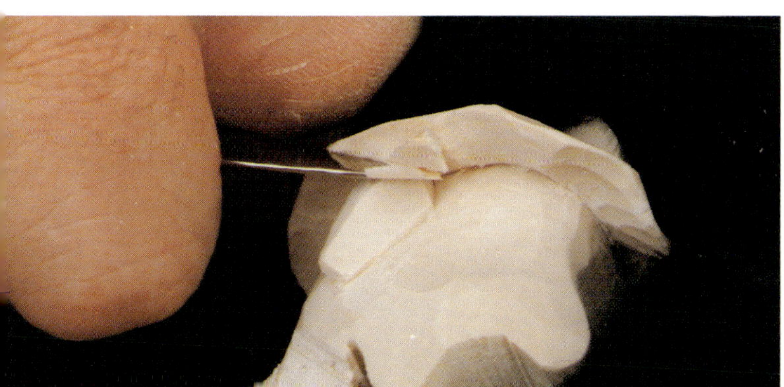

With your knife tip at about a 30 degree angle to the side of the head, remove the front edge of the ear mound.

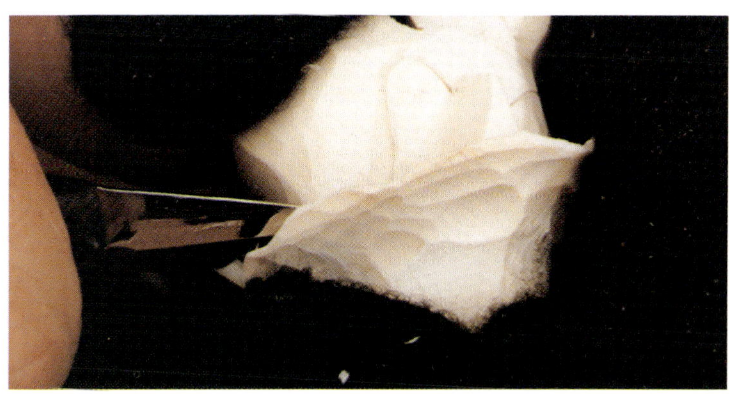

Relieve the side of the head to the depth of the scored line.

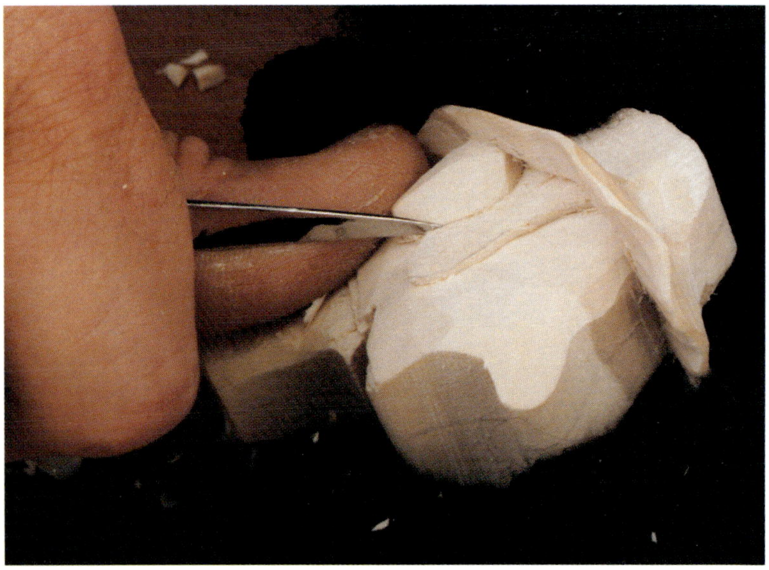

Score along the front of the ear to the same depth as the scored front of the sideburn.

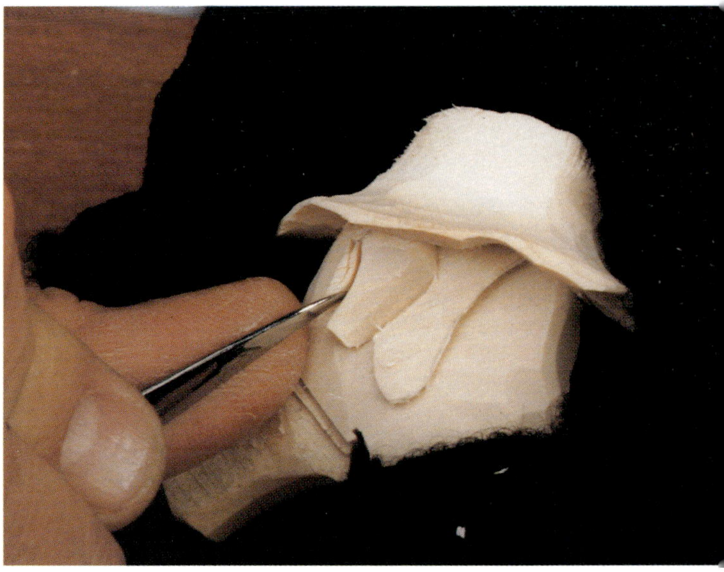

Let's also cup the back of the ear so that it looks a little like a question mark.

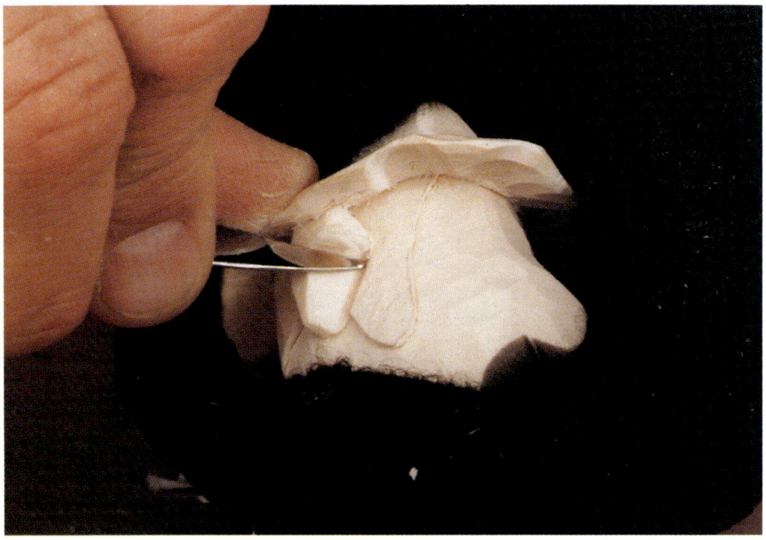

Remove wood along the ear to the depth of the newly scored line.

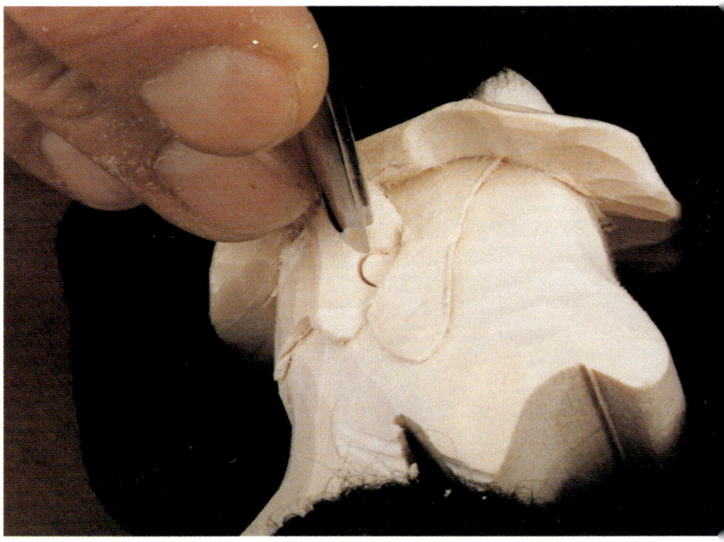

With a 3/16" deep gouge push directly into the ear, forming the tragus.

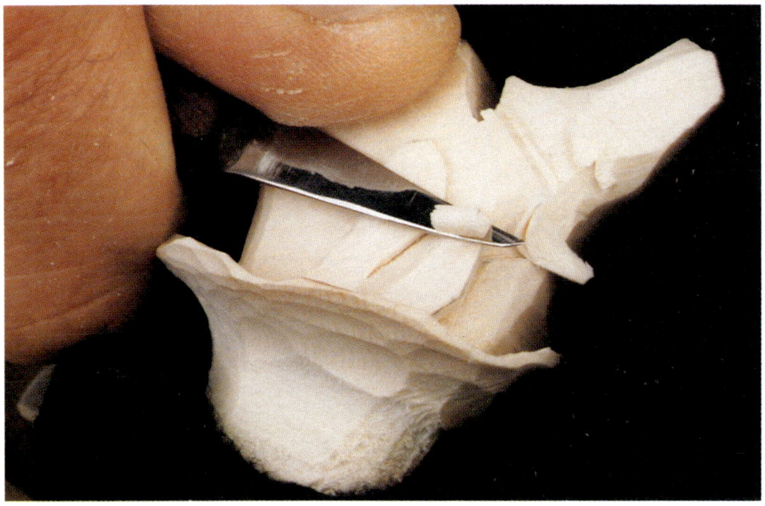

With the detail knife, cup the side of the ear to give it a little character when viewed from the front.

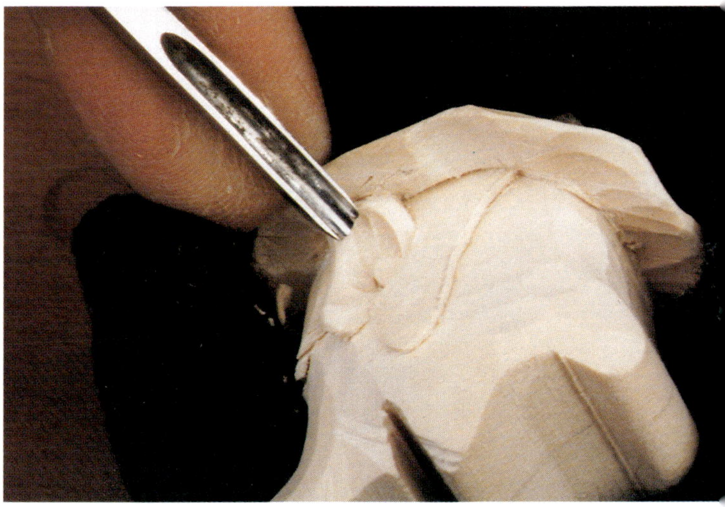

Using the same gouge, relieve the inside of the ear to the depth of the tragus gouge cut.

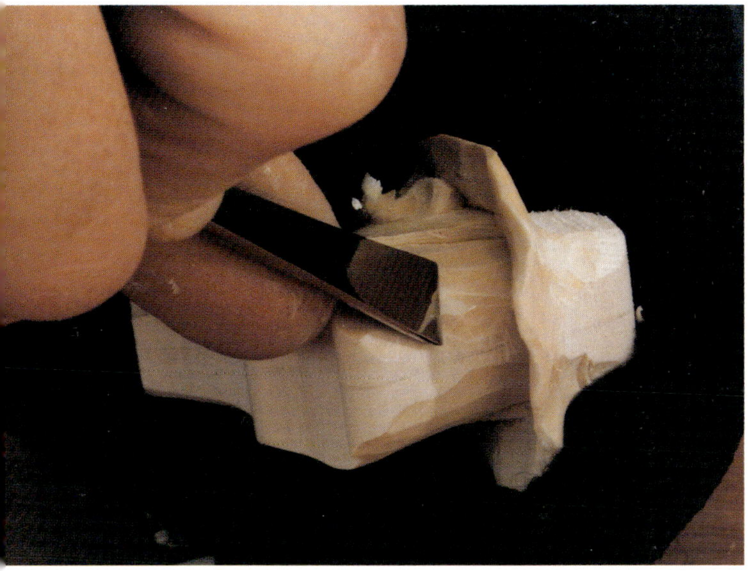

With a 1/2" fishtail gouge, finish forming the front of the head into an oval.

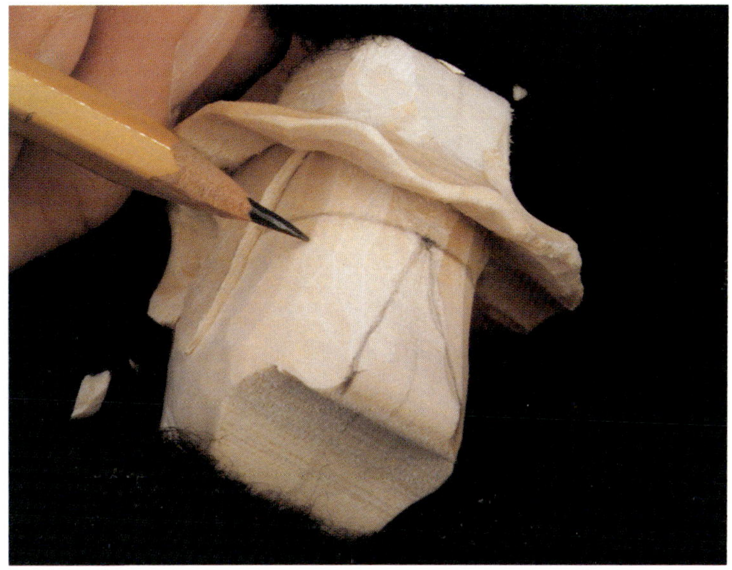

Draw the eyebrow line from the centerline of the head to each sideburn as shown.

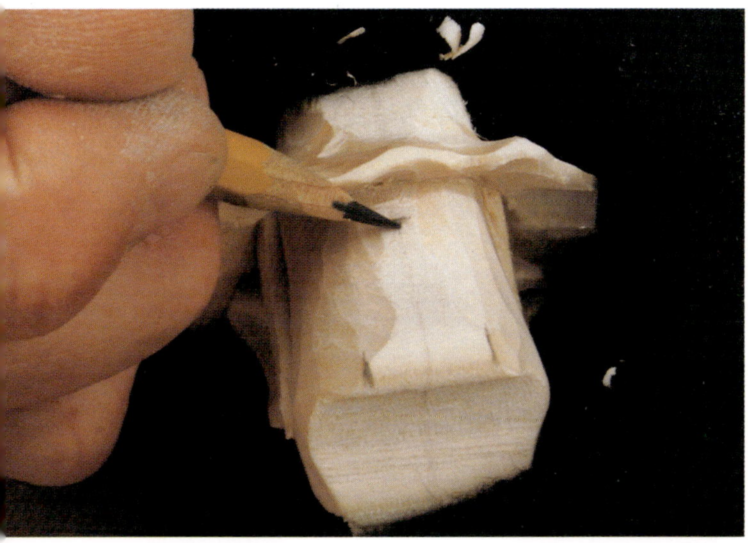

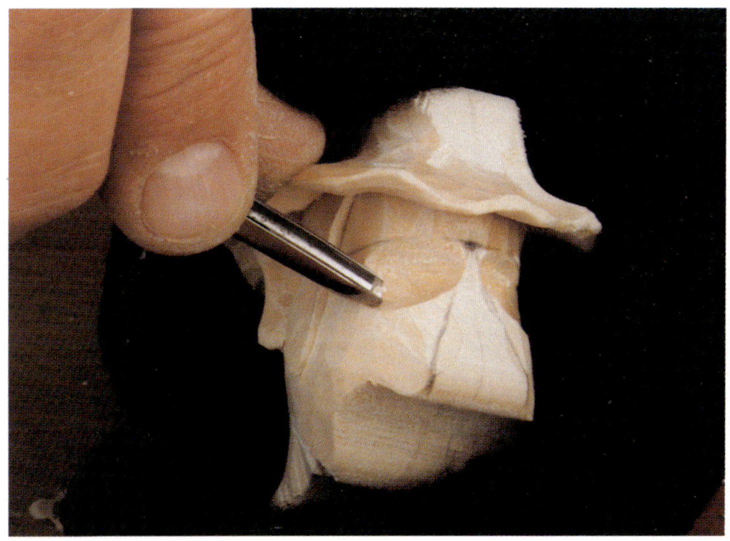

Using the 3/16" deep gouge, form the cavities below the eyebrows and along the sides of the nose into which the eye will eventually be carved.

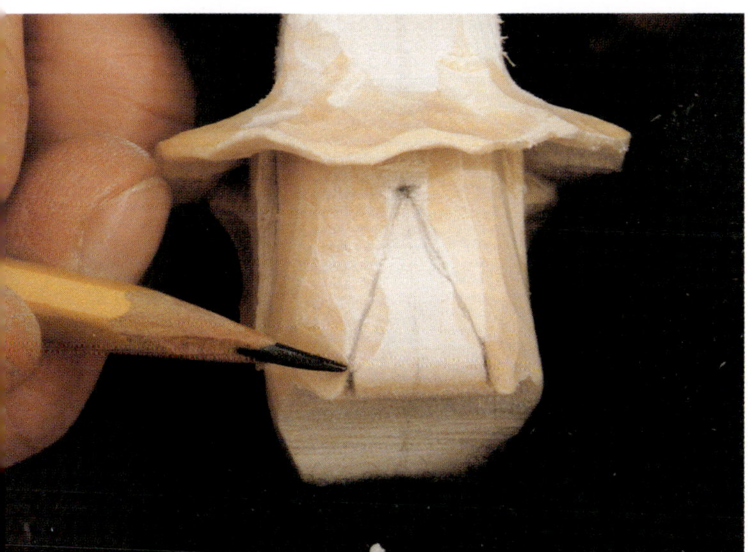

Place a point about 3/16" below the edge of the hat brim along the centerline of the face. Mark the width of the nose below. Connect these three points to form the triangle shown.

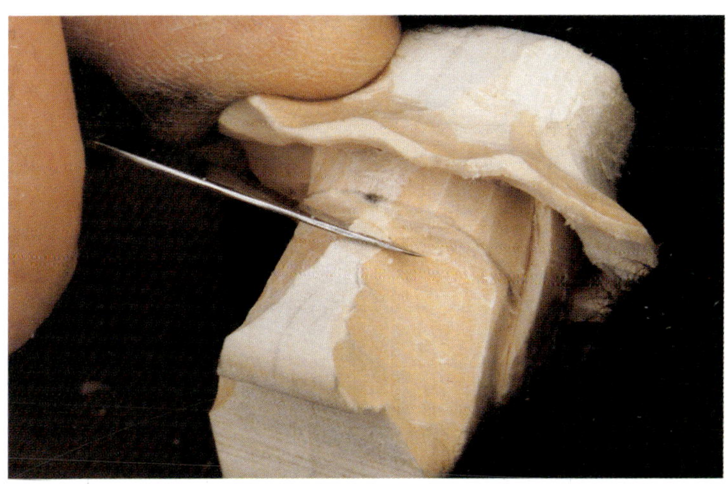

Notch the upper part of the nose to form the bridge.

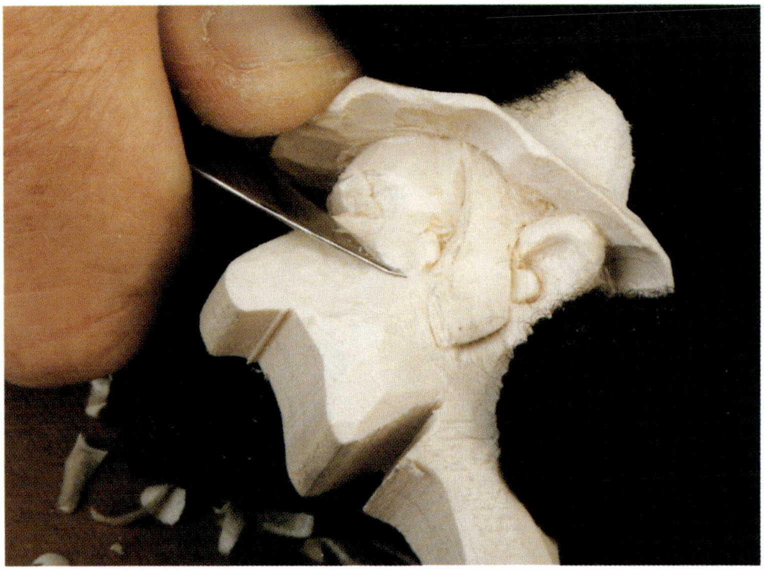

Begin rounding the cheek area on either side of the mouth and along the sideburns.

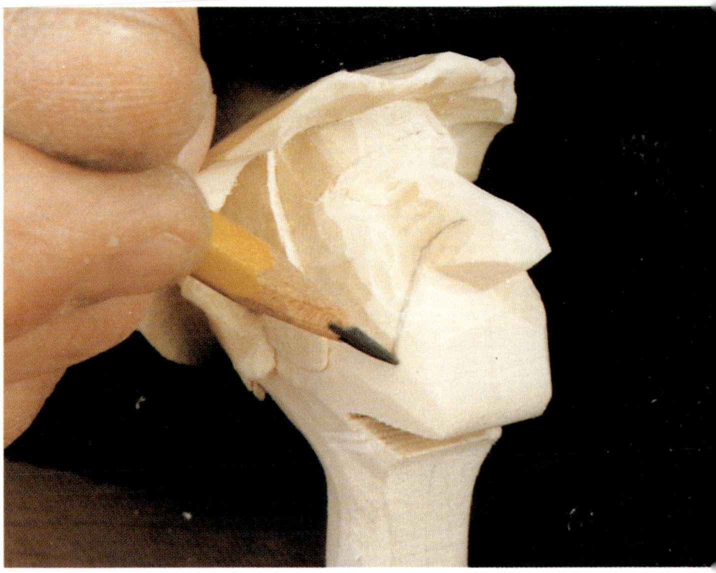

Sketch in smile lines.

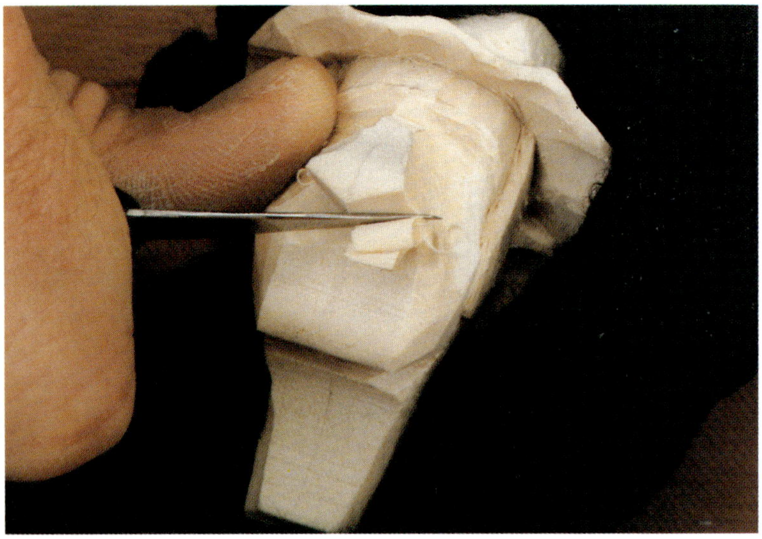

With the detail knife, clip the bottom of the nose at the angle shown.

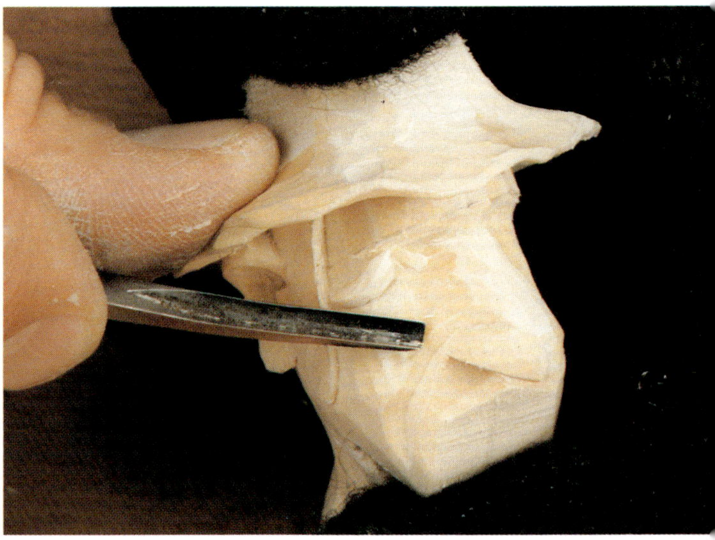

Using the V tool, follow these smile lines into the side of the nose as shown.

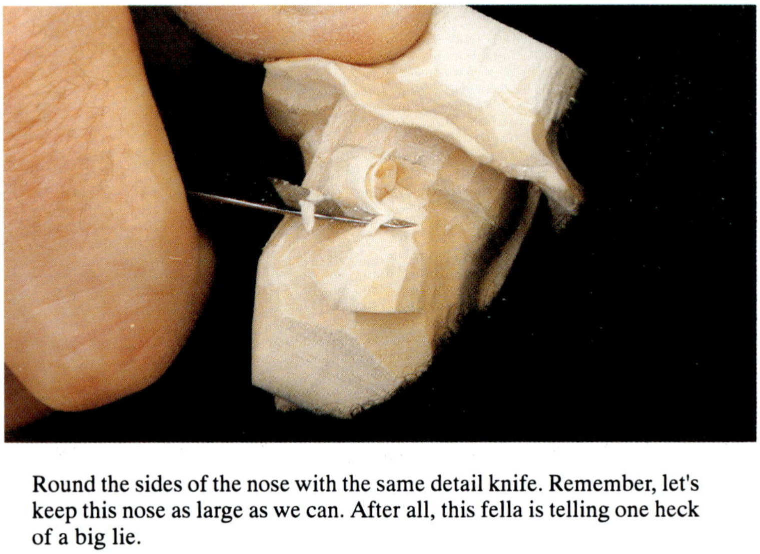

Round the sides of the nose with the same detail knife. Remember, let's keep this nose as large as we can. After all, this fella is telling one heck of a big lie.

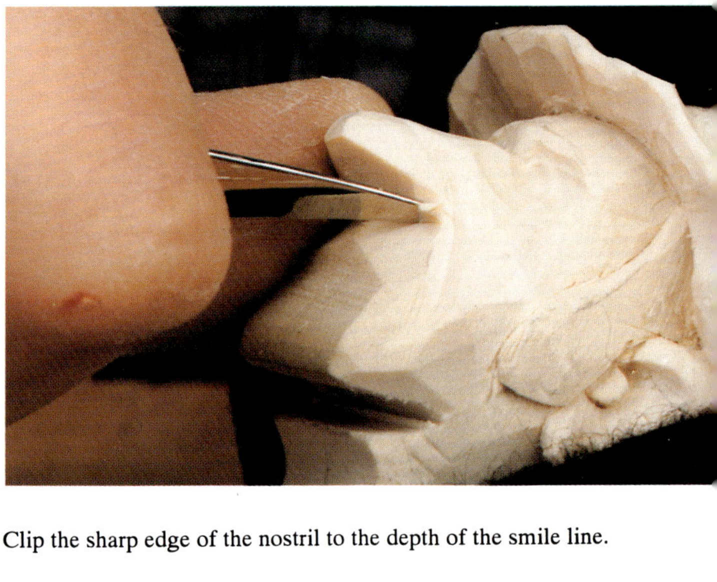

Clip the sharp edge of the nostril to the depth of the smile line.

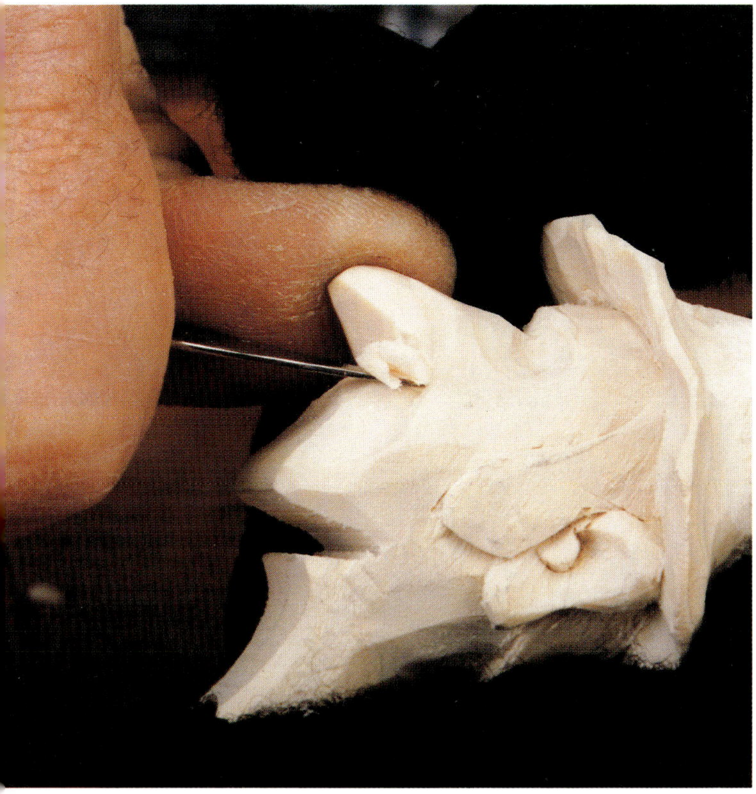

With the tip of your detail knife, remove wood from the area of the mouth (up to the nostrils) to the depth of the smile line.

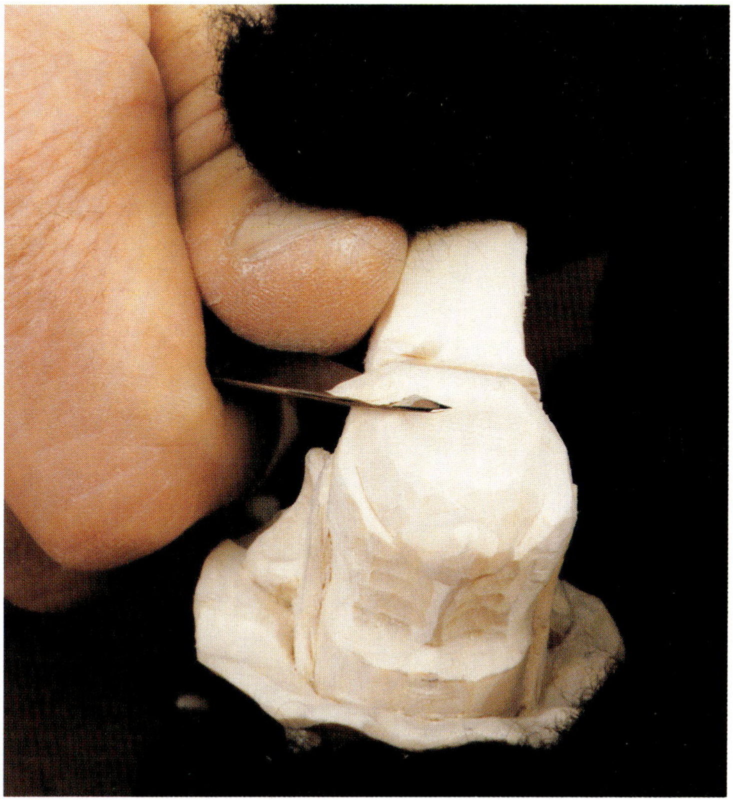

Begin to shape the chin.

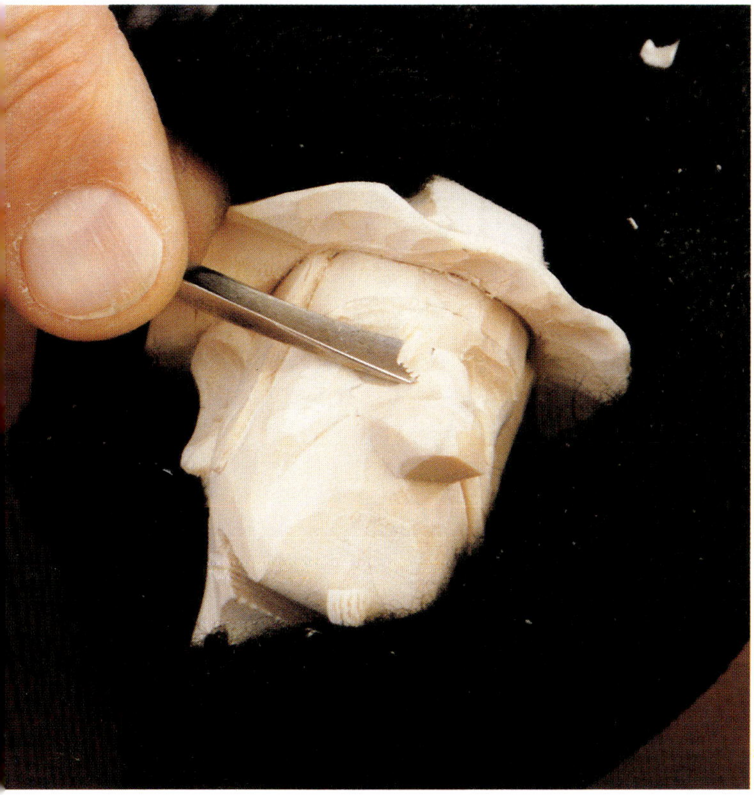

With your shallow gouge, remove wood from the eye sockets above the nostrils.

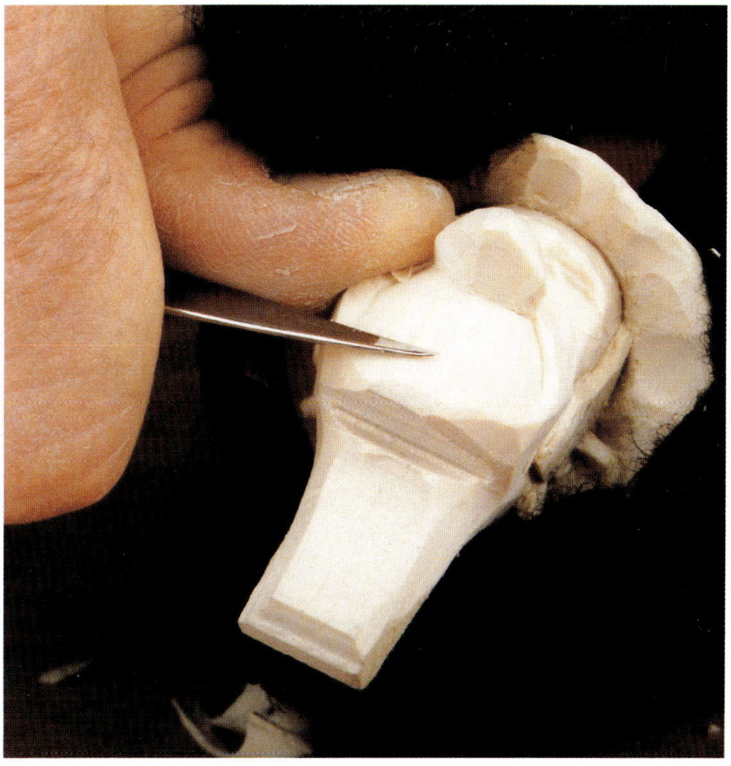

Shaping the chin and mouth area.

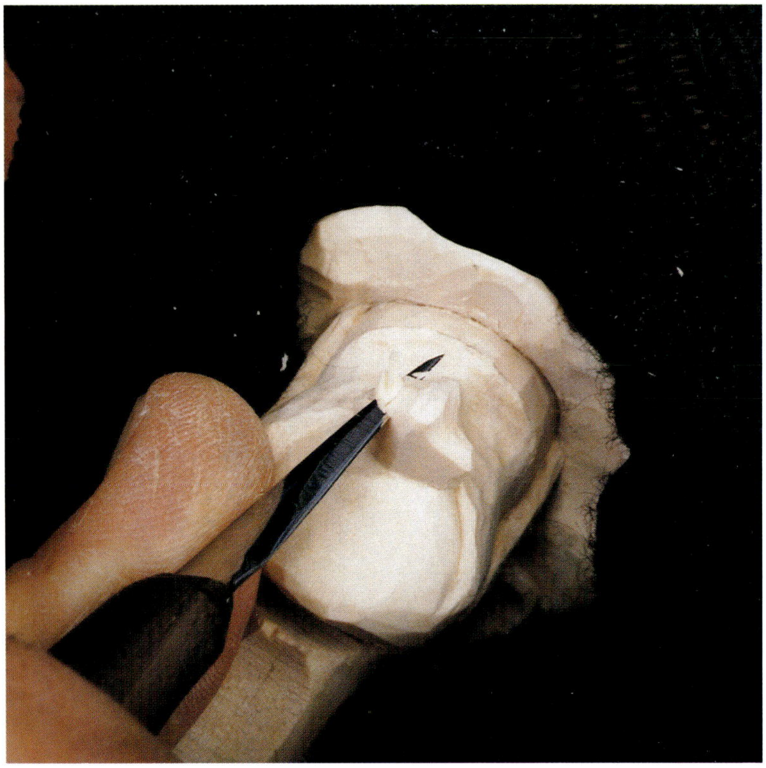

With your knife tip, complete forming the outer surfaces of the nostrils.

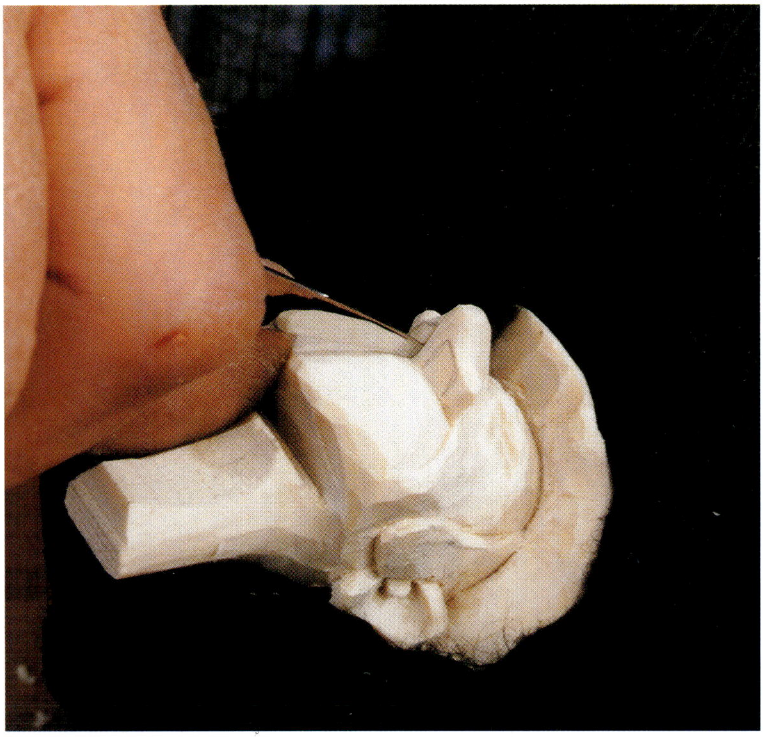

Note that I've drawn in the septum lines on either side of the centerline of the nose. Stick your knife tip 1/8" deep into the nose, along the septum line, parallel to the center line of the nose. Be sure to use a very thin, sharp detail knife or you will clip the nostril off.

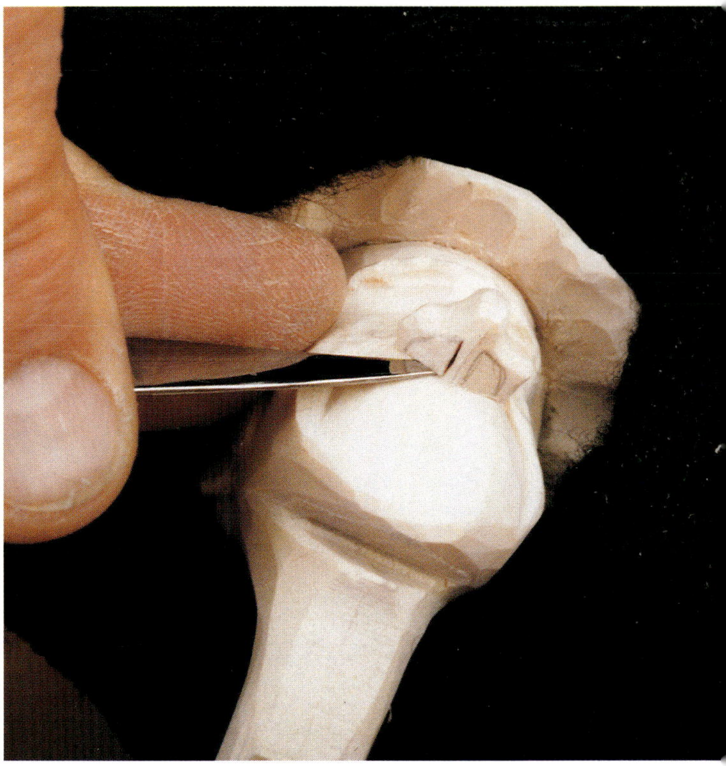

With your detail knife flush with the plane of the mouth, slip the knife tip into the bottom of the nose as shown.

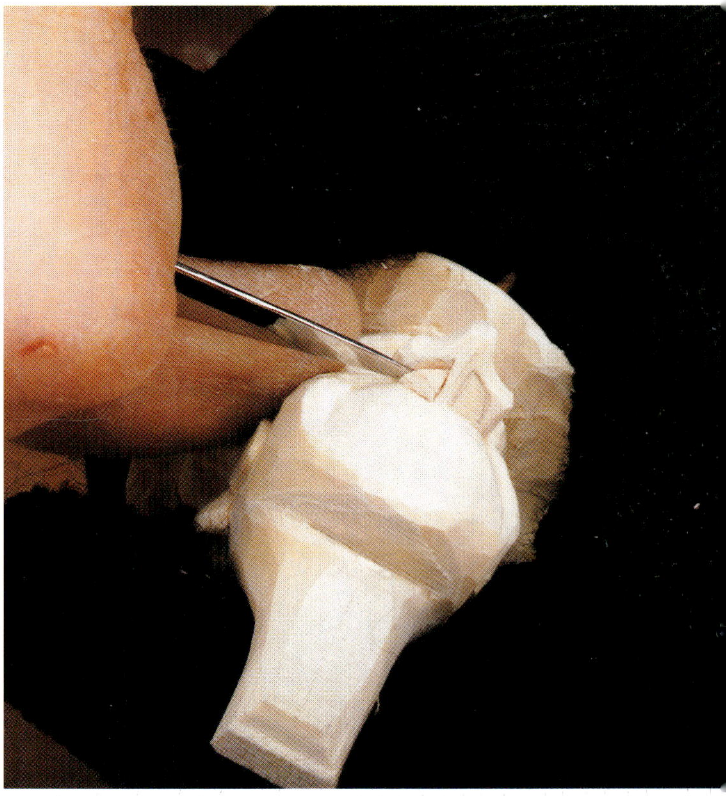

Form a triangular cut with your knife tip by connecting the outermost ends of the two former cuts. Remove the small triangle of wood.

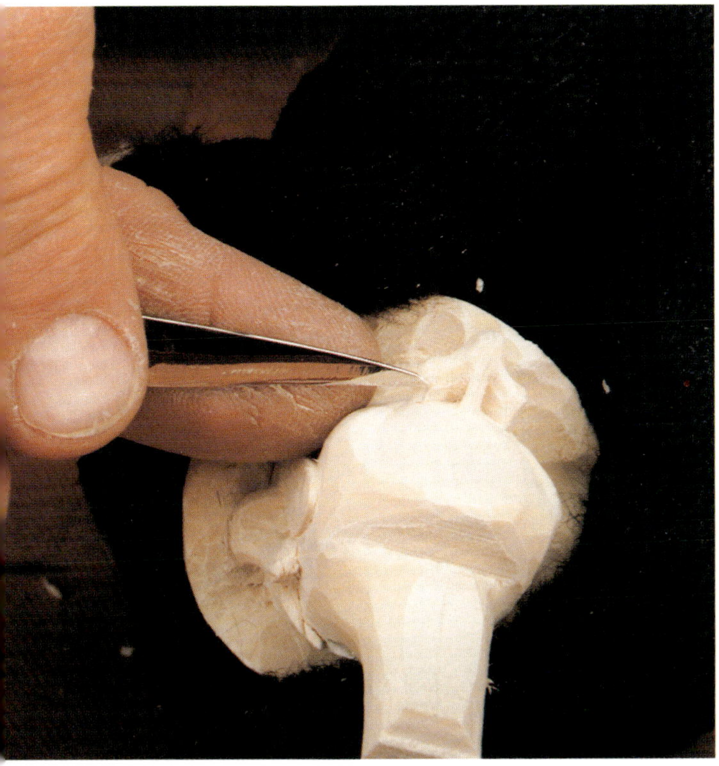

The completed nostrils. Remove or leave remaining "fuzzies" inside the nostrils — depending on the age of your fisherman.

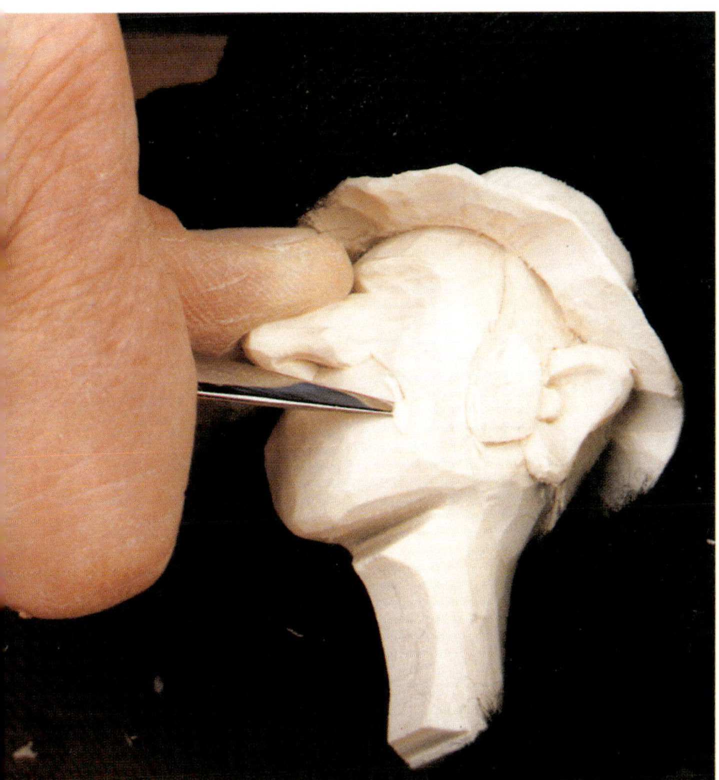

To accent the depth of the smile line, insert the knife tip along the bottom of the smile line V tool cut as shown.

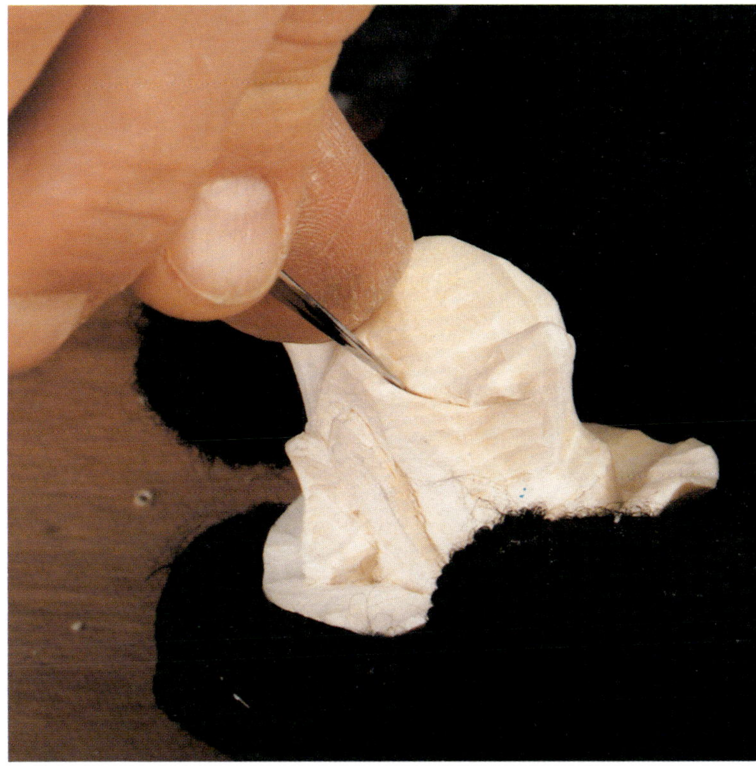

Undercut the smile line with the knife tip at an angle of about 45 degrees.

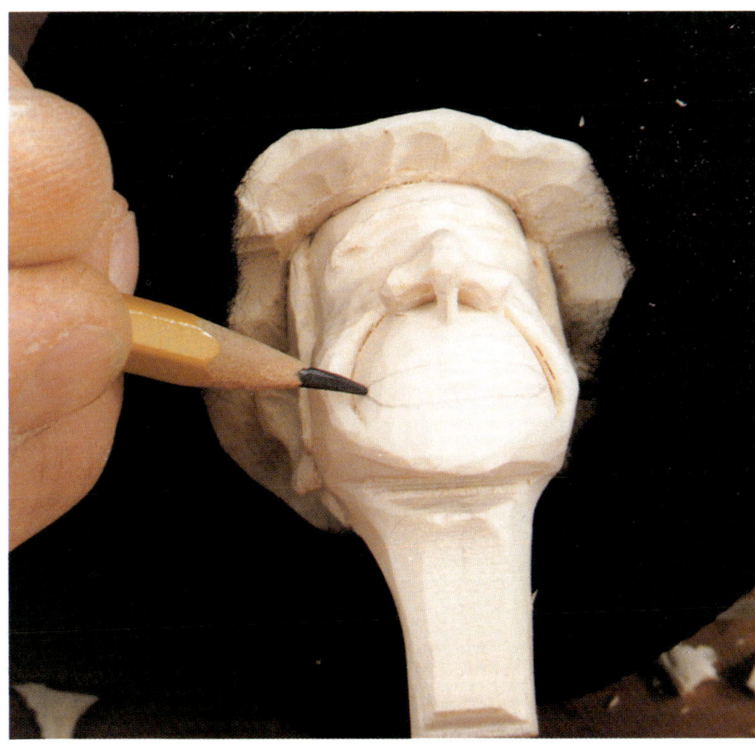

Sketch in a mouth with a forced smile expression. This expression usually displays the upper lip as a straight line and the lower lip roughly parallel to that upper lip.

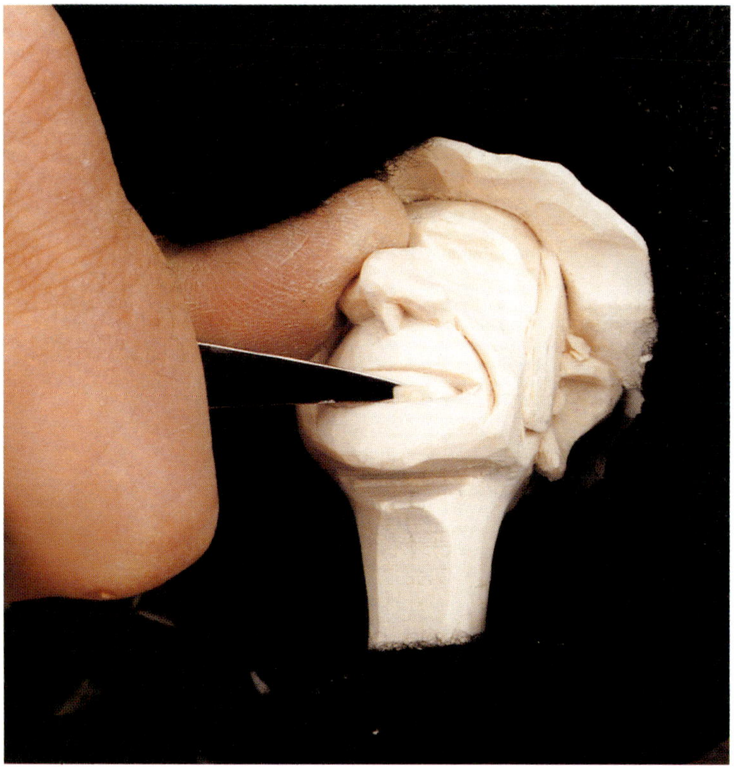

Remove wood to a depth of about 1/8" between the upper and lower lips.

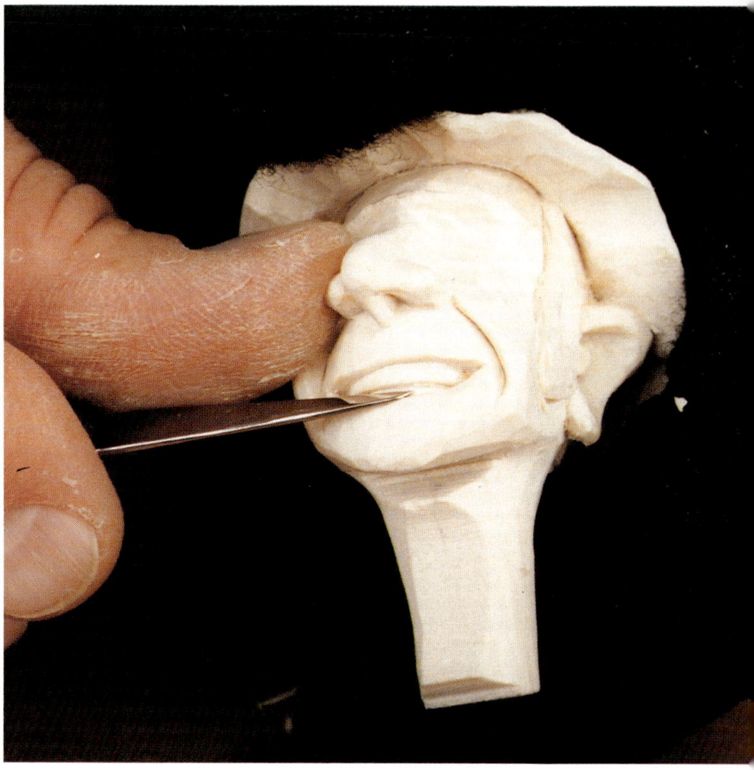

Relieve the lower teeth from the lower lip to this scored line.

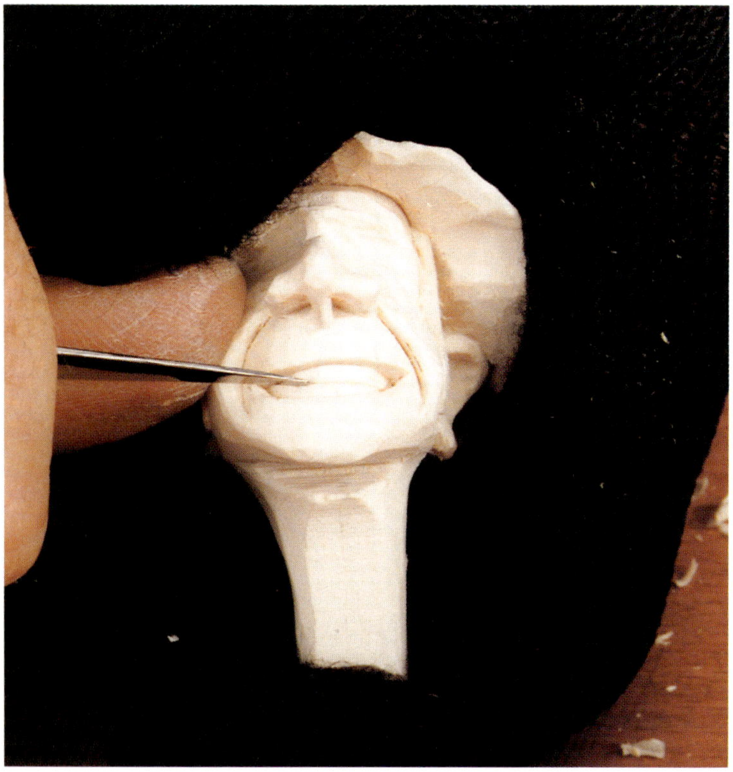

Score a line across his mouth area that will become the separation of the upper teeth from the lower teeth.

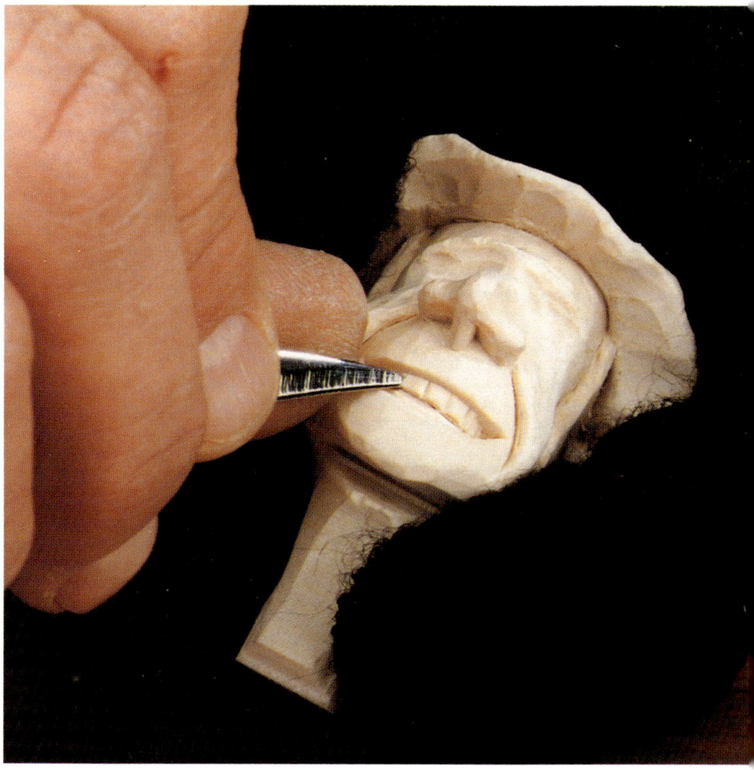

With your knife tip, begin to make shallow V cuts between individual teeth.

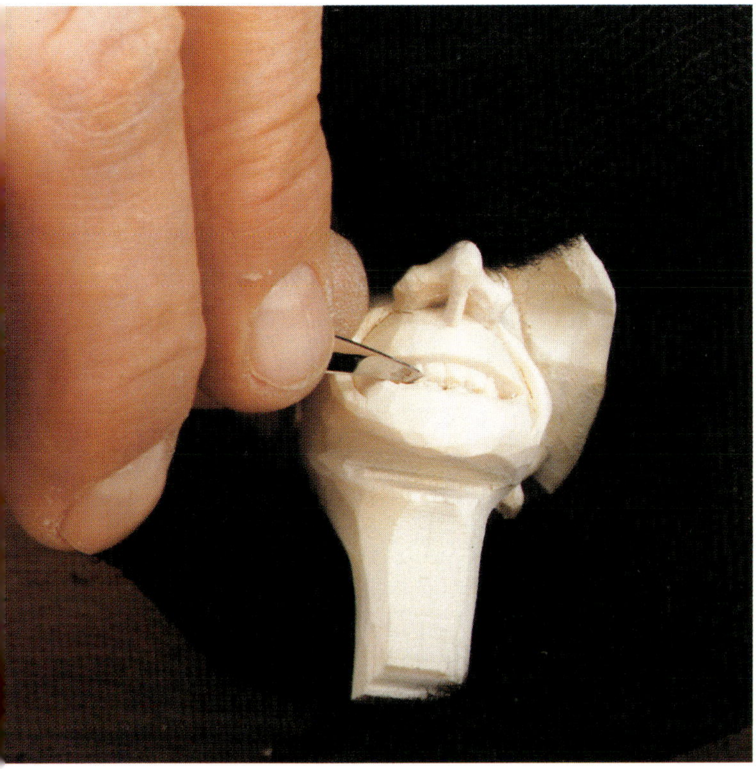

With your knife tip clip the corners from each individual tooth.

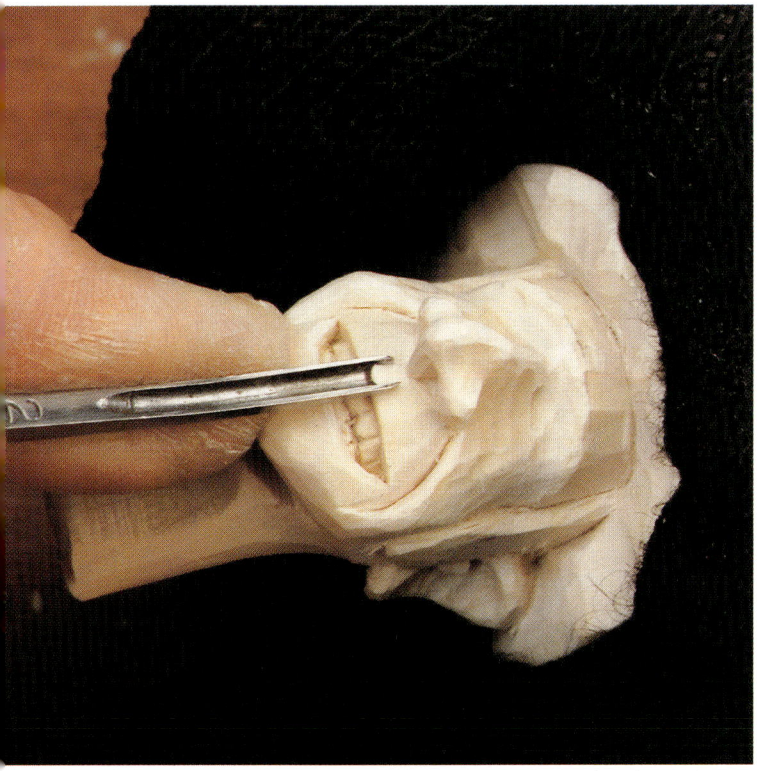

With one of your deep gouges carve the filtrum from the upper lip to the septum.

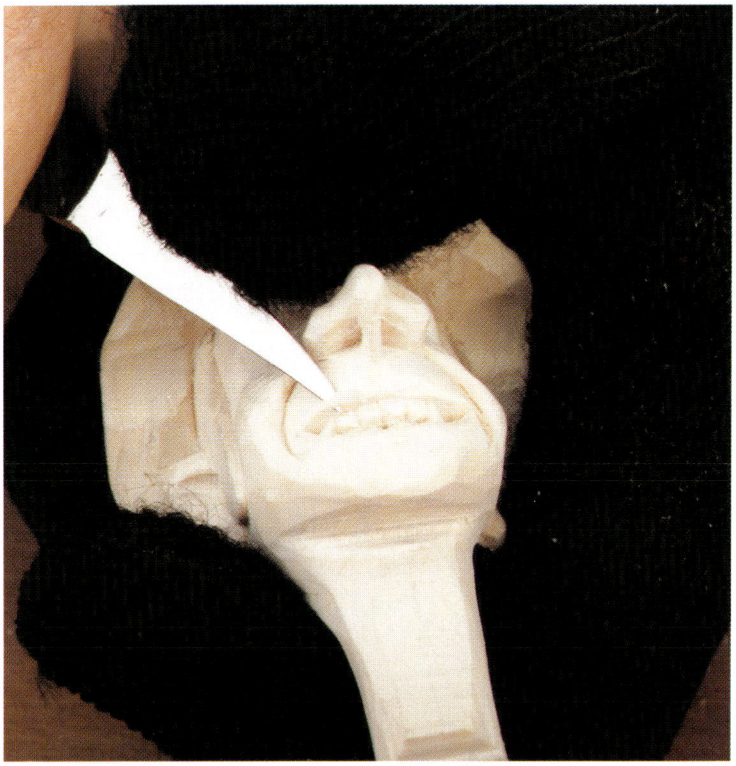

At an angle of about 60 degrees, remove wood along the upper lip from each side of the philtrum to the outside corners of the mouth.

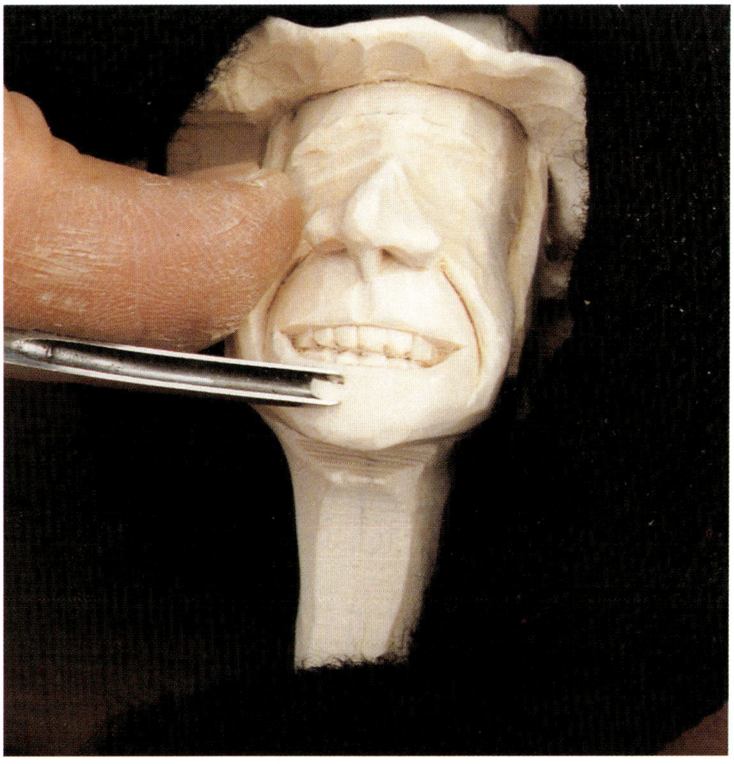

With one of your deeper gouges, carve a very shallow line beneath the bottom lip. We do not want a lot of lip because with this fake smile expression the lips are pulled tight across the teeth.

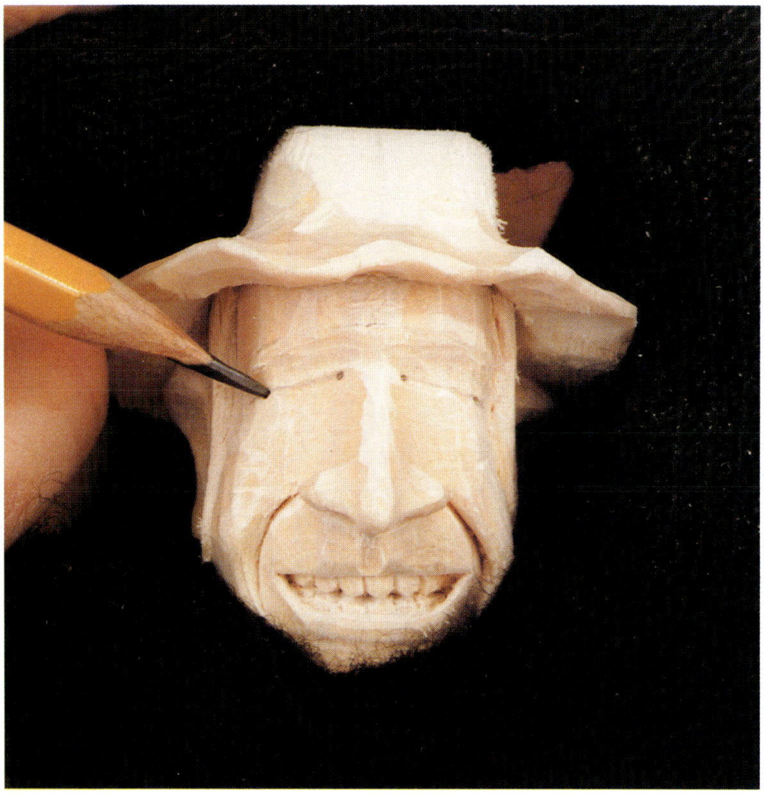

I always save the most difficult part of carving the face to the last, the carving of the eyes. I do this not because I dislike carving eyes, rather it is because the eyes play such an important role in portraying the desired expression. To begin the layout of our eyes, locate the inside and outside corners of the eyes, marking each with a small dot. Connect the dots with a straight line as shown.

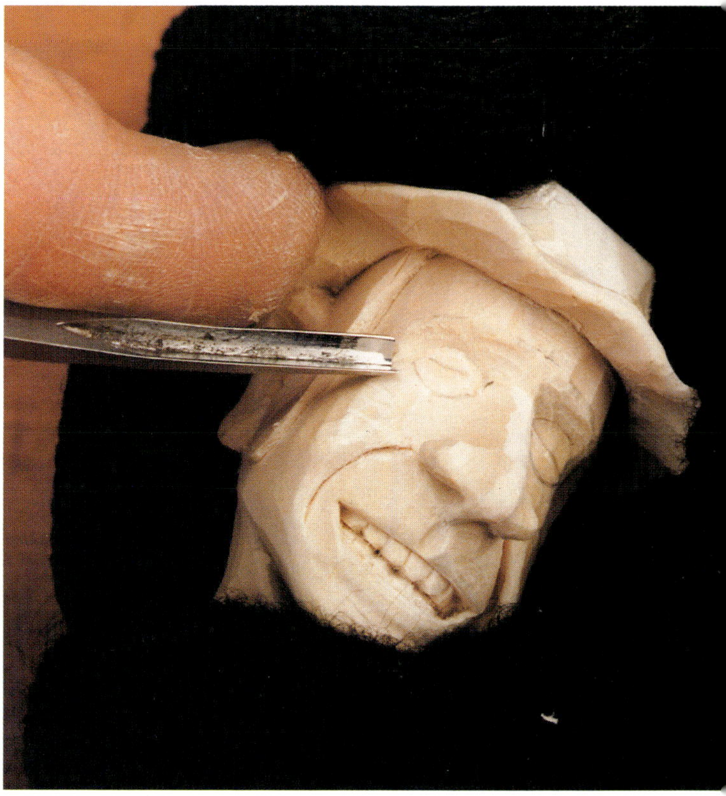

With a small V tool, follow the upper part of the ellipse from the outside corner of the eye to the inside corner of the eye. As you approach the nose with this V tool cut, slightly increase the pressure to the tip of the V tool, causing it to cut a little deeper at the inside corner of the eye.

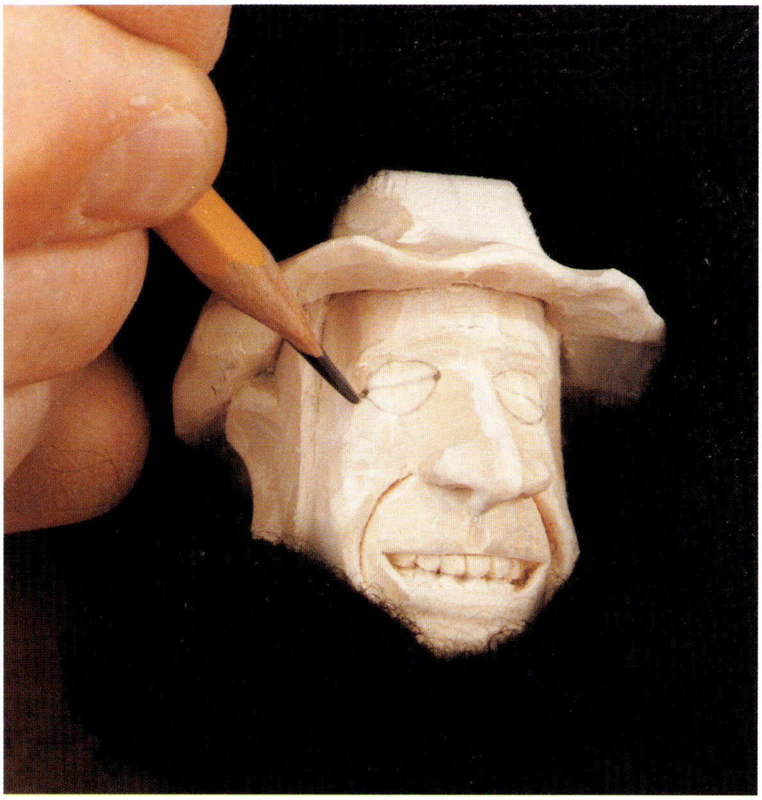

Using the inside and outside dots as the ends of the major axis, sketch an ellipse indicating the general shape of the eyeball.

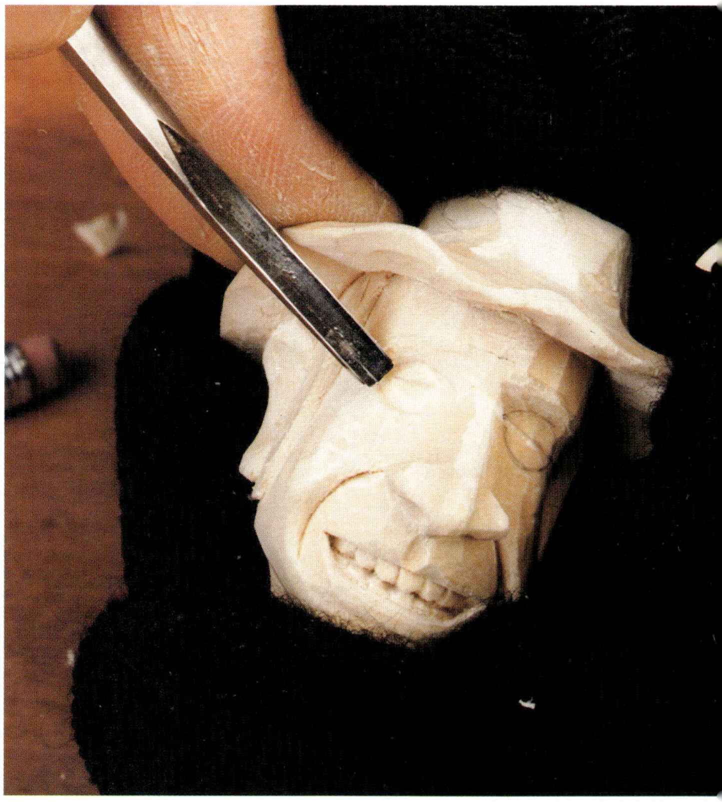

With the same V tool, trace along the bottom part of the ellipse and once again apply a little more pressure to the V tool as you approach the inside corner of the eye.

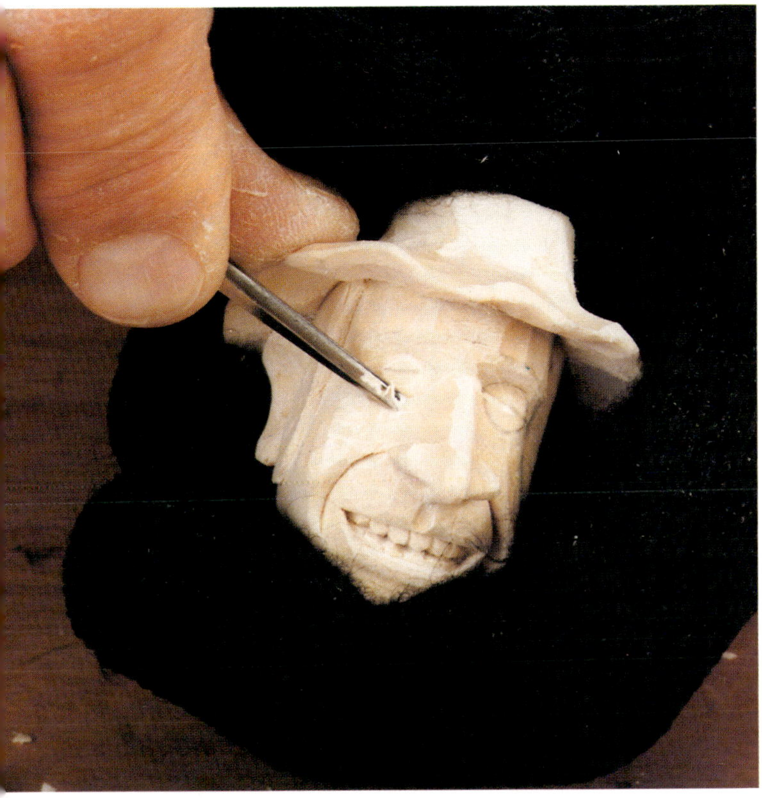

With a small, shallow gouge, remove some of the wood immediately below this last V tool cut.

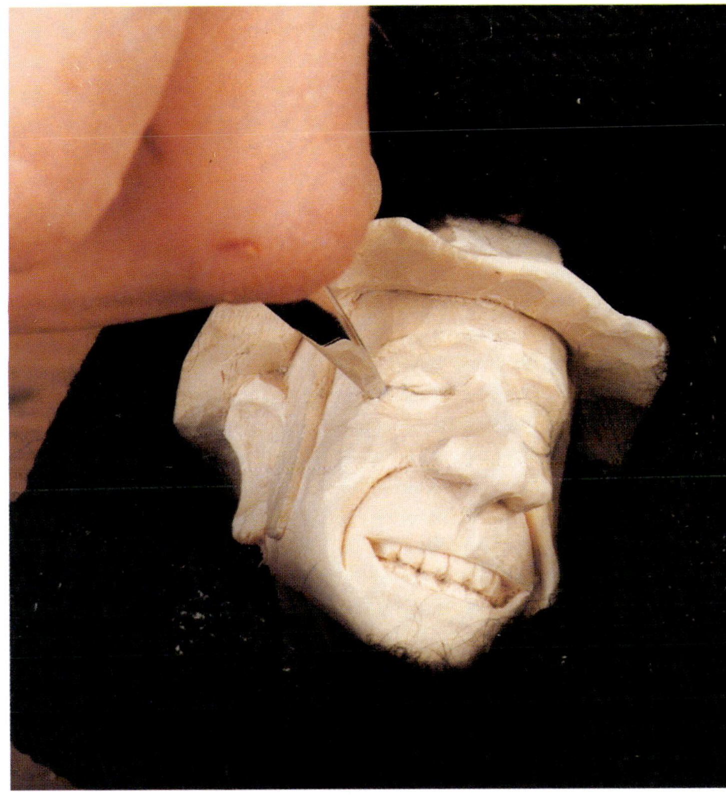

With your knife tip, score along this upper eyelid.

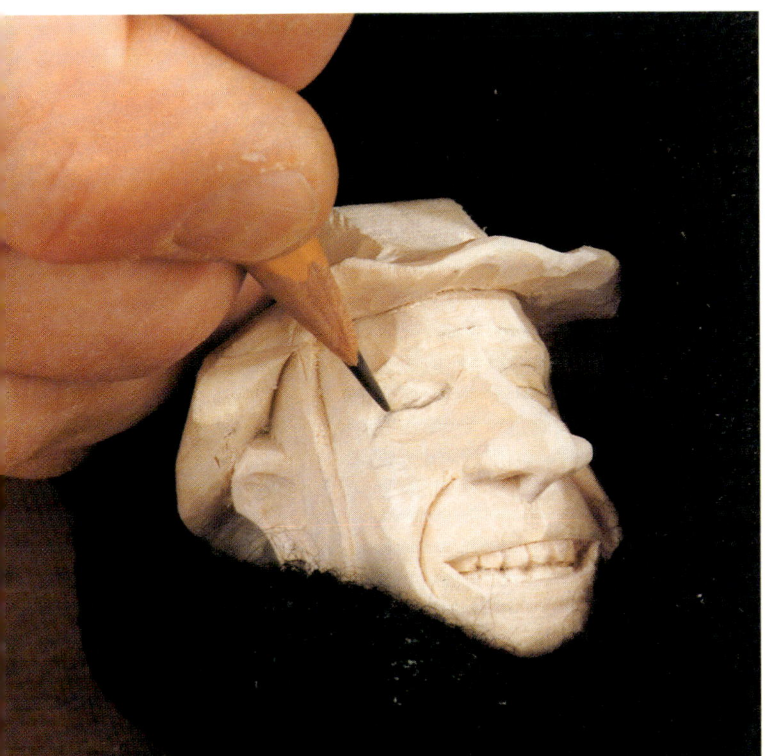

The upper eyelid is the part of the eye that portrays the most expression. Raising the eyelid generally will indicate expressions of surprise. Lowering the eyelid gives the expression of shiftiness or sleepiness, shyness, bashfulness, etc. This old guy is telling a big fib. His subconscious is relaying a message to his eyelids to cover as much of the pupil as possible — because the pupil dilates when one prevaricates. Therefore we'll sketch the upper lid so it sags somewhat.

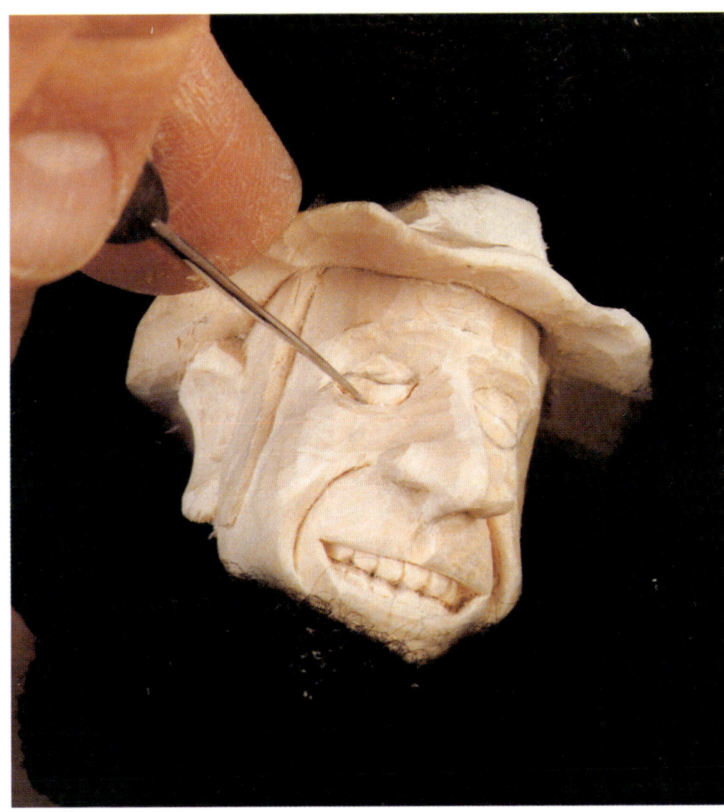

Score along the bottom lid, following the bottom of the V tool cut previously made along the perimeter of the ellipse.

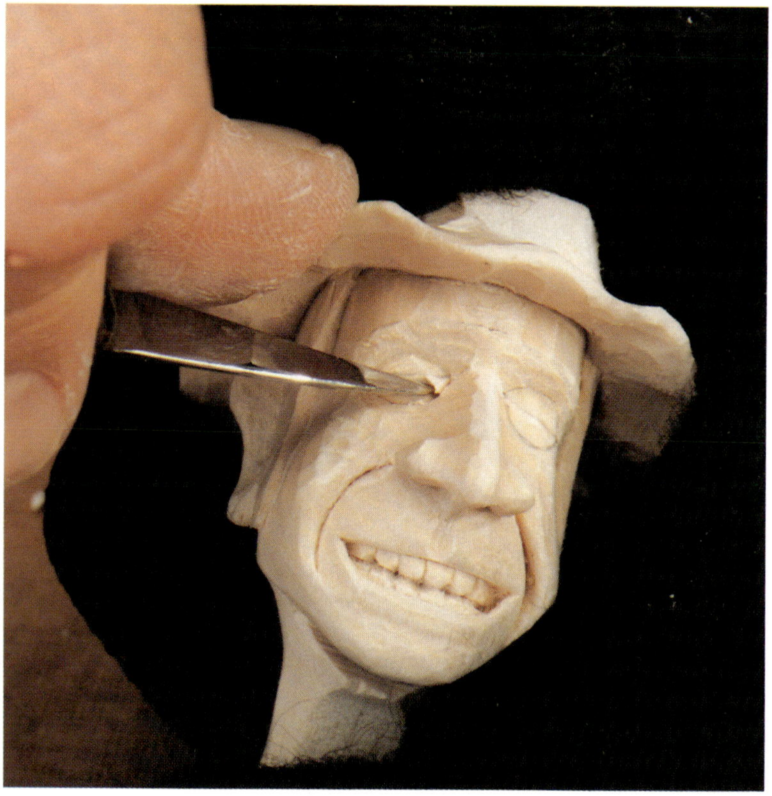

With your knife tip, remove the small triangle of wood formed by the intersection of the knife cuts at the inside and outside corners of the eye.

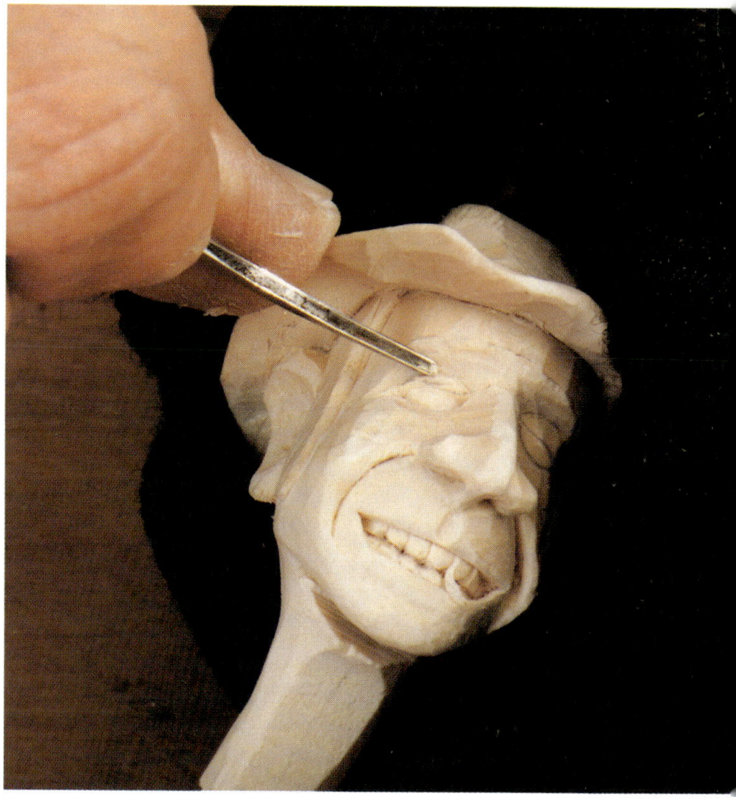

As you remove this wood, shape the eyeball to appear as a ball. With the smallest of your V tools, form the upper lid to overlap the bottom lid at the outside corner of the eye.

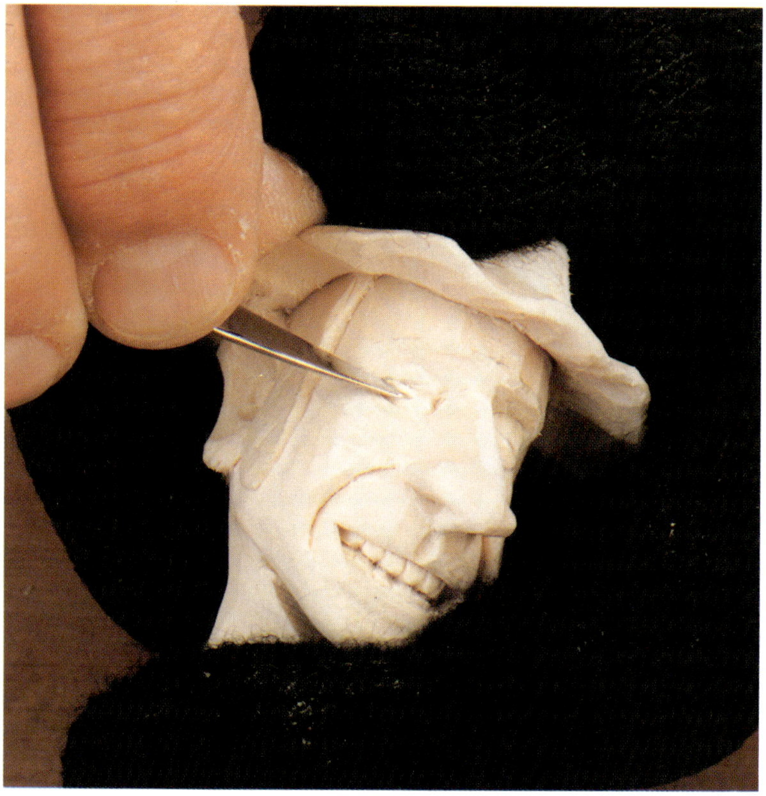

Gently remove wood between the upper and lower eyelids.

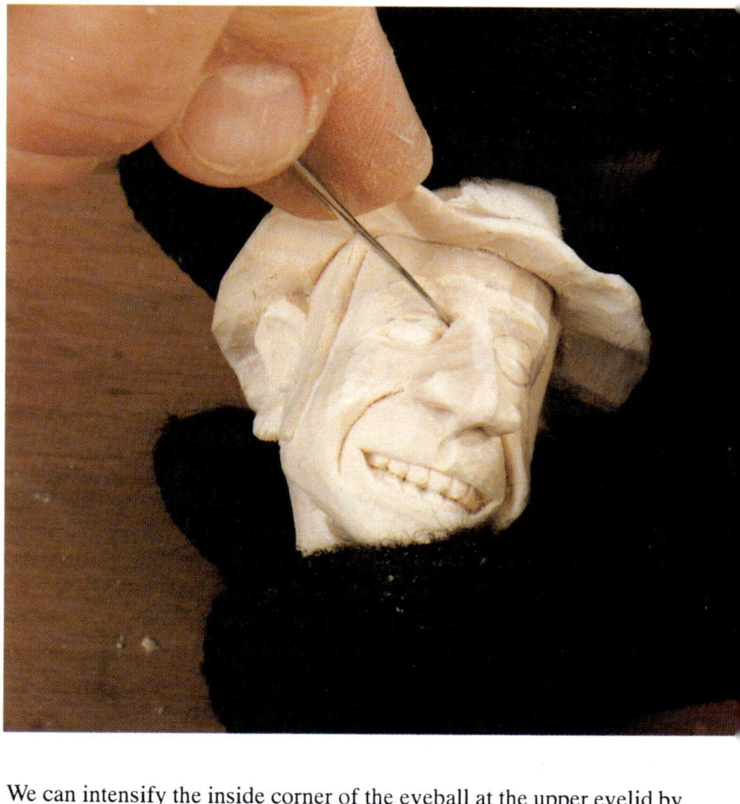

We can intensify the inside corner of the eyeball at the upper eyelid by removing a small triangle of wood as shown.

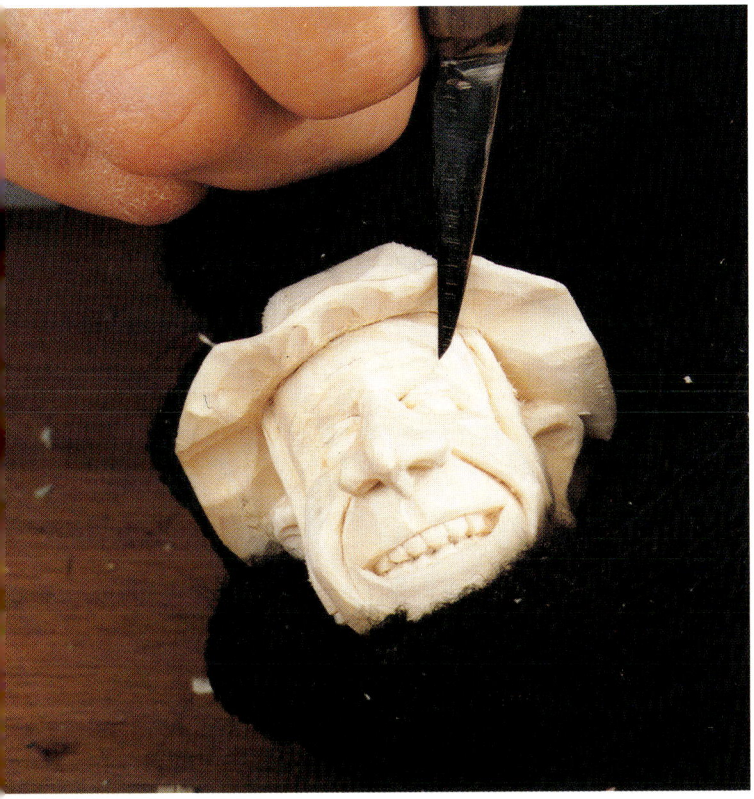

Using the same procedures, carve the character's left eye. Note that we carved this character's right eye first. For a right handed carver, the right eye is the most difficult to carve because it is carved with the head upside down. Note too that I have arched the upper eyelid on the characters left eye, indicating a slight sneer.

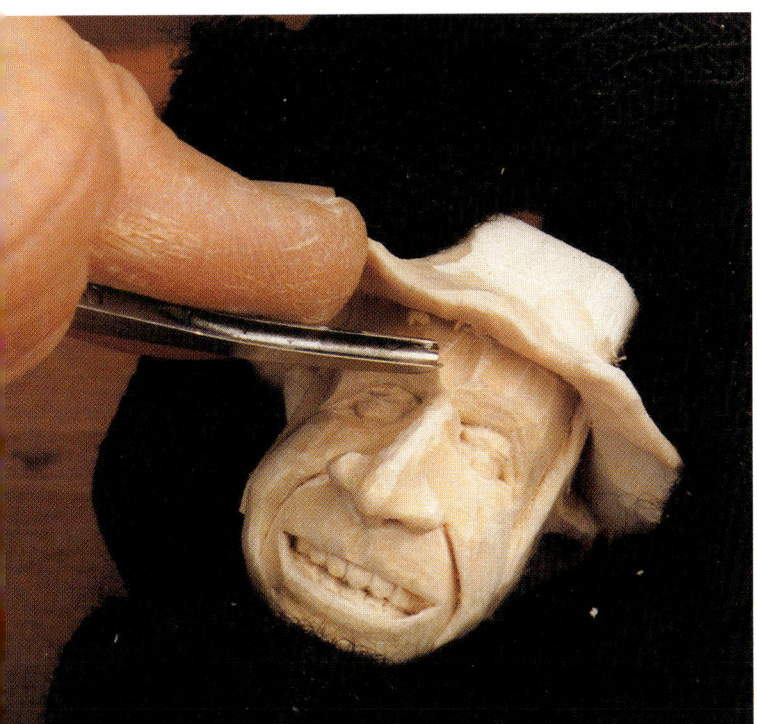

With a small, deep gouge, separate the eyebrow by forming a trough immediately above the bridge of the nose.

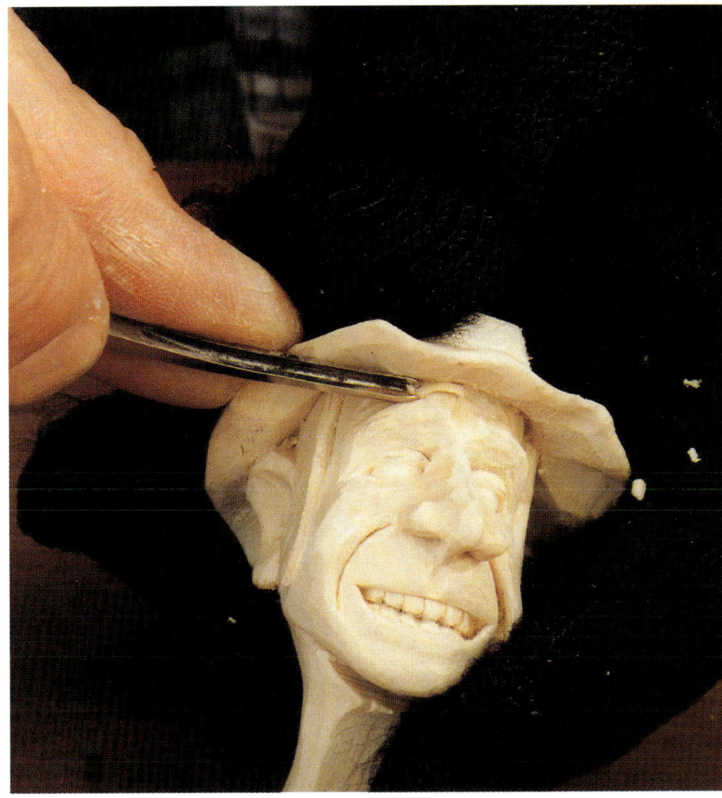

Using your small V gouge, form a mound upon which we will carve hair for the eyebrow. Remove the wood above this mound to the hat brim.

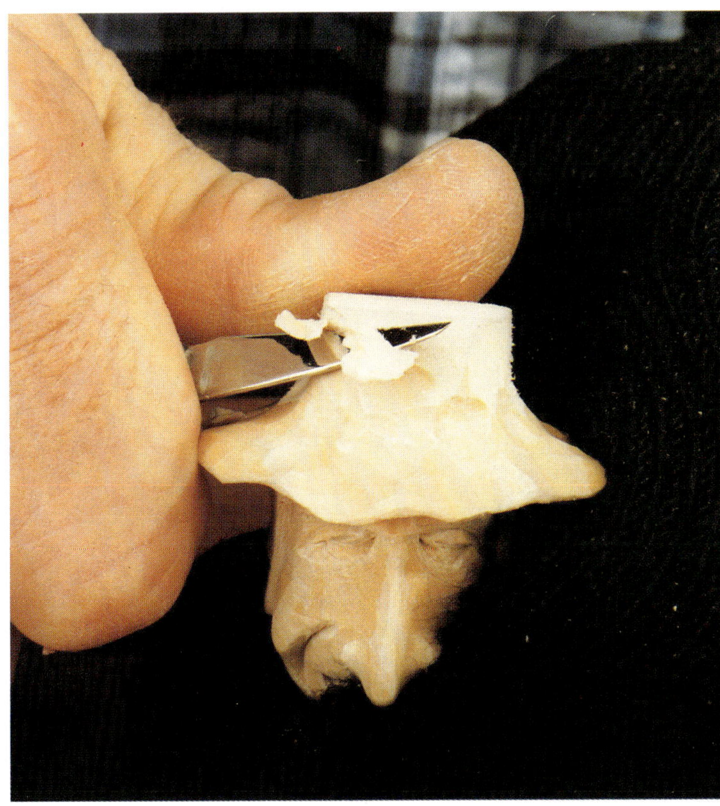

Using your detail knife, finish carving the crown of hat.

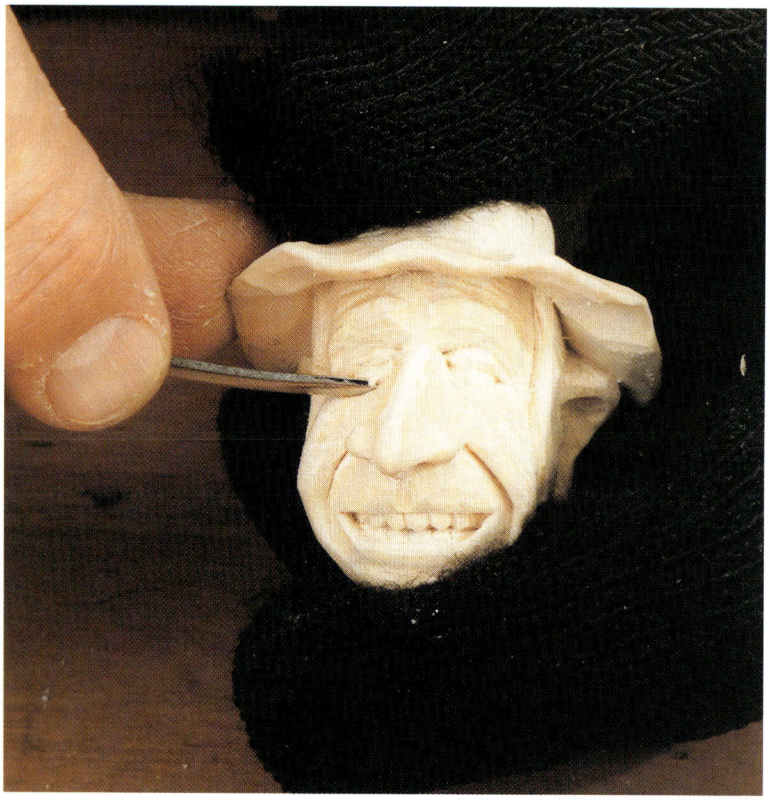

Using the smallest of your V tools, add wrinkles below each eye, in the outside corners of each eye, and along the brow. These lines while very shallow are irregular in depth, length, and orientation to each other.

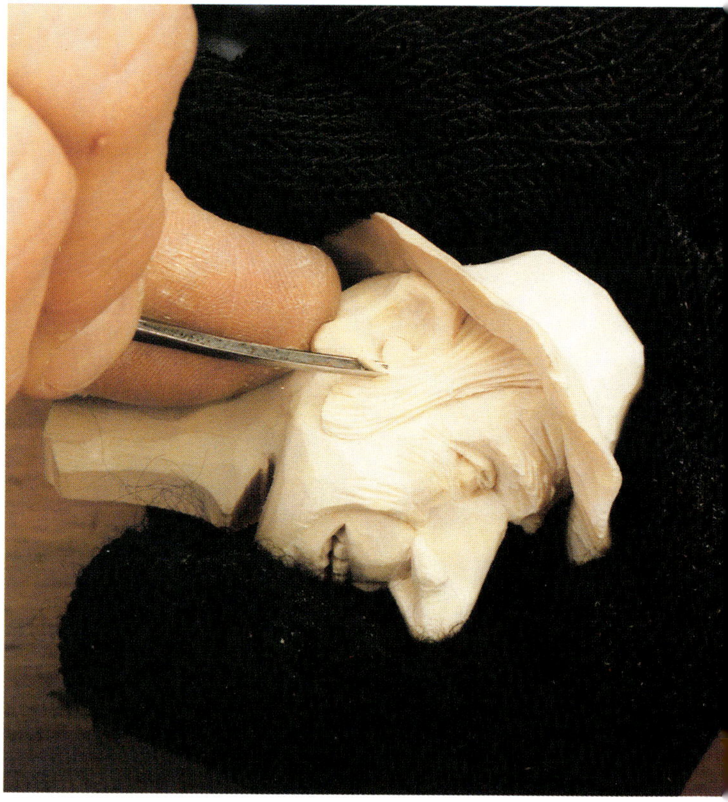

Continue carving hair for the sideburns and the back of the head.

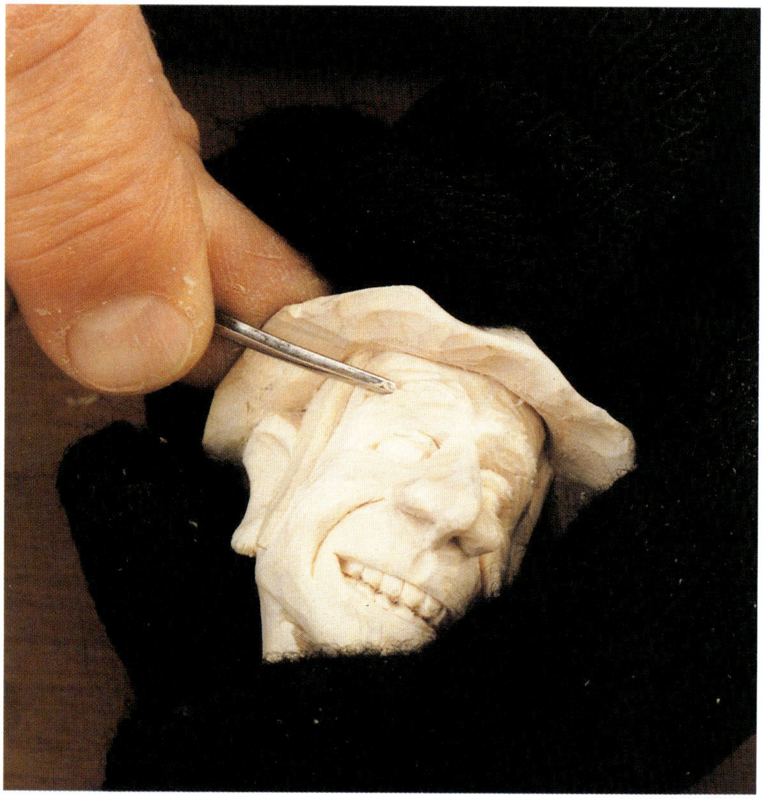

Using the same small V tool, begin forming hair along each eyebrow. Again these hairlines are very irregular in depth, as well as skew.

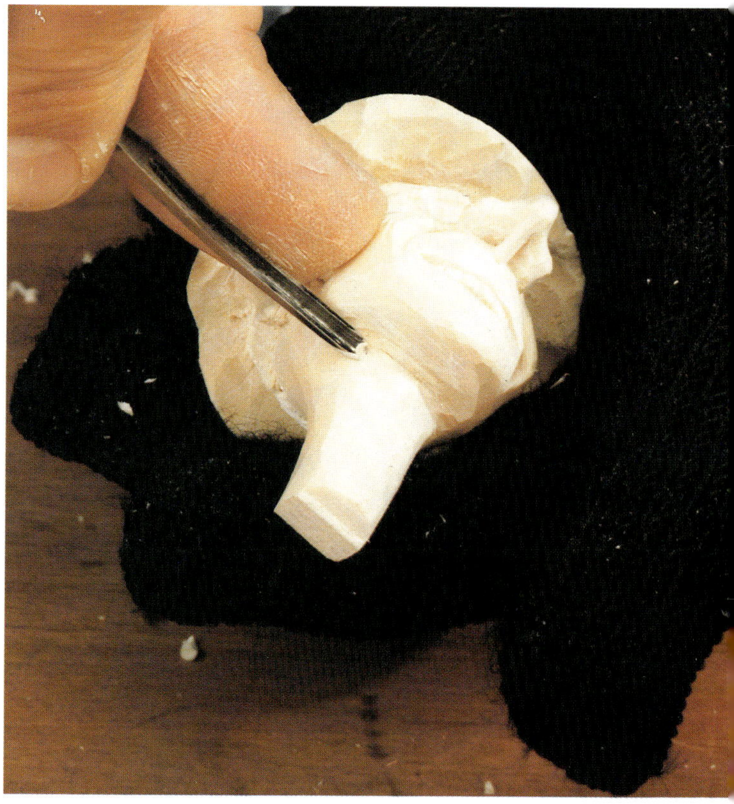

Finally, finish the head by shaping the neck so that it fits into the 1/2" hole drilled into the body.

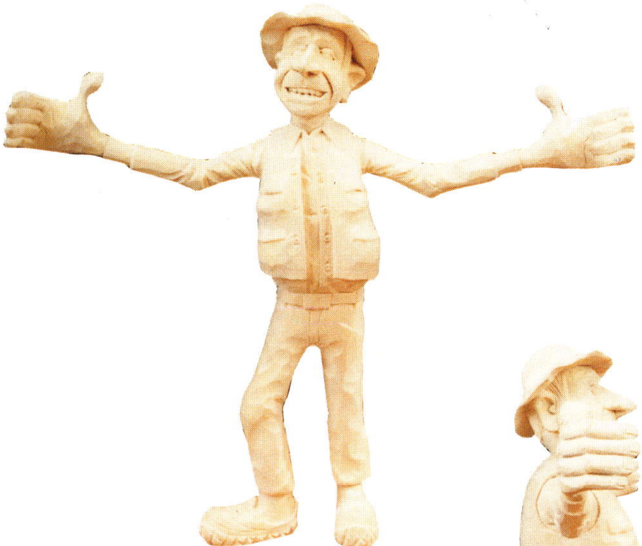

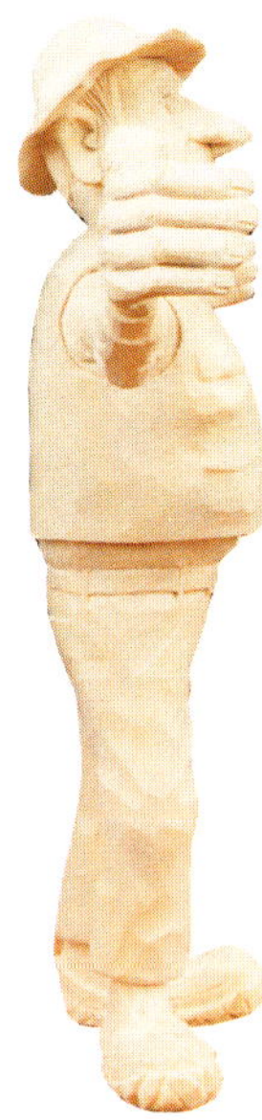

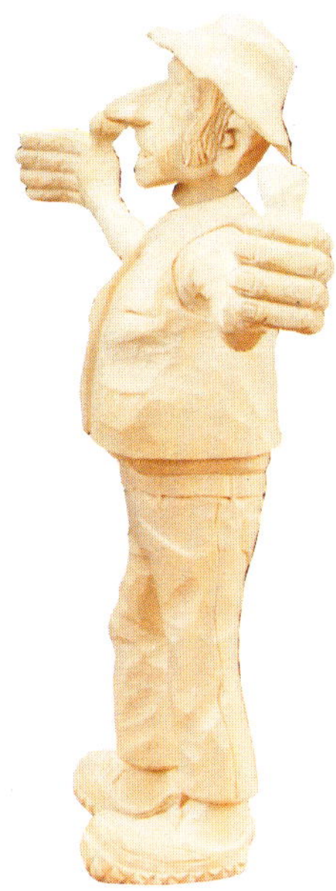

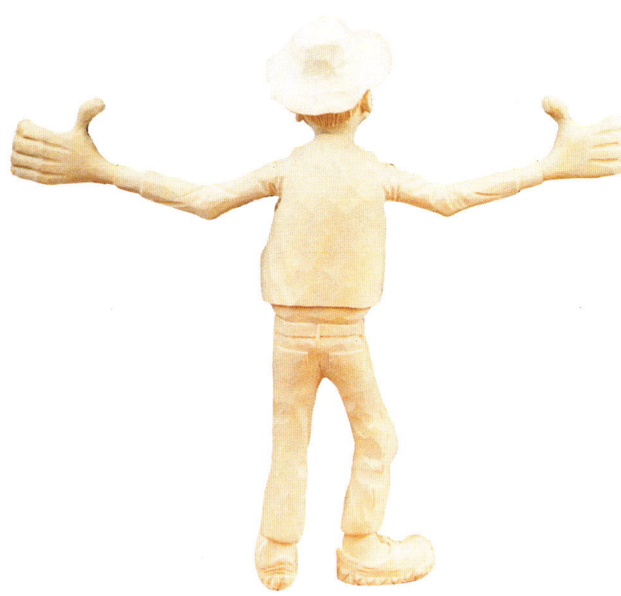

The finished carving.

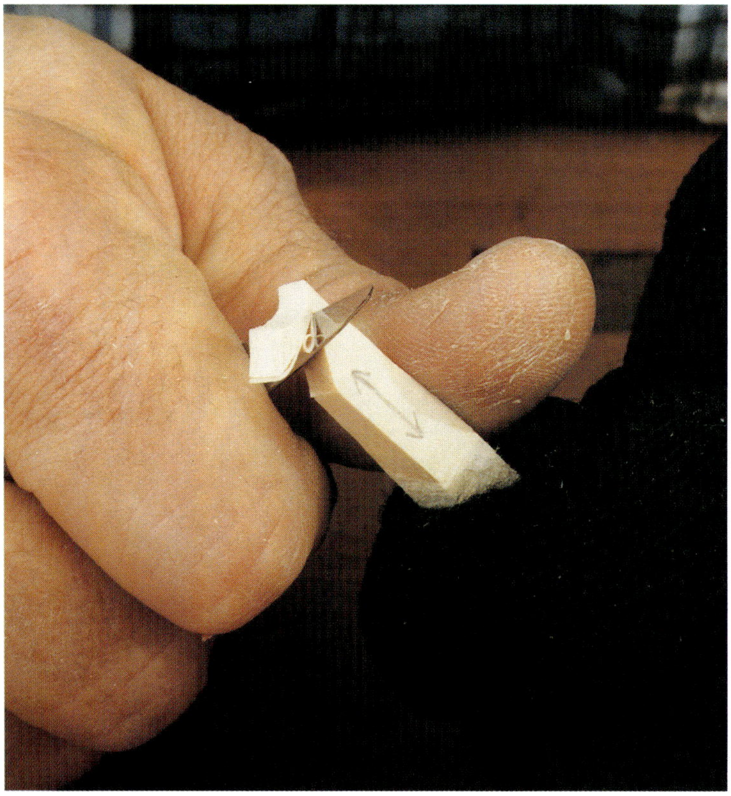

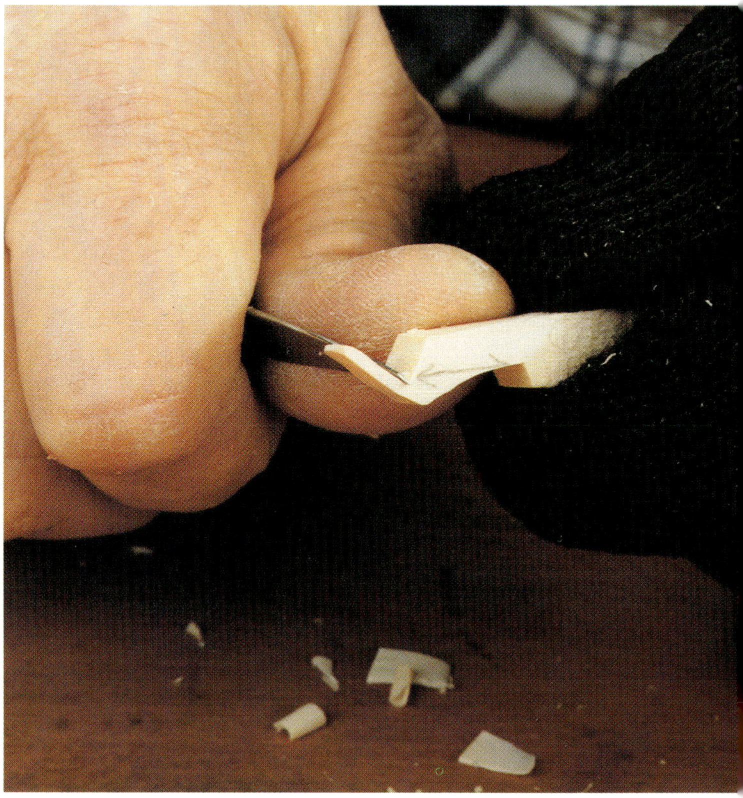

Let me show you how I carve the little fishing lures that I glue onto the caps and vests of my fishermen. Take a thin piece of wood about 1/4" wide by 1/4" deep. Clean off the saw marks. With the grain of the wood oriented in the direction indicated by the arrows, cut a 30 degree incline at end of your carving stick.

With your detail knife, very gently make the diving plate of the lure about 1/16" thick.

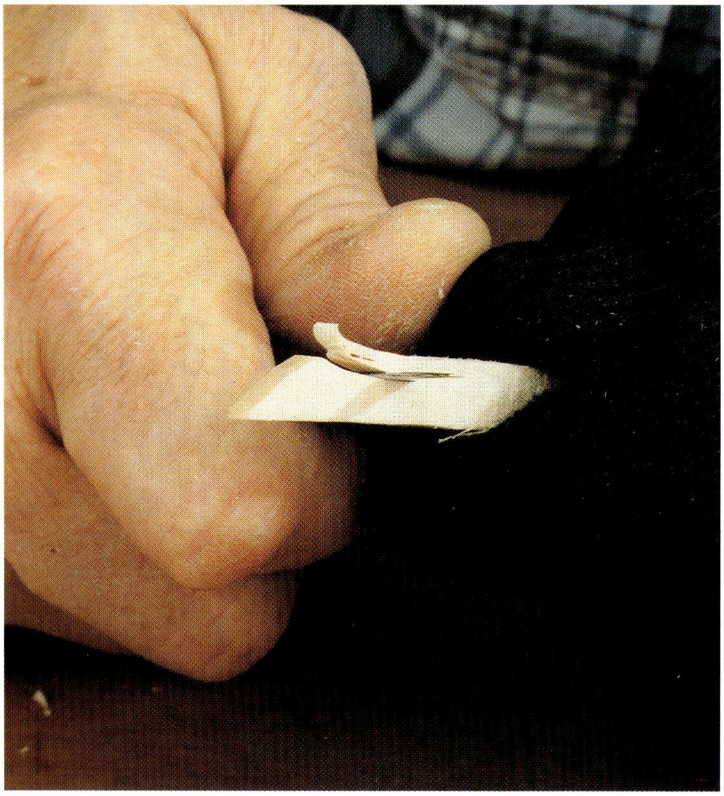

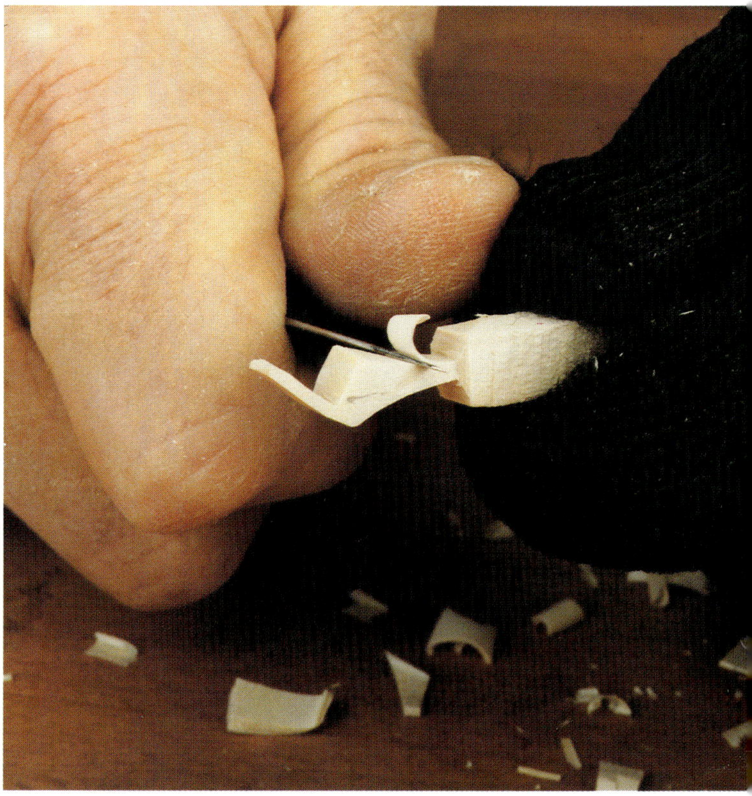

Along the top of that inclined surface hollow out the top of the lure as shown.

Slope the bottom of the body toward the back of the lure.

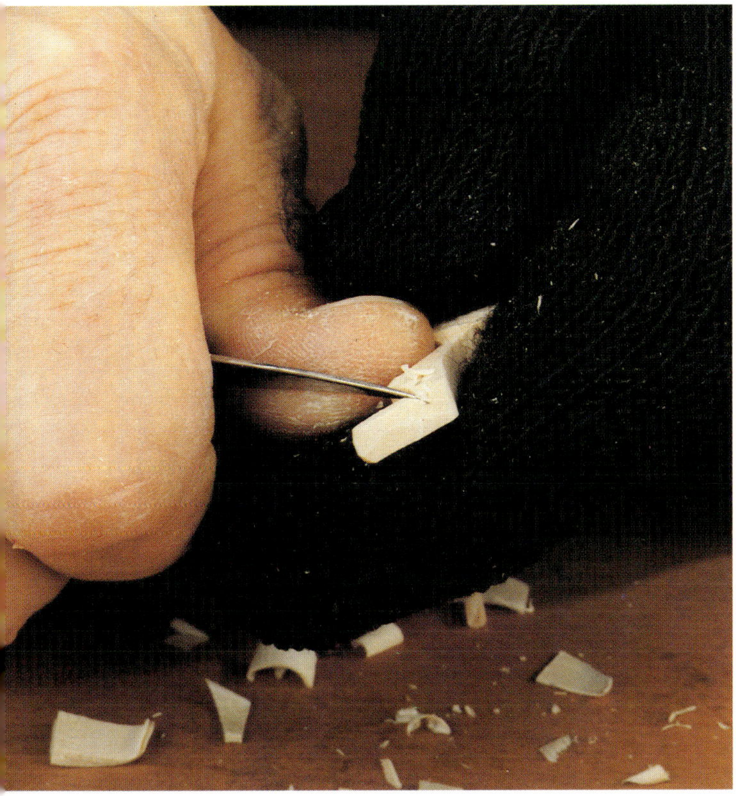

Notch the diving plate as shown.

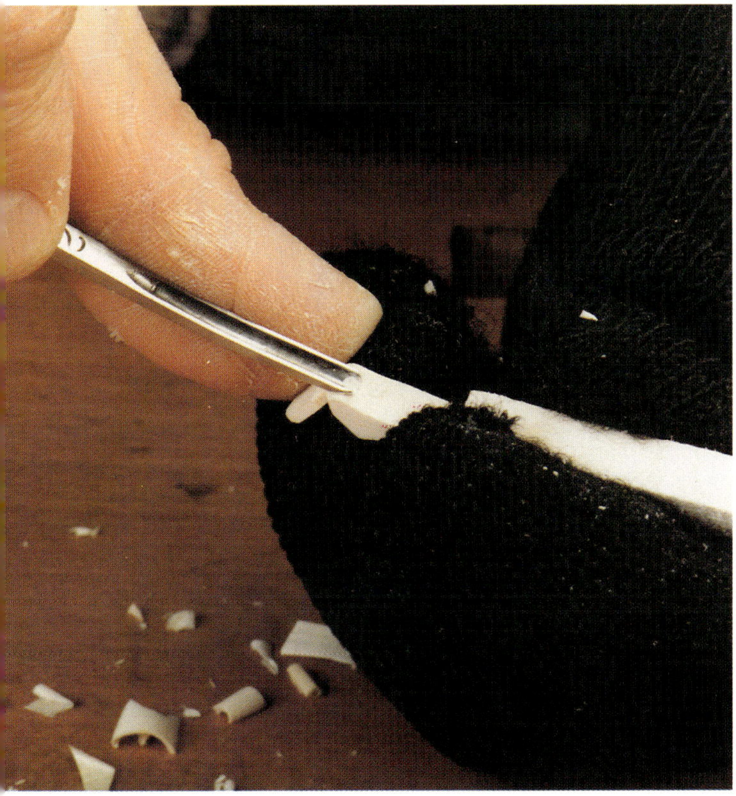

With a small deep gouge, separate the eyes along the top of the body.

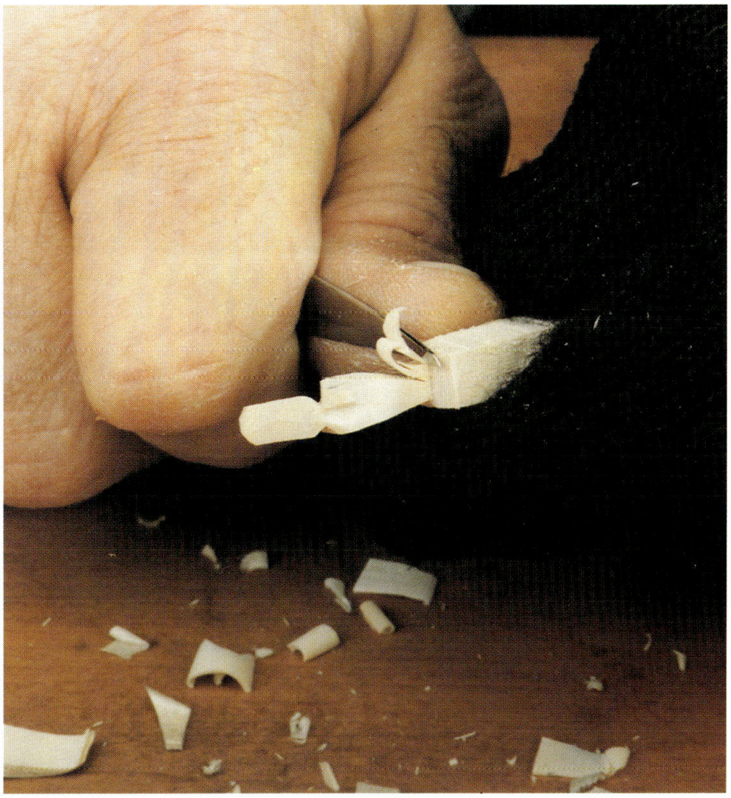

Slope the sides of body toward the lure's tail.

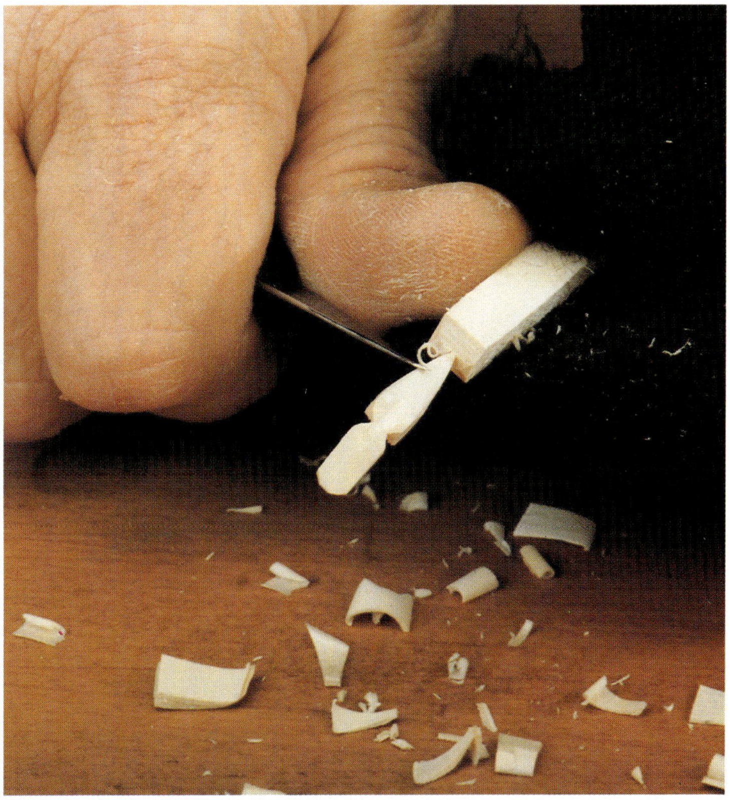

Remove sharp corners from the body of the lure.

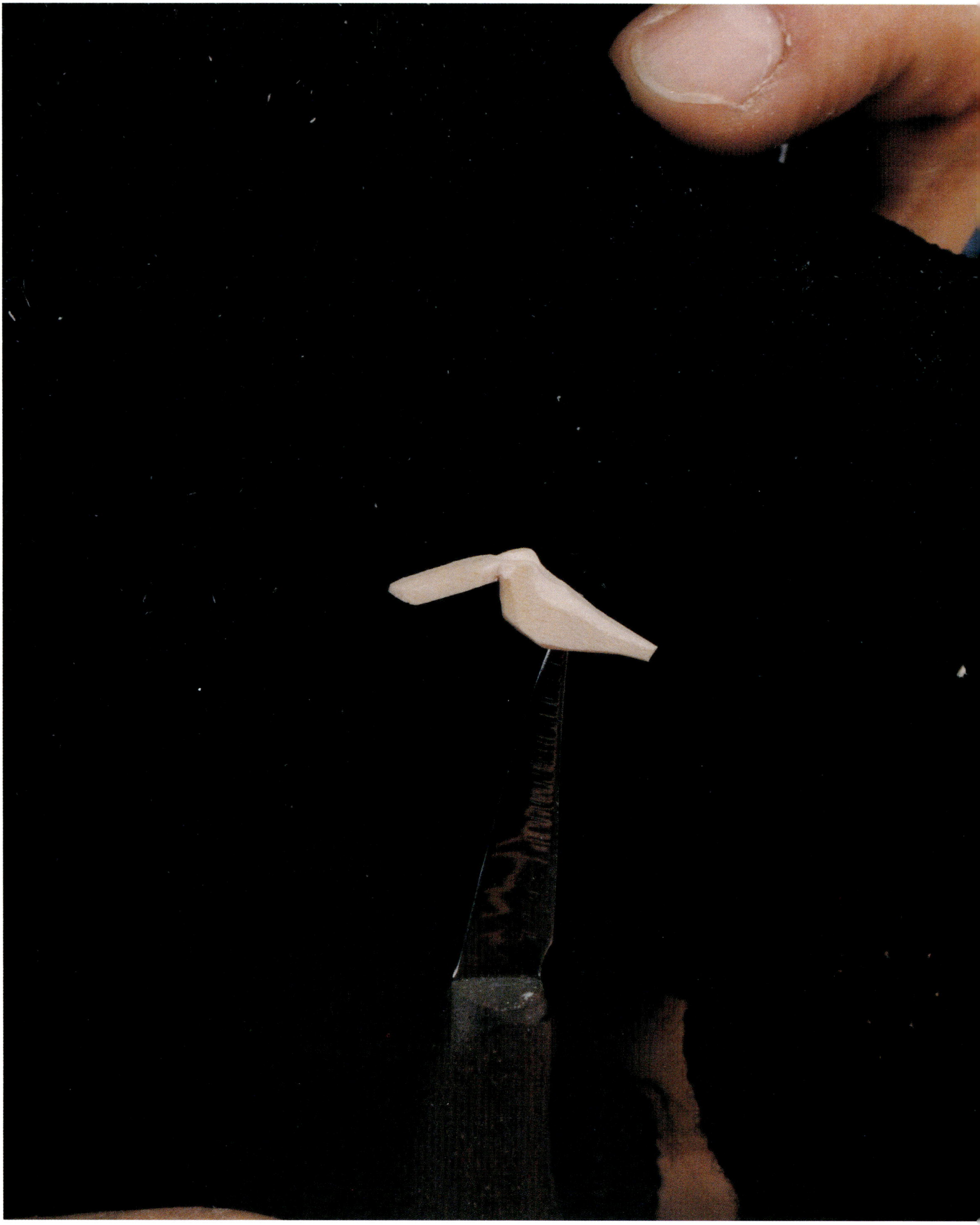

The finished lure. Now it's time to paint.

Painting the Fisherman

To paint the fibbing fisherman you will need the following Ceramcoat colors:
Caucasian Flesh #2029, Medium Flesh #2126, Midnight Blue #2114, Seminole Green #2009, Yellow #2504, Golden Brown #2054, White (no number), Black (no number), Brown Iron Oxide #2023, Fire Red #2083, Silver #6003, and Blue Haze #2122.

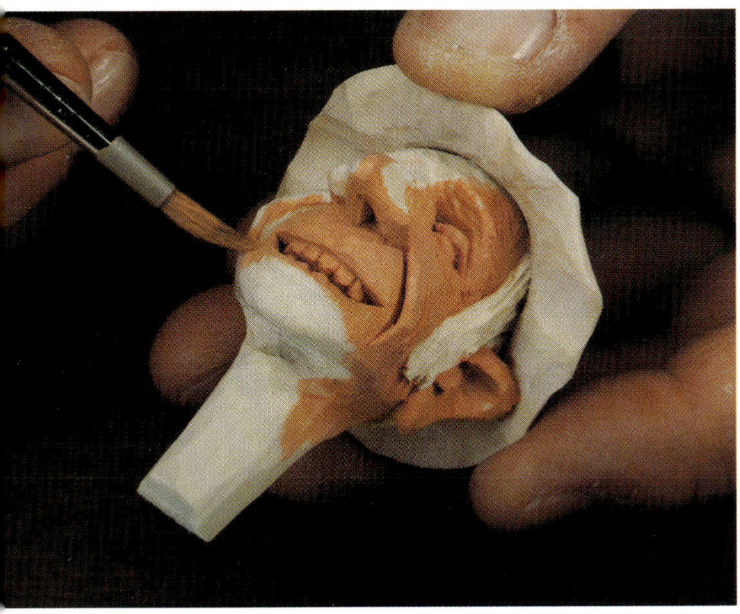

Mix four parts Caucasian Flesh #2029, one part Medium Flesh #2126, and about 6 parts water. Stir well and paint all flesh areas of the head. Cover the eyeballs and the mouth—including teeth—with this flesh mixture. We will use undiluted white at a later time to cover the eyeball and the teeth.

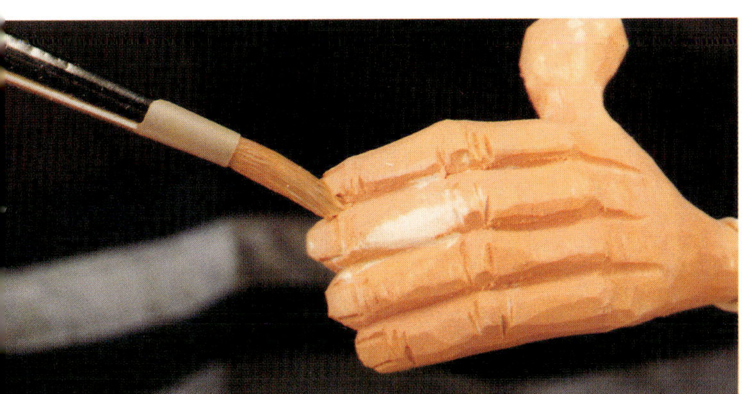

Paint the hands with the flesh mix as well.

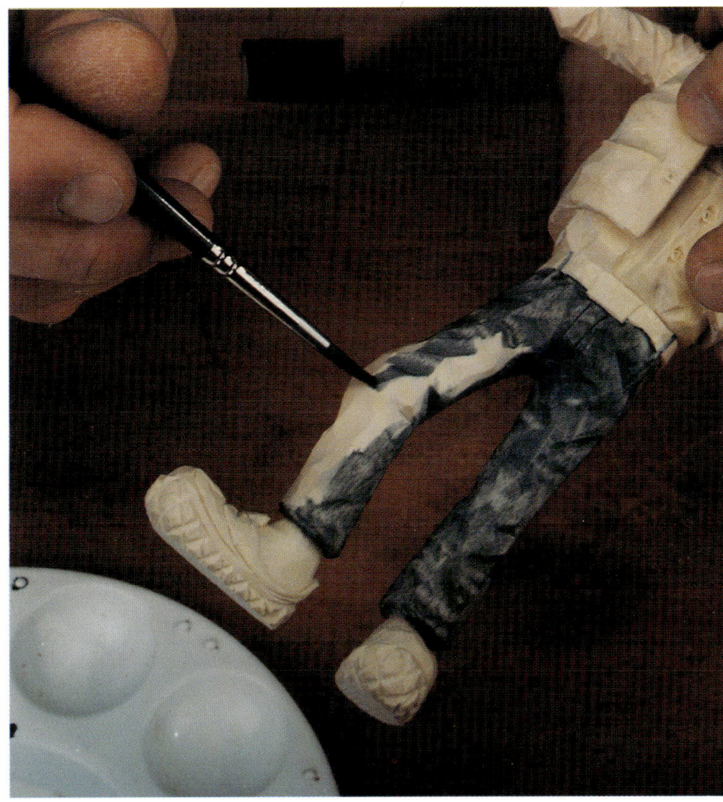

Mix one part Midnight Blue #2114 with four parts water and paint the jeans.

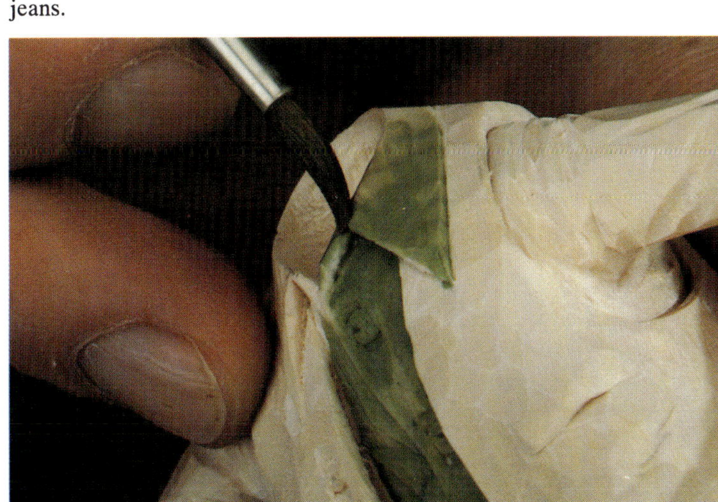

I'm using Seminole Green #2009 to paint the shirt.

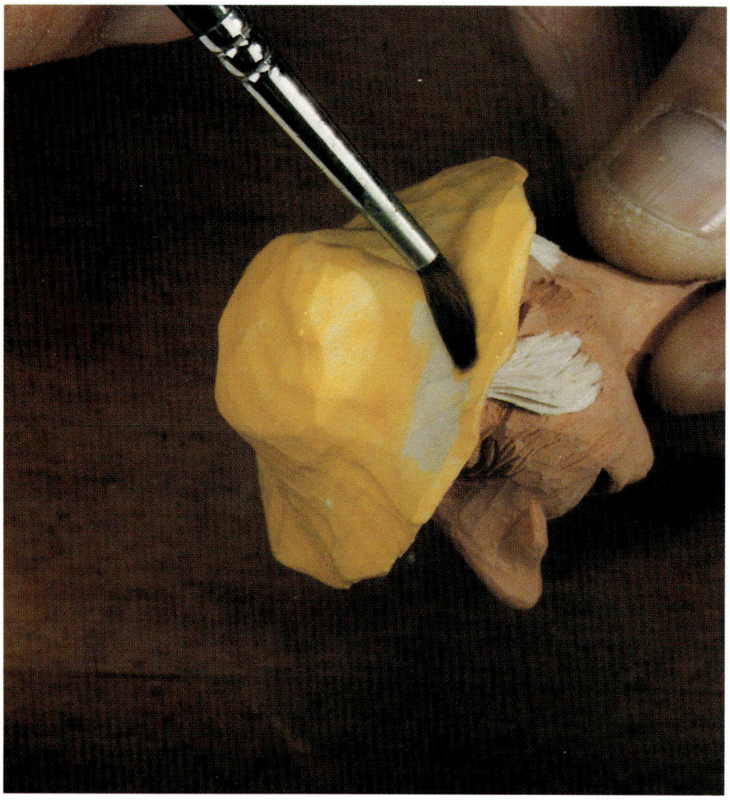

To paint the fisherman's hat, use one part Yellow #2504 and six parts water.

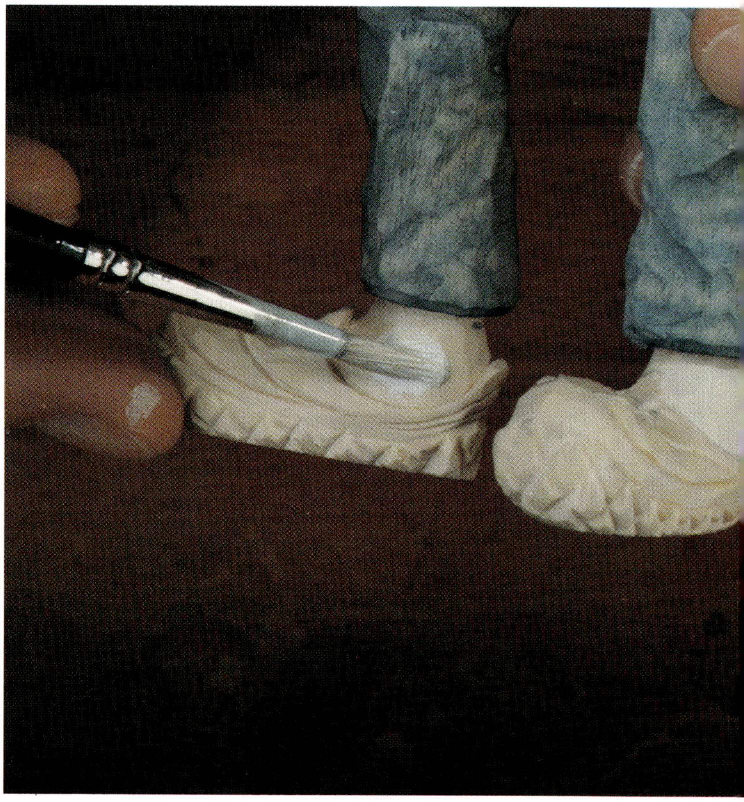

Using one part White and one part water, we're going to paint the fisherman's socks.

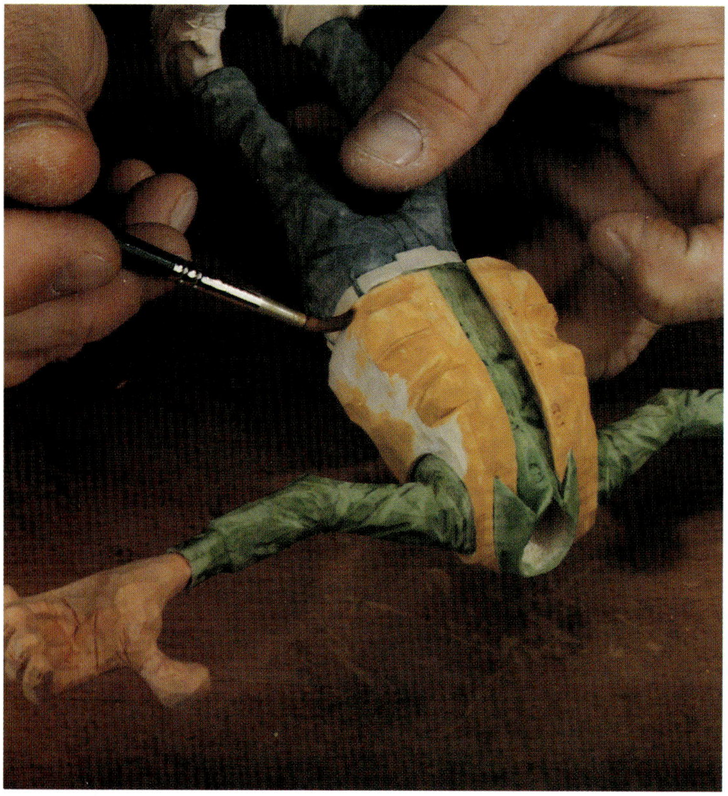

Let's paint the vest with Golden Brown #2054.

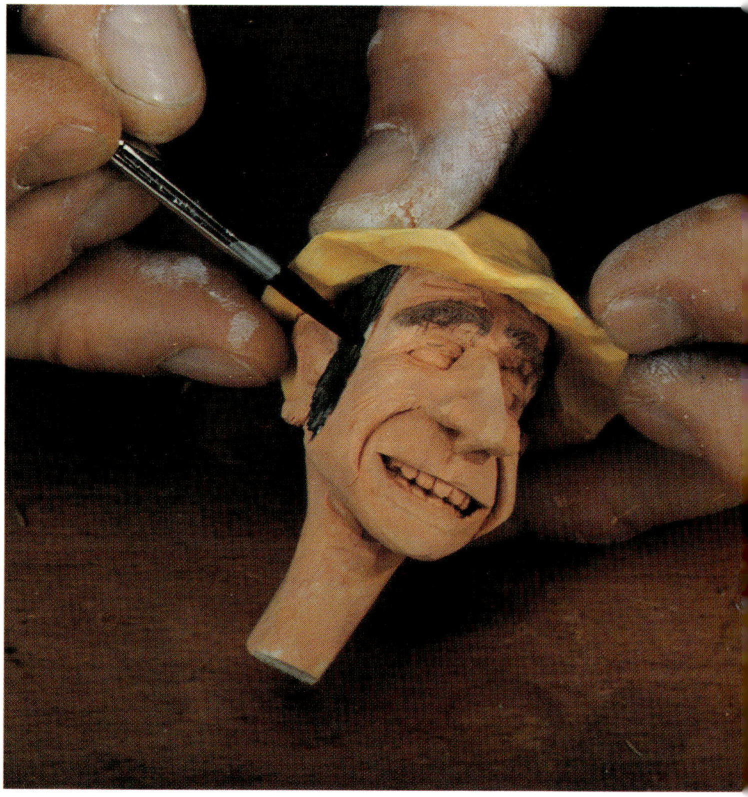

Paint the fisherman's hair with one part Black and six parts water.

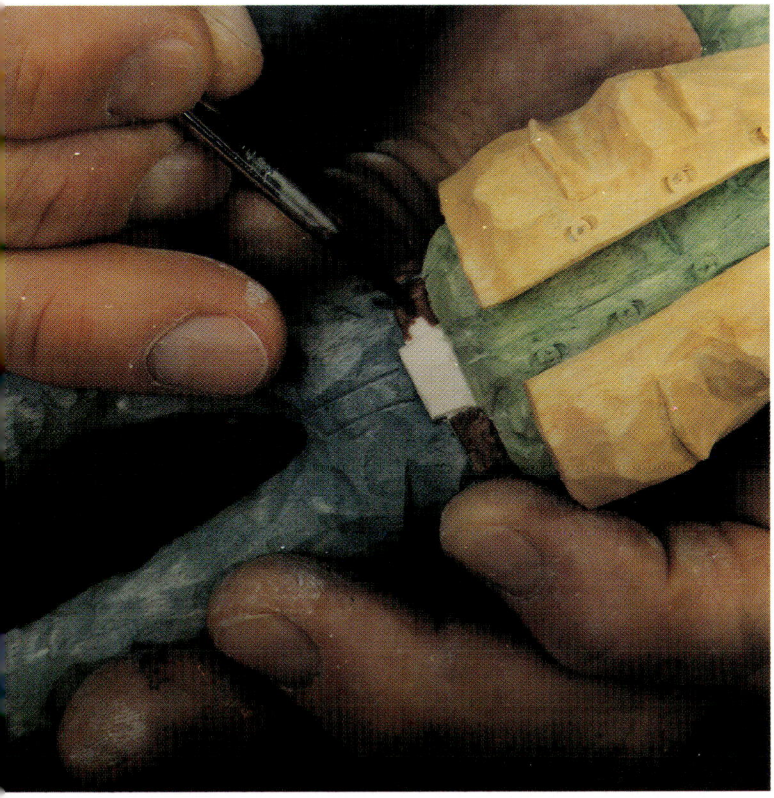

Mix one part Brown Iron Oxide #2023 and six part water and use to paint the fisherman's belt ...

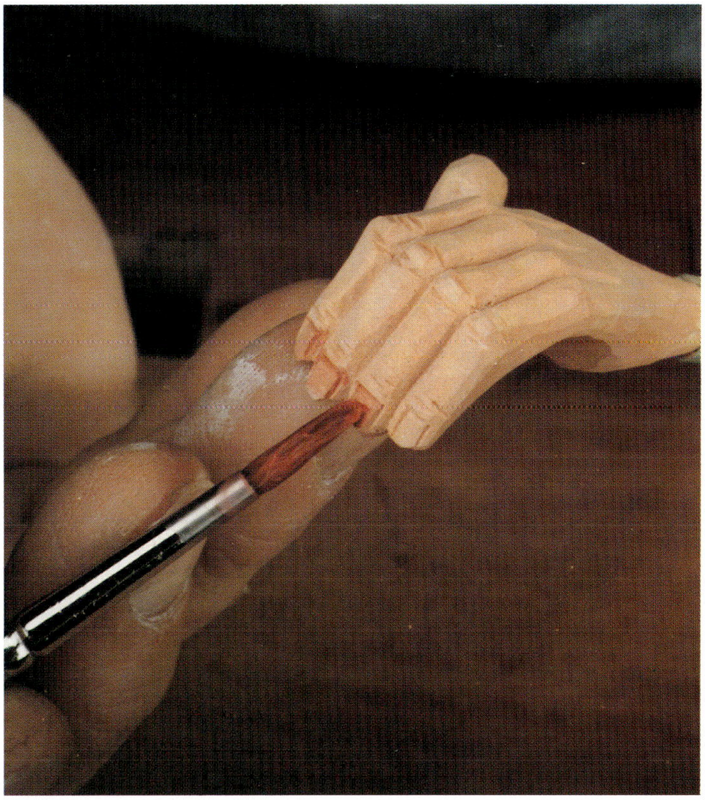

Mix one part Fire Red #2083 with six parts water. Use this to paint the fisherman's finger nails.

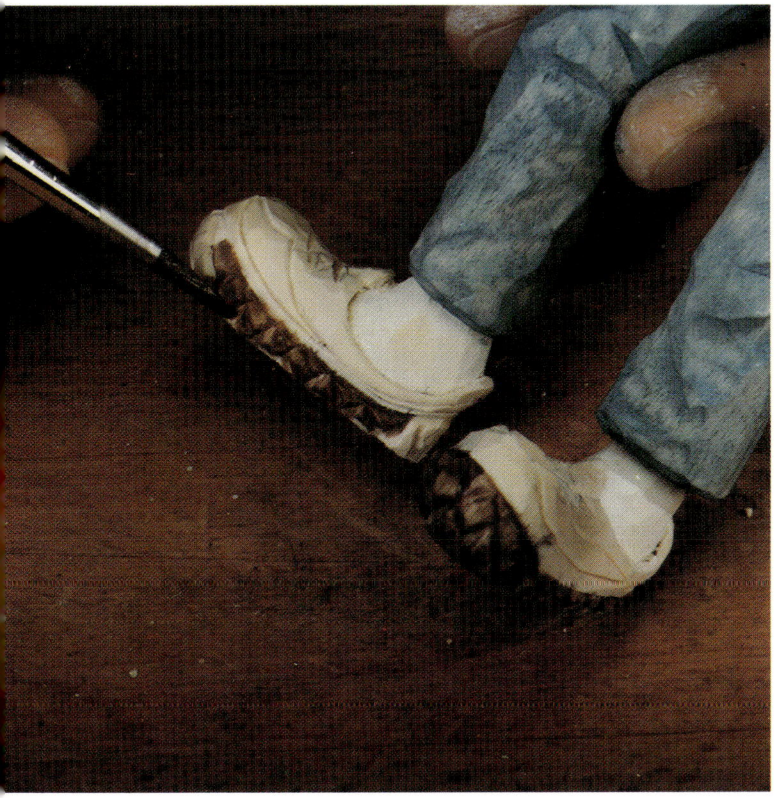

... and the soles of his deck shoes.

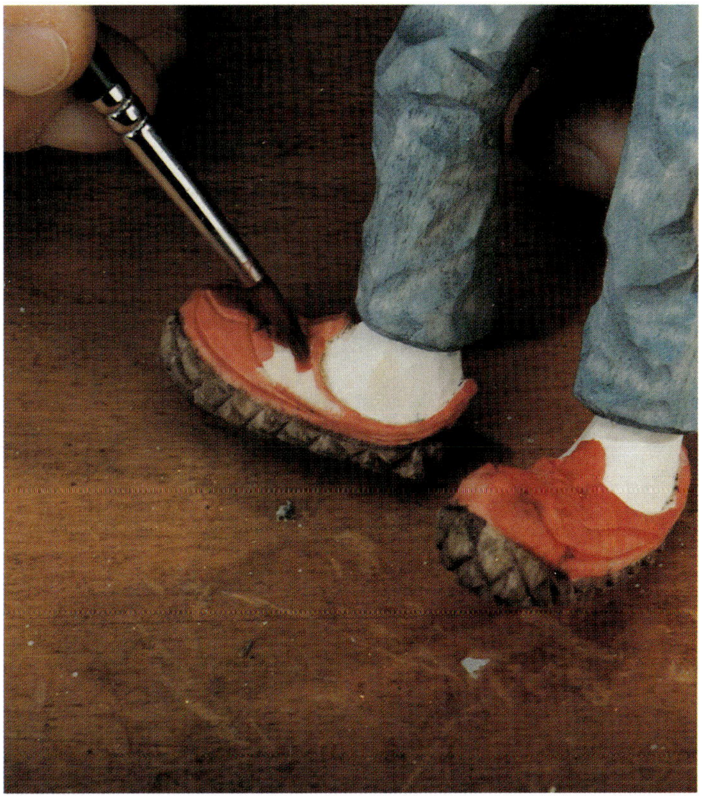

Let's paint the uppers on the fisherman's shoes with this red. I realize that most tennis shoes are white but, in this case since the socks are also white, we'd like a contrast between the shoes and the socks.

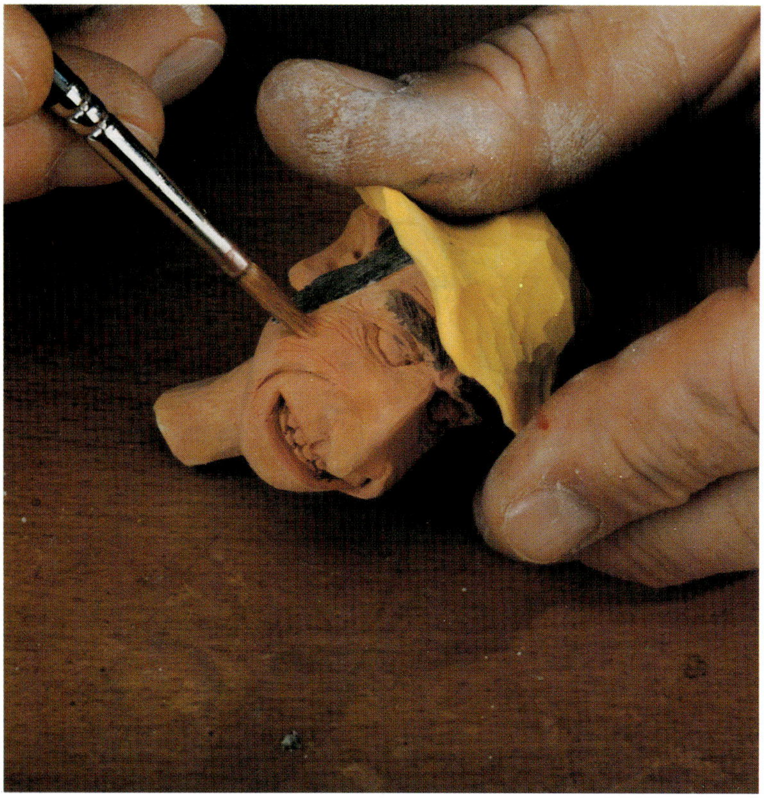

Mix a small amount of this red with flesh tone and paint lips of the fisherman and his cheeks.

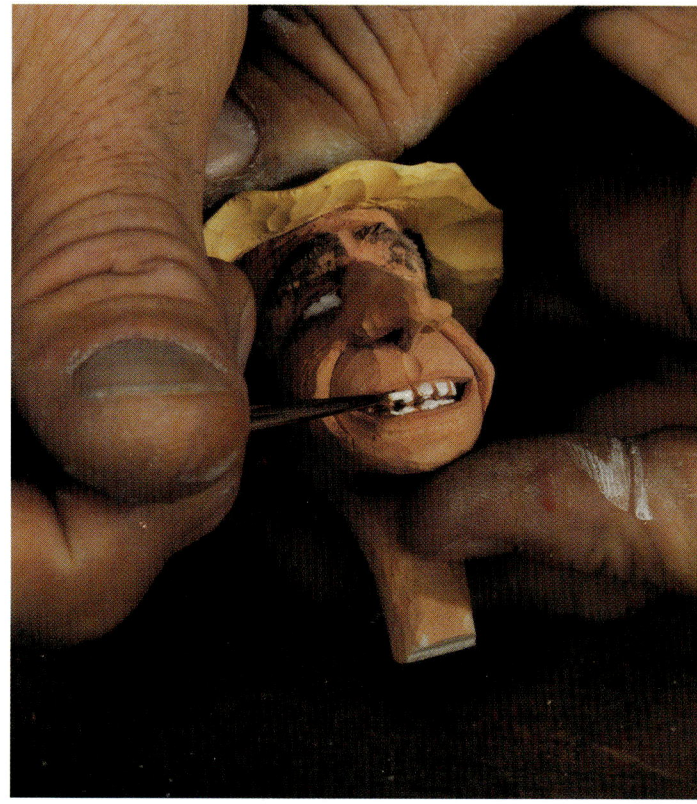

Using undiluted white and a #000 brush, paint the eyeballs and the teeth.

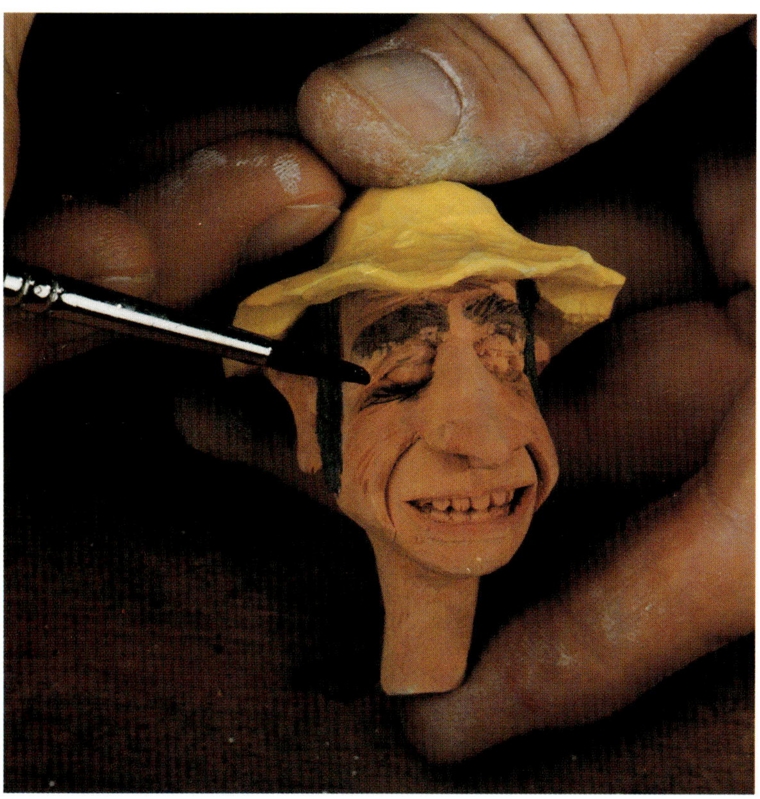

With clean water, moisten the underside of the eyes. Load your paint brush with Black and lightly touch this wet area. The black paint will spread through the wrinkles, producing an interesting effect.

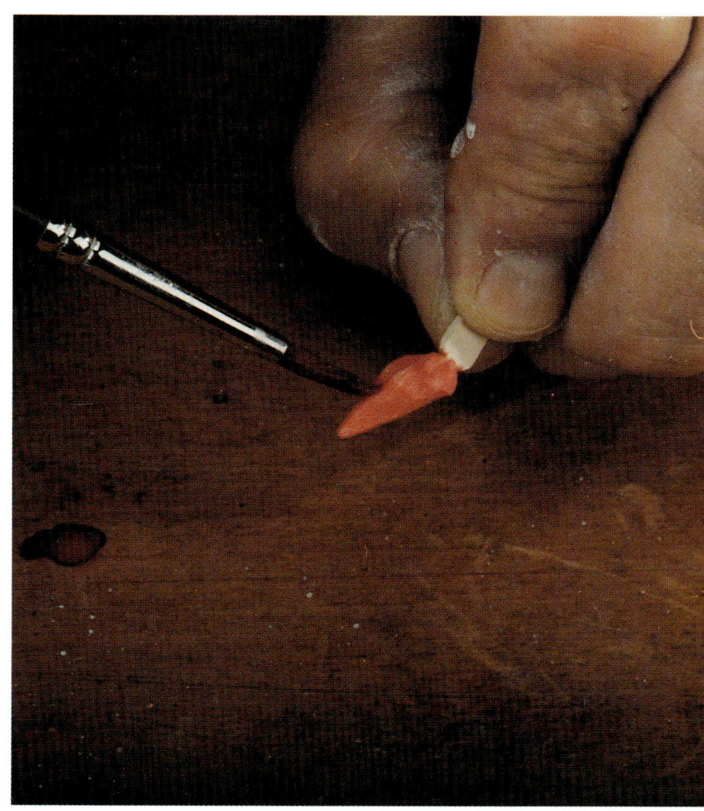

Paint the deep diving lure any color that will contrast with the hat.

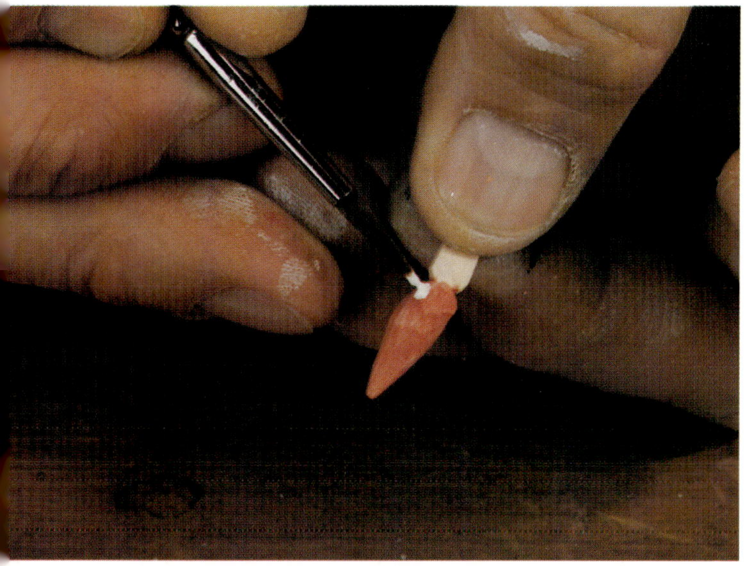

Paint the eyes white.

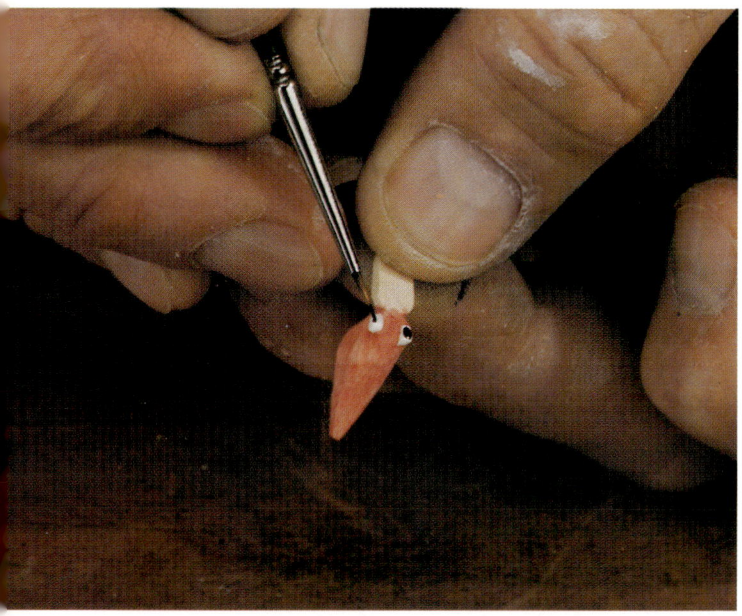

Place a dot of undiluted black at the center of each eye.

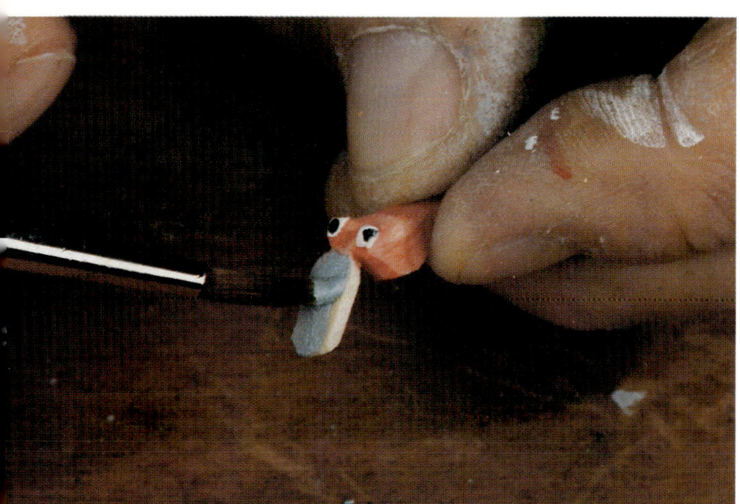

Use undiluted Silver #6003 to paint the metal nose of the lure.

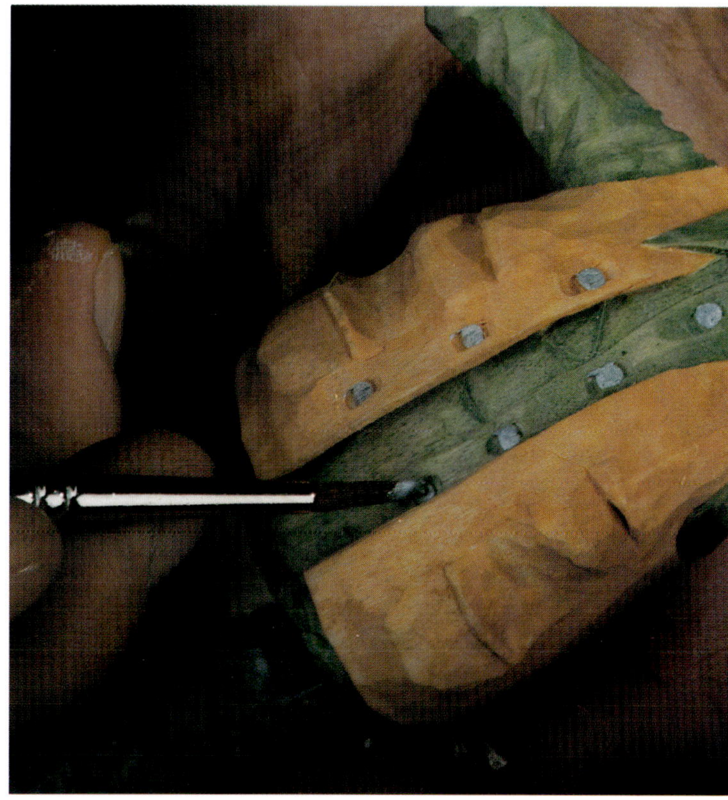

Use undiluted Silver #6003 to paint the buttons ...

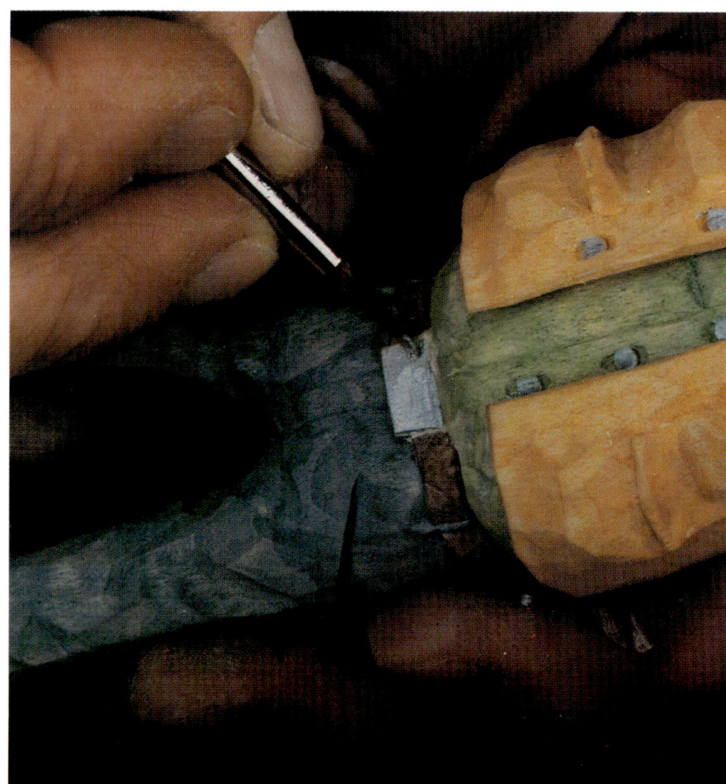

... and the belt buckle as well.

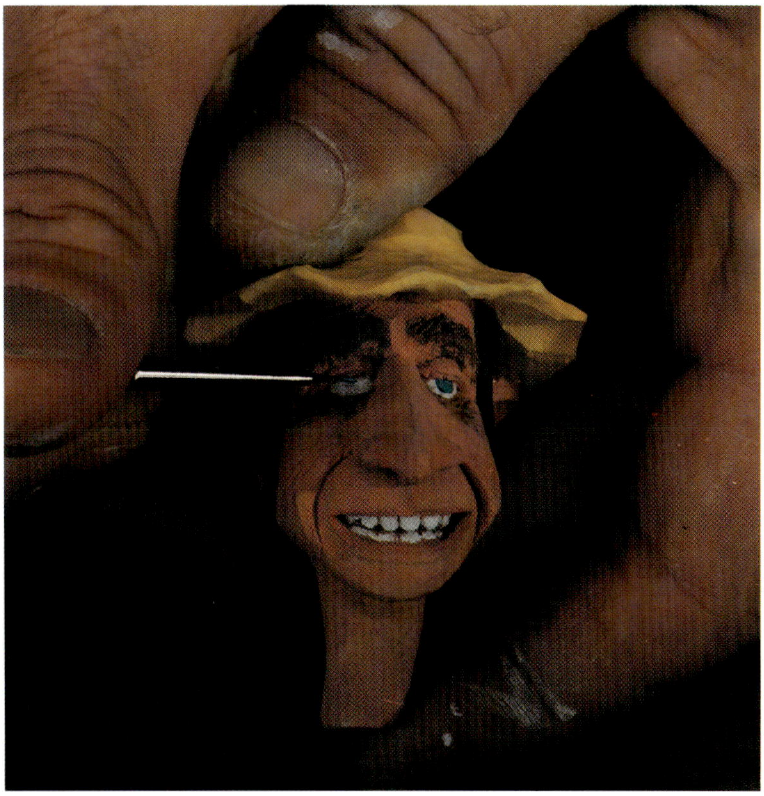

Use undiluted Blue Haze #2122 to paint the iris.

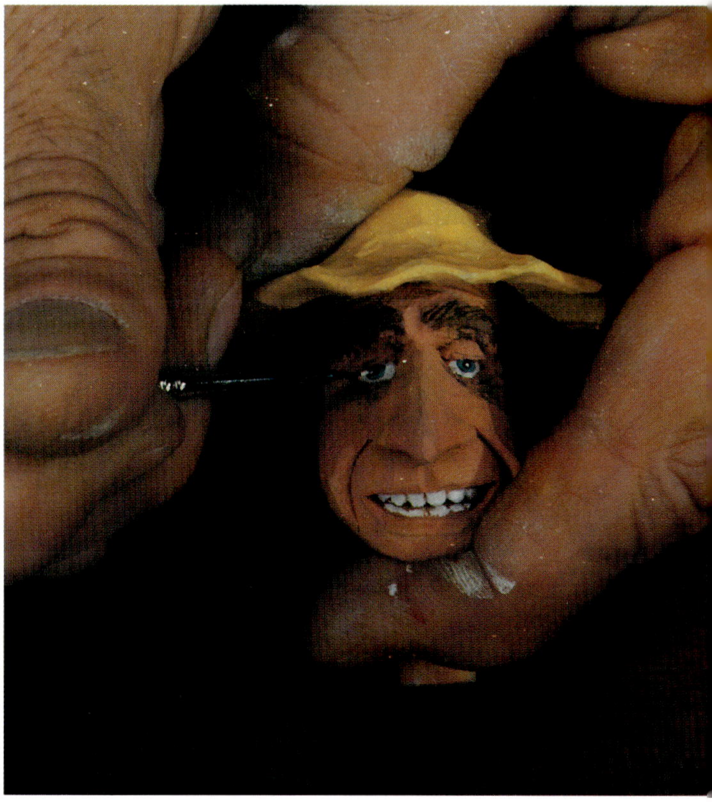

Using undiluted White, place a tiny dot on each pupil to simulate the reflection of light off the eyes.

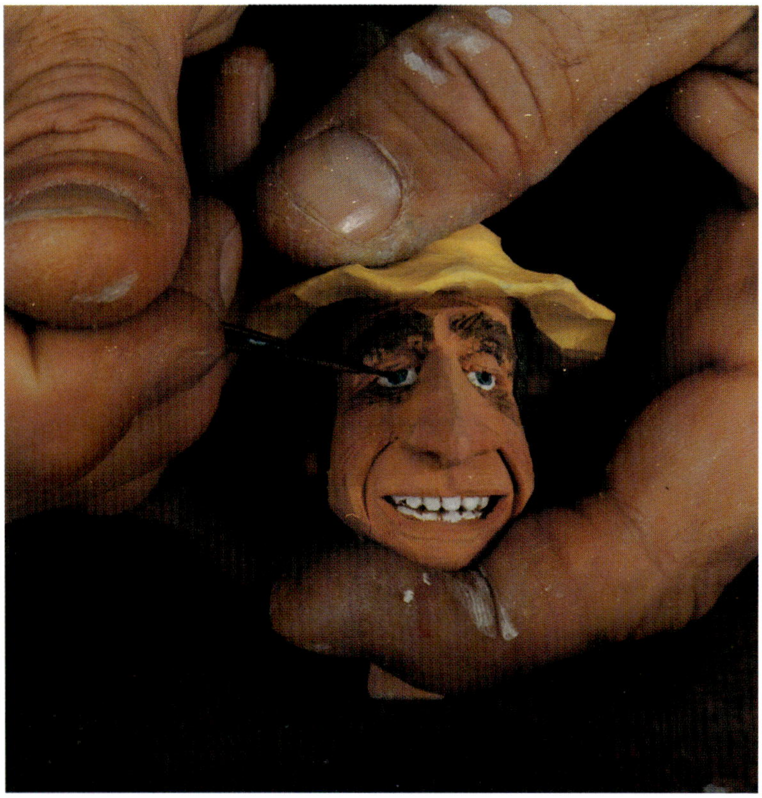

Using undiluted Black, paint the small pupils on the fisherman.

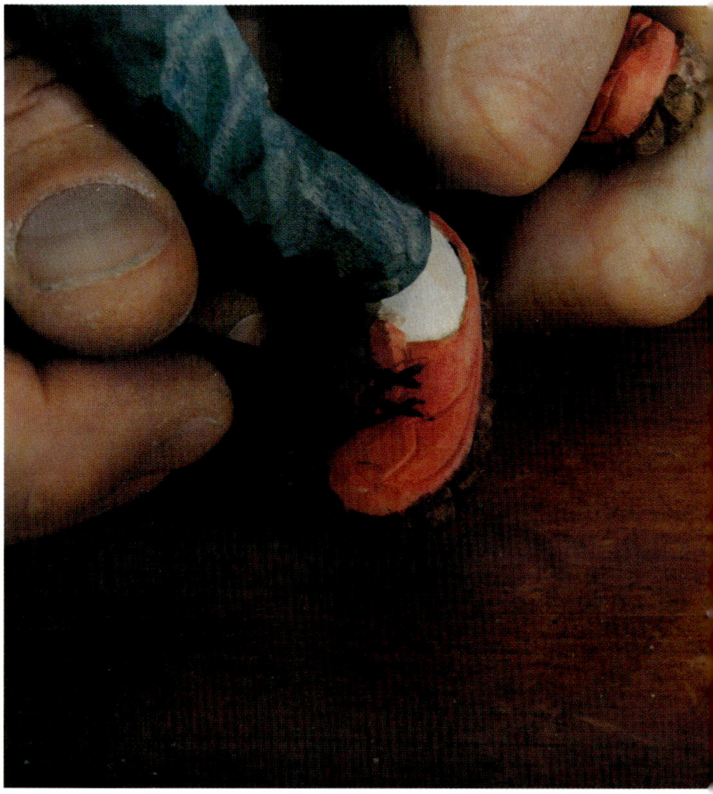

Use a black, fine tip ink pen to draw shoe laces on the deck shoes.

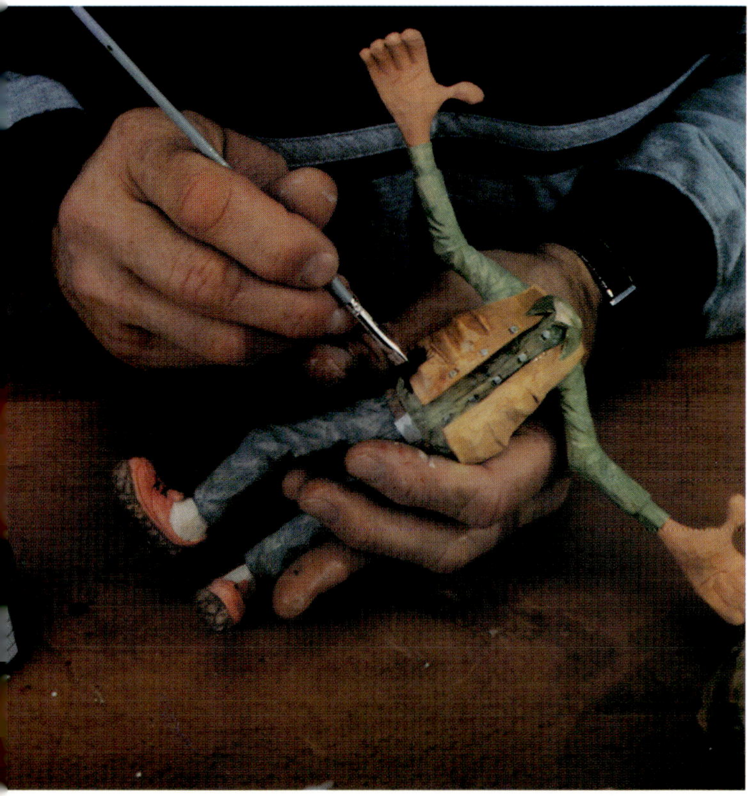

I use a mixture of 10 parts boiled linseed oil to 1 part dark walnut Minwax stain as a combination sealer/antiquing finish. Use an old, worn out brush to apply this mix liberally to all of the carvings. Wipe excess solution from the carving. The rag or paper towel used to wipe this solution should be disposed of immediately in an airtight container because this solution has a tendency to spontaneously combust.

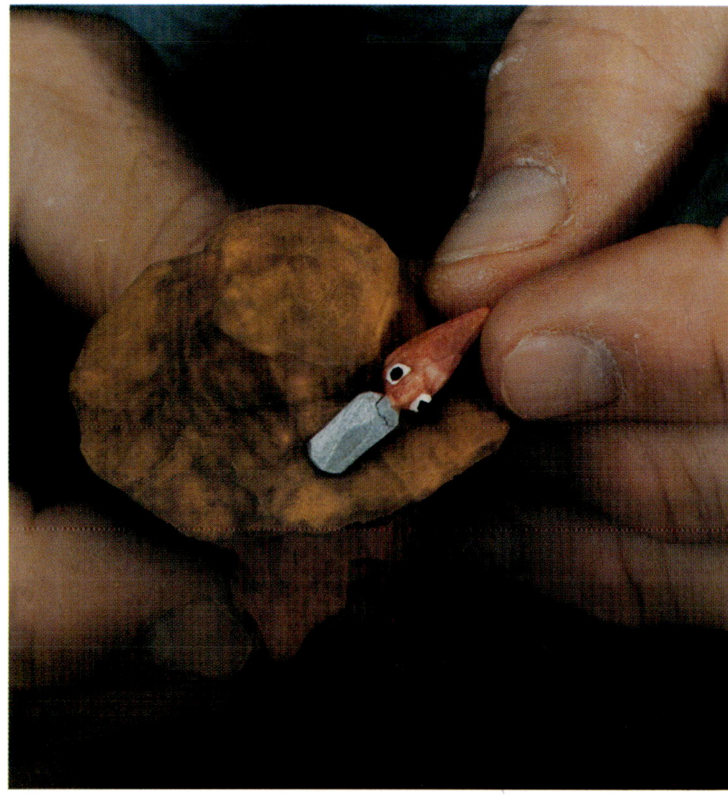

To complete the fisherman, we'll glue the deep diving lure to his hat ...

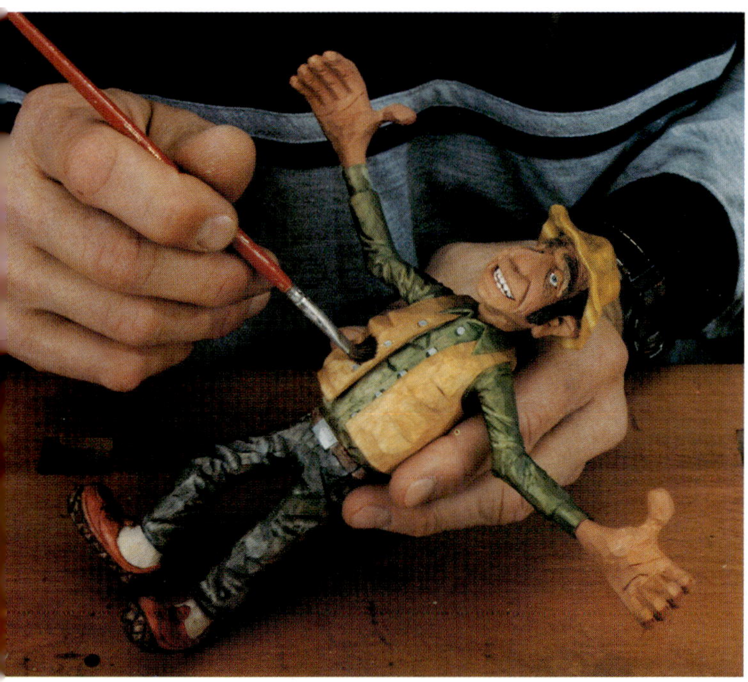

The final finish that we will apply to this carving is a water base clear matt varnish. The particular brand I am using presently is Right-Step. Apply this varnish sparingly so as not to create a shine.

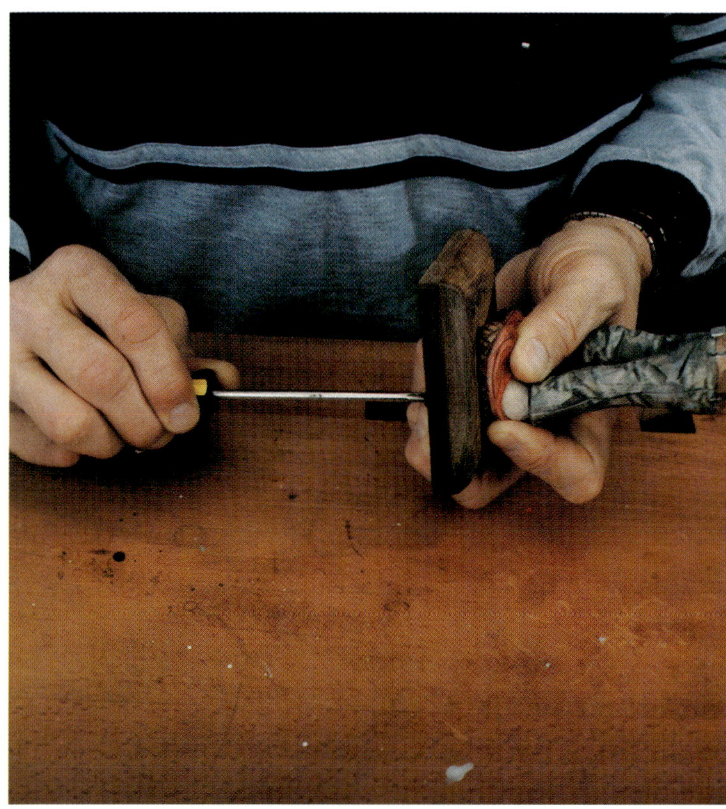

... and attach a base on which the fisherman will rest. I use a drywall screw and a counter-sunk hole in the base. Drive the screw through the foot and into the leg.

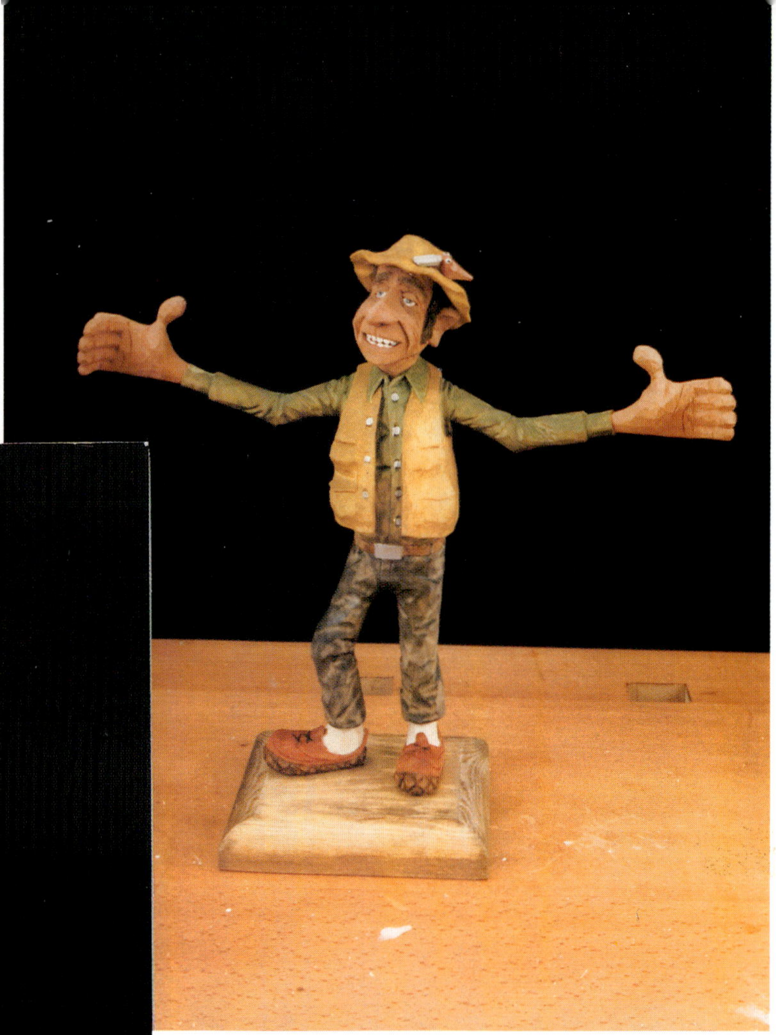

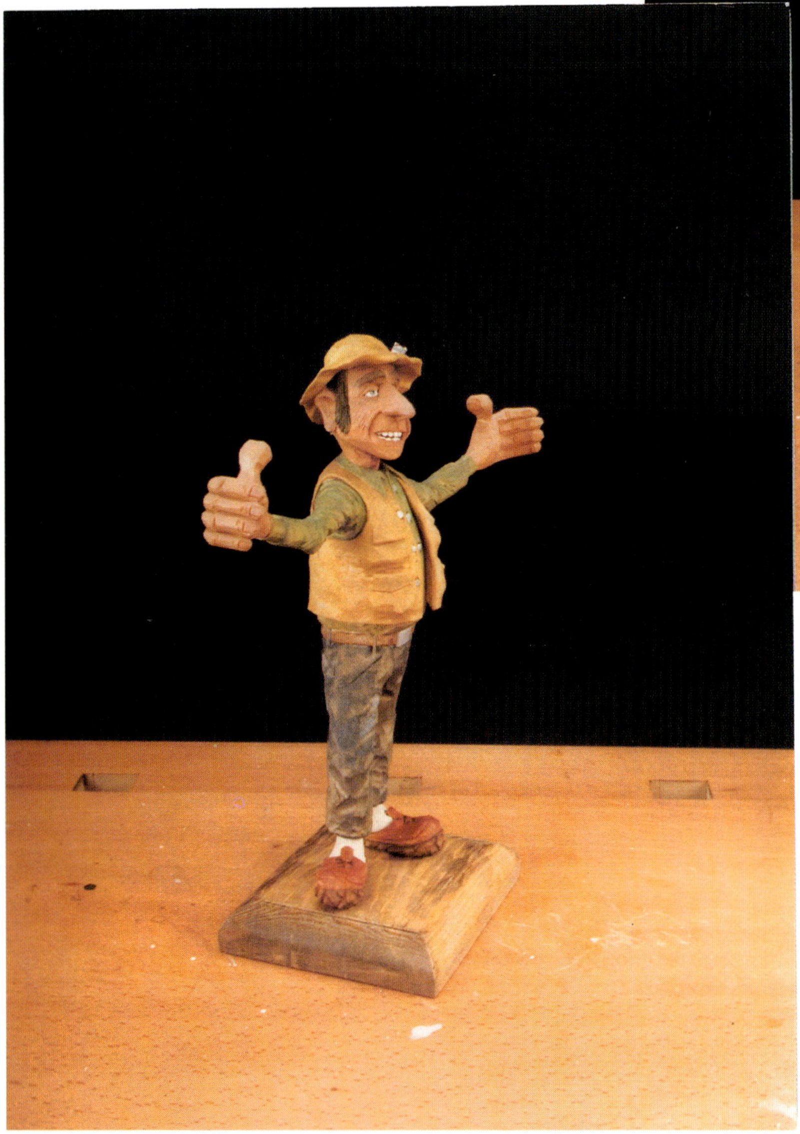

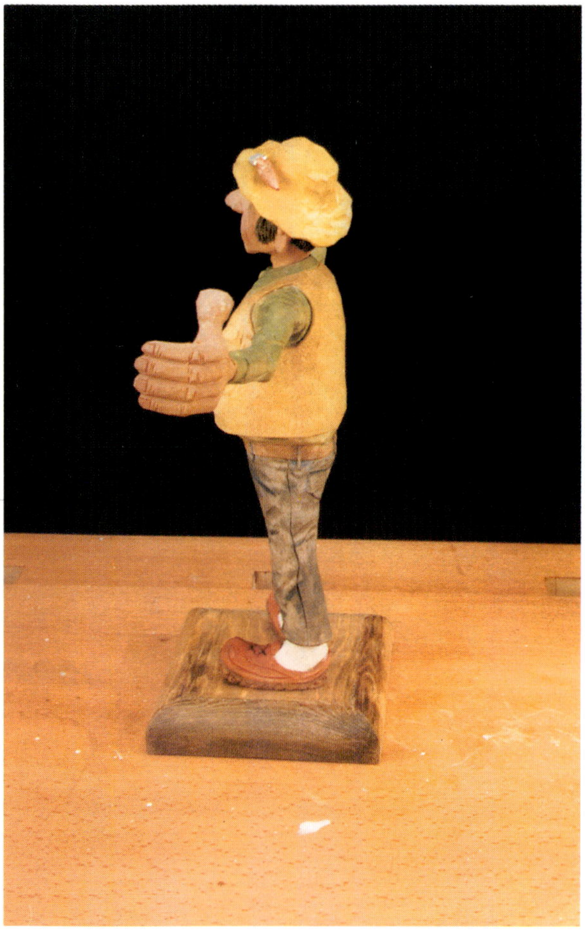

Final shots of the completed fisherman.

The Gallery

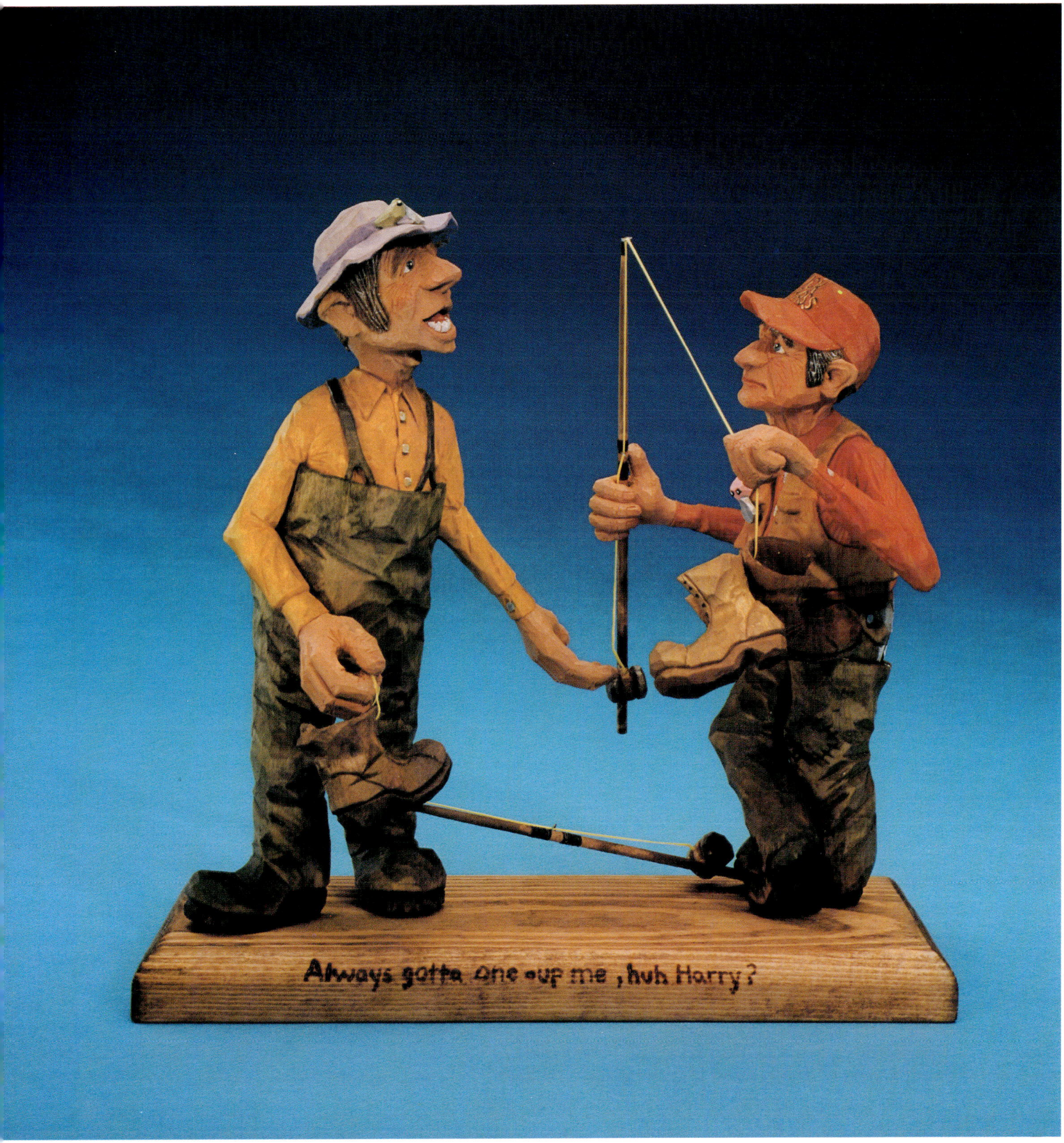

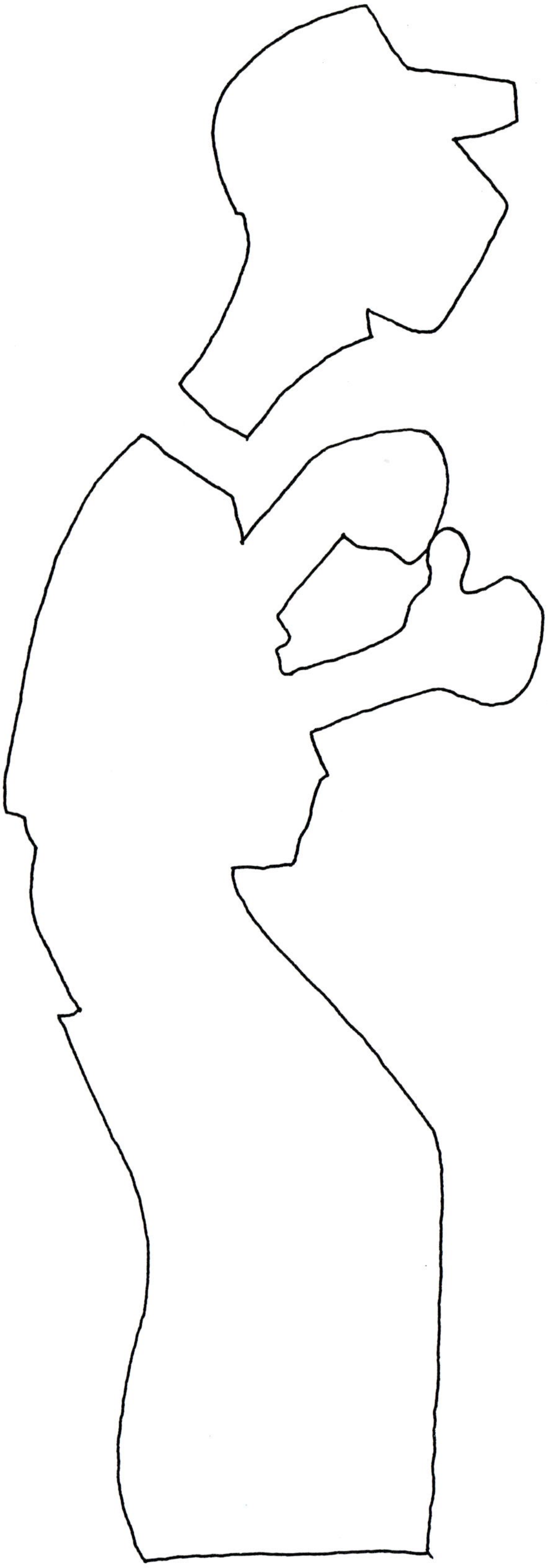

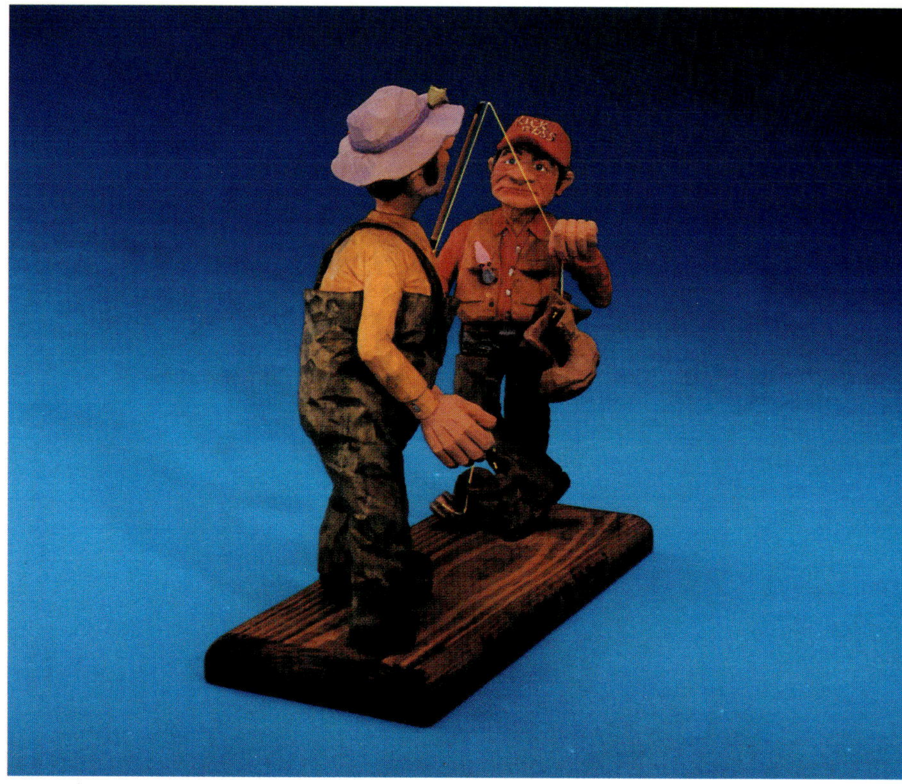

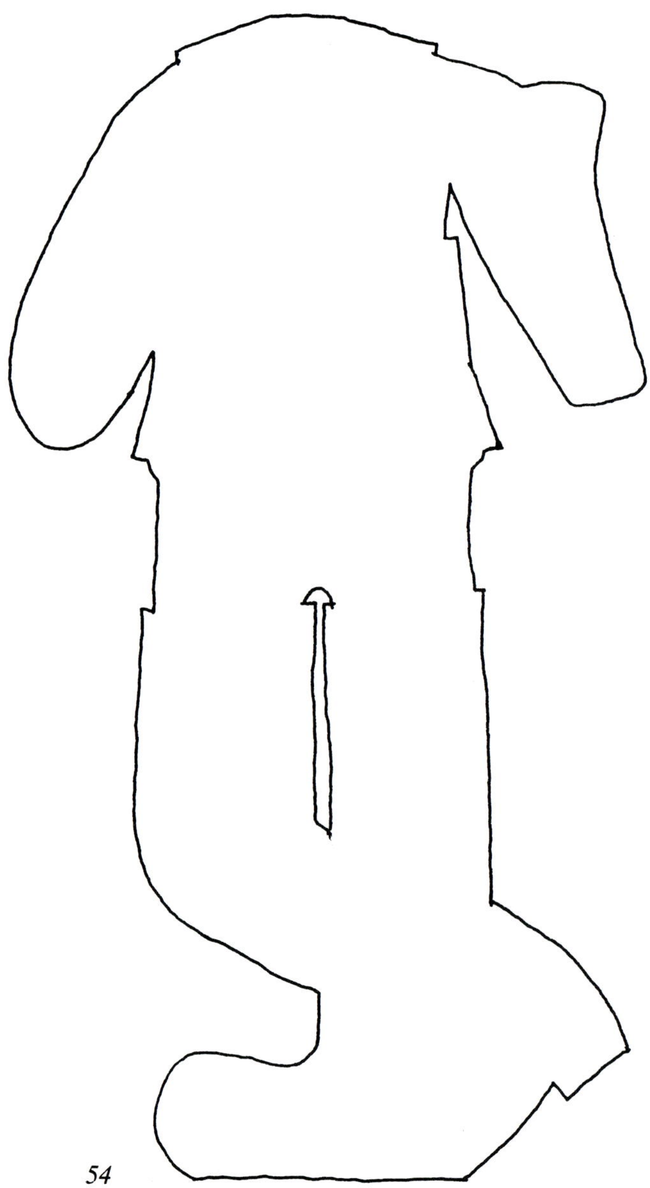

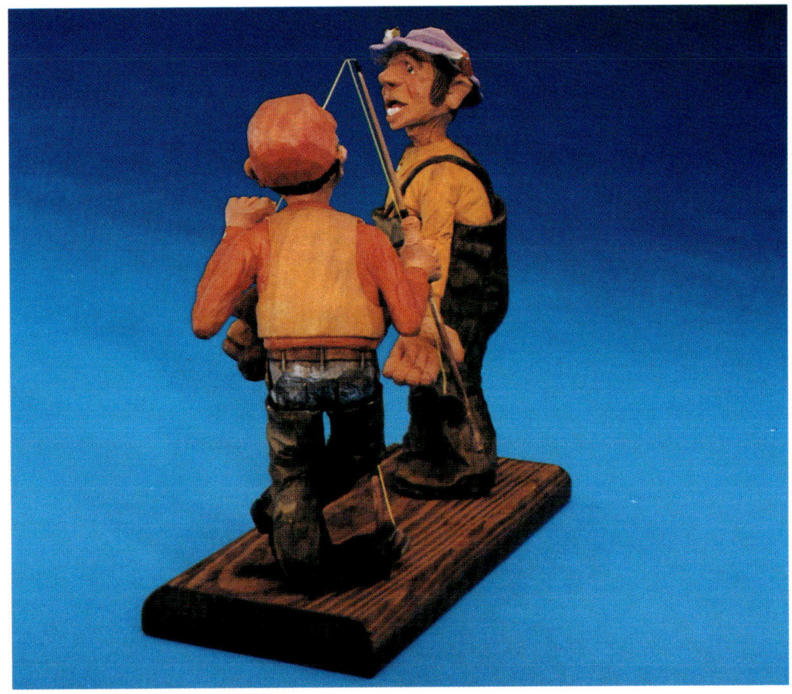

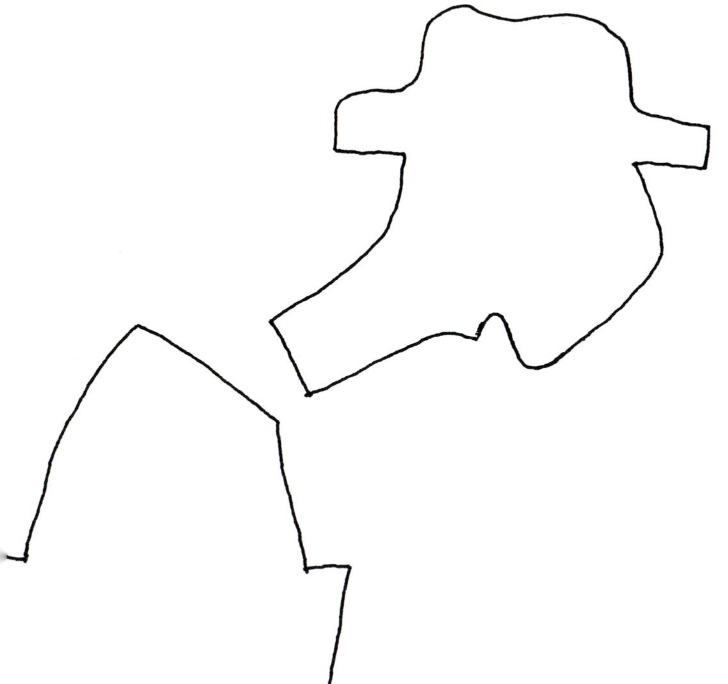

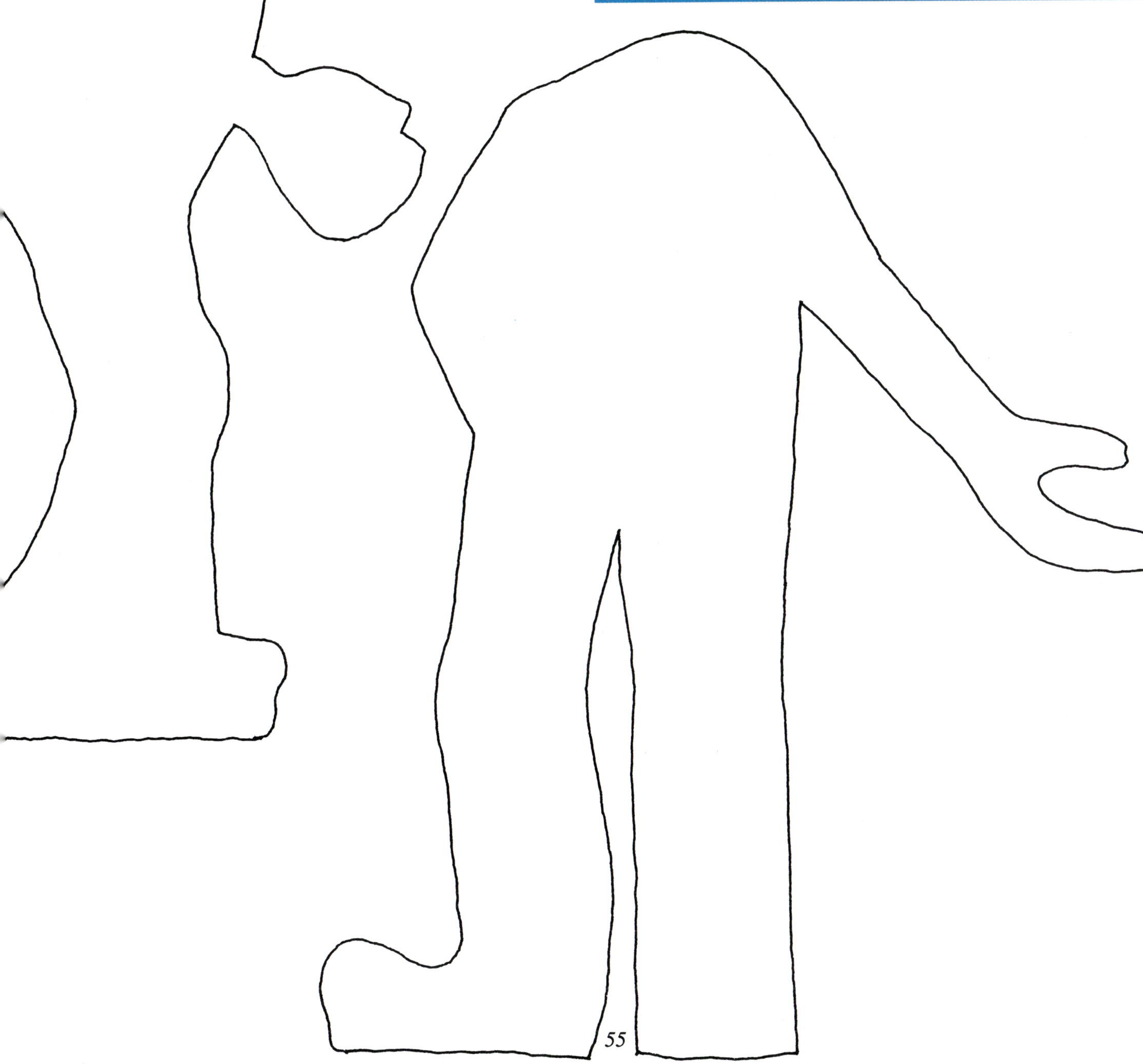

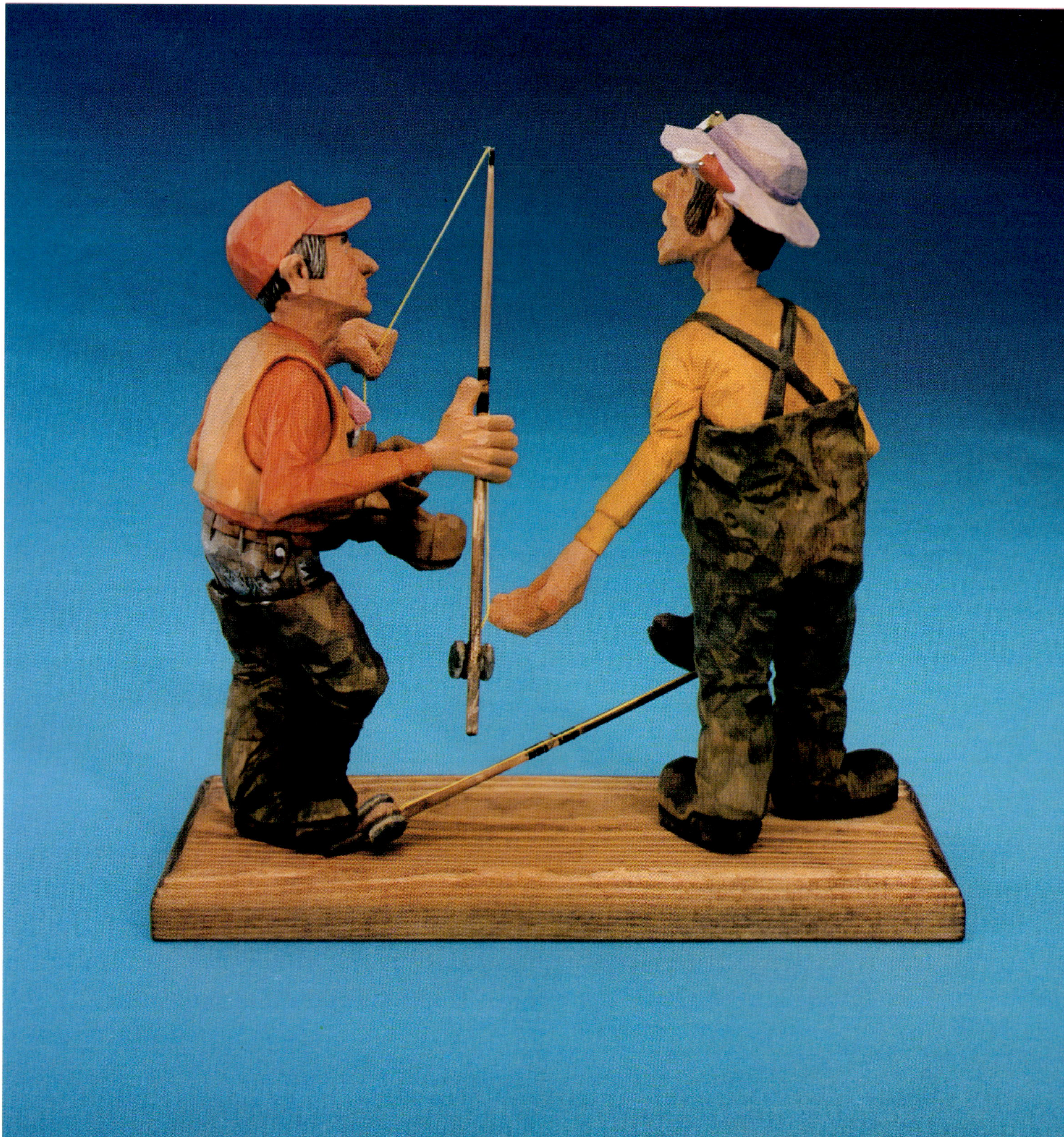

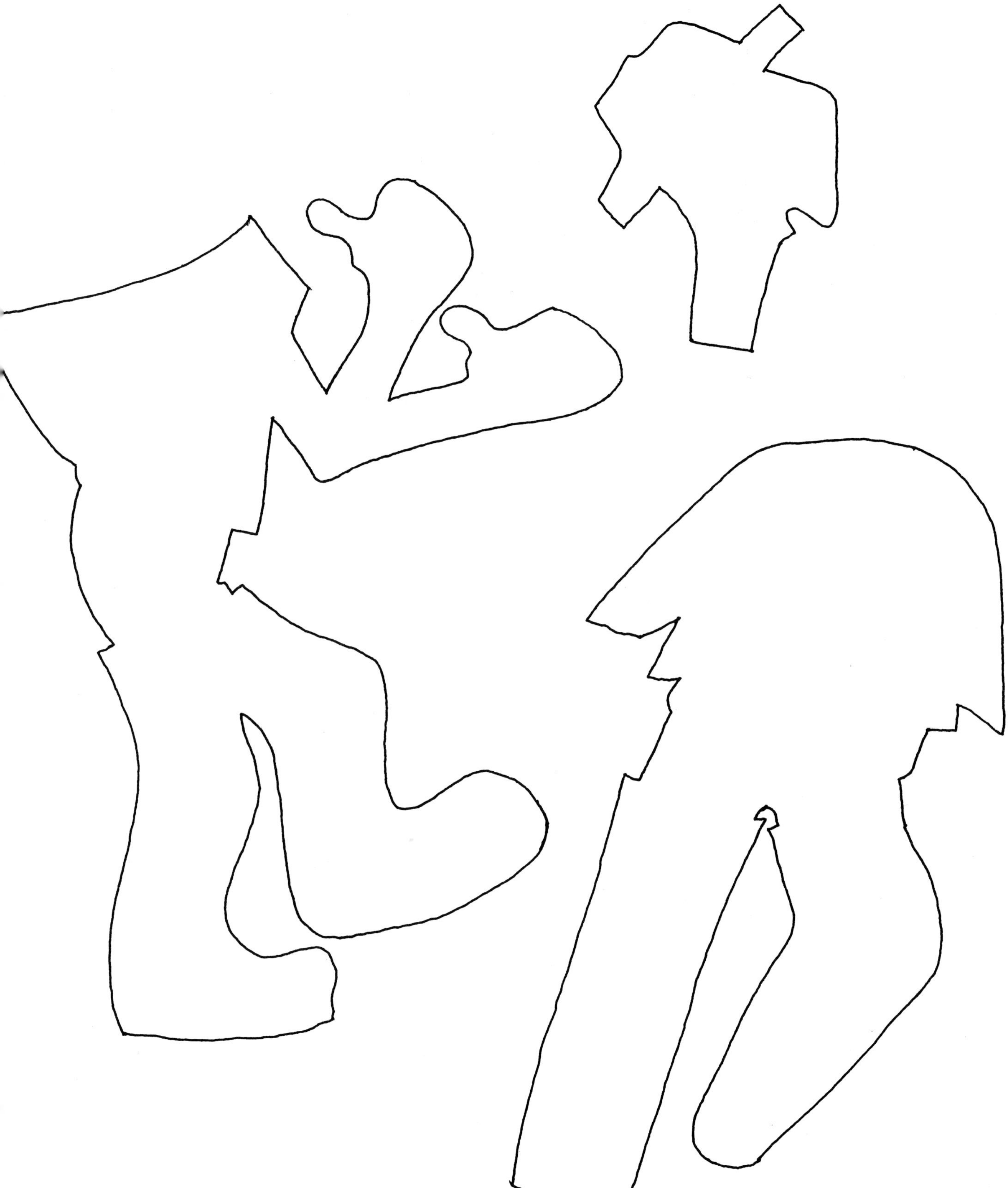

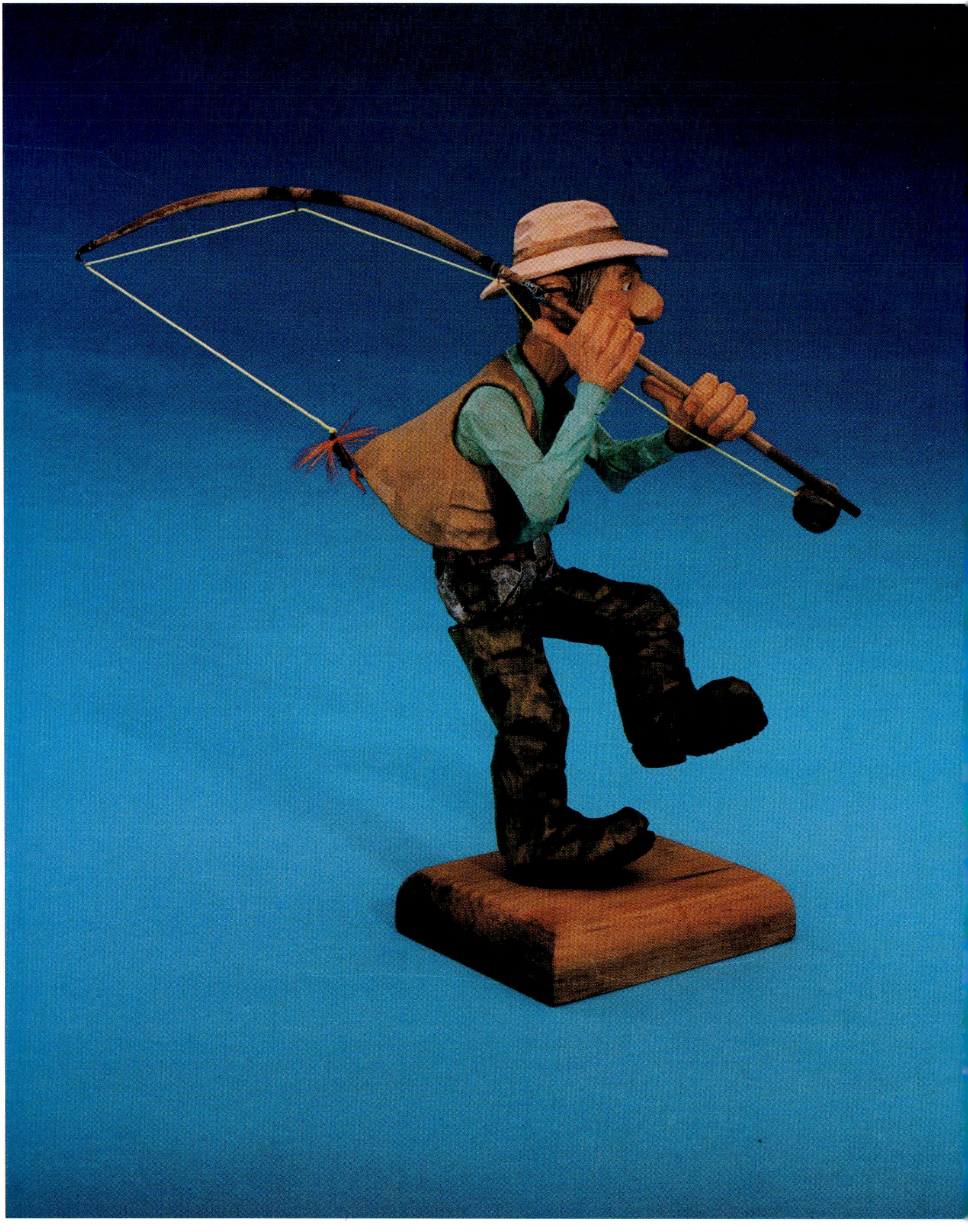

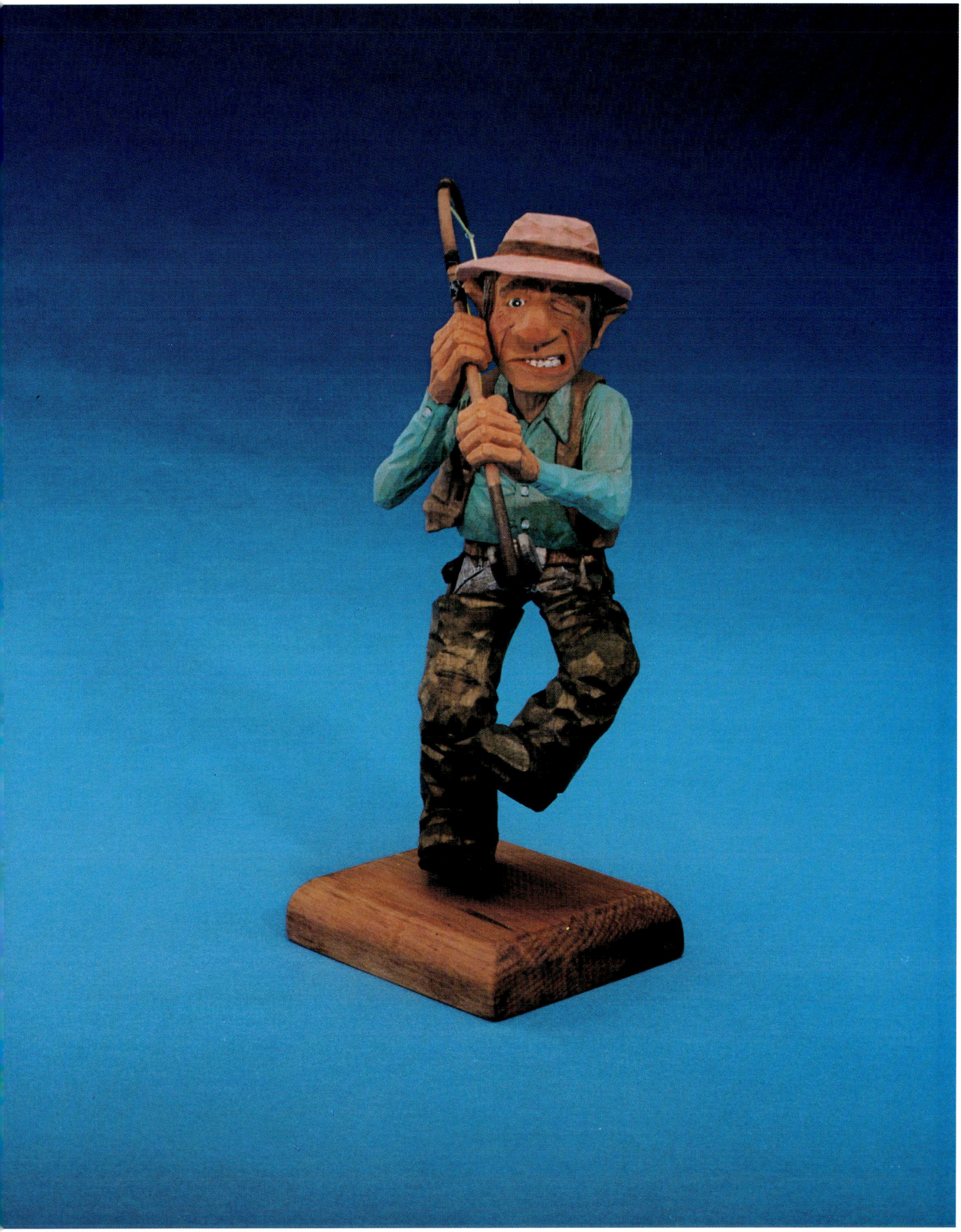

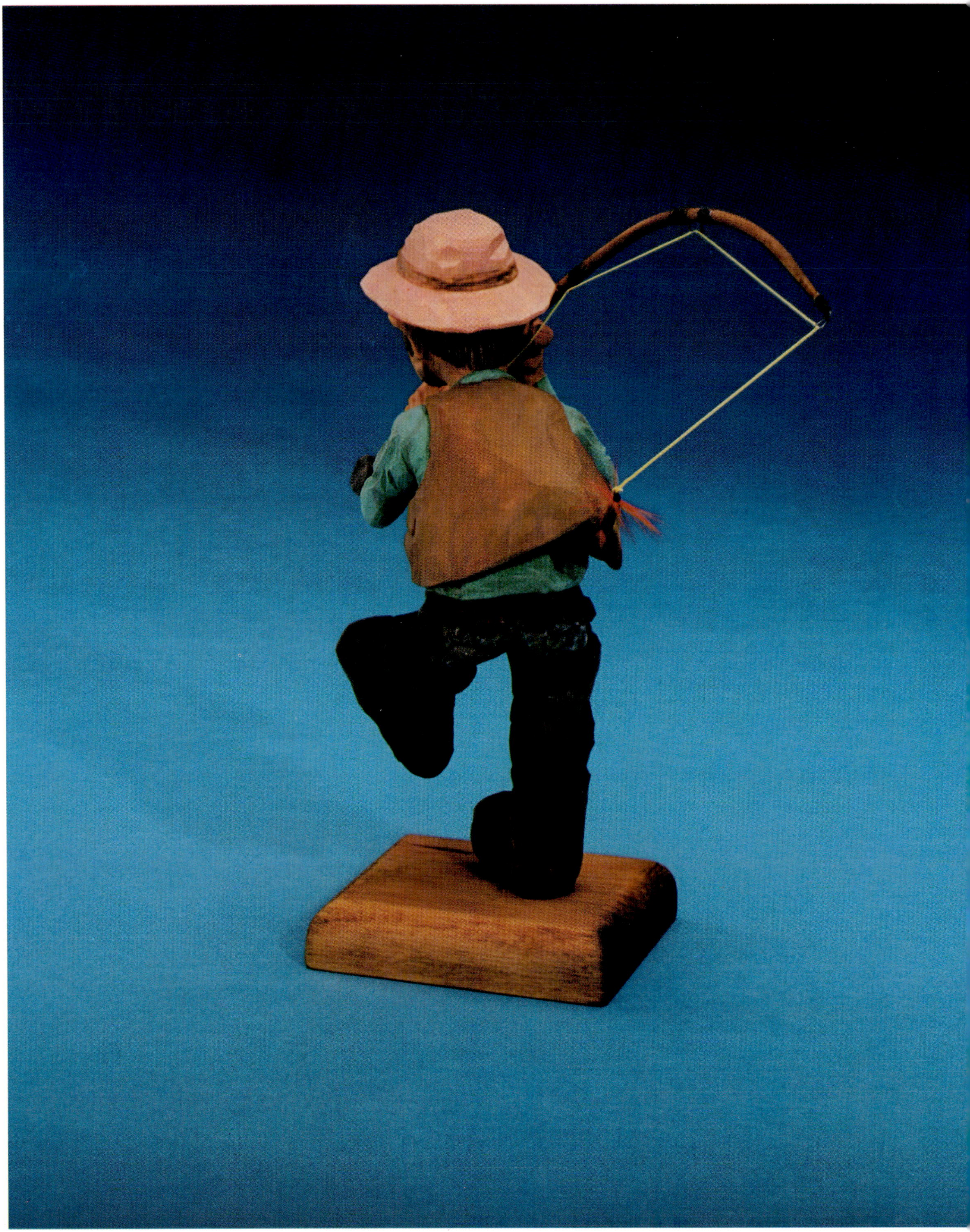

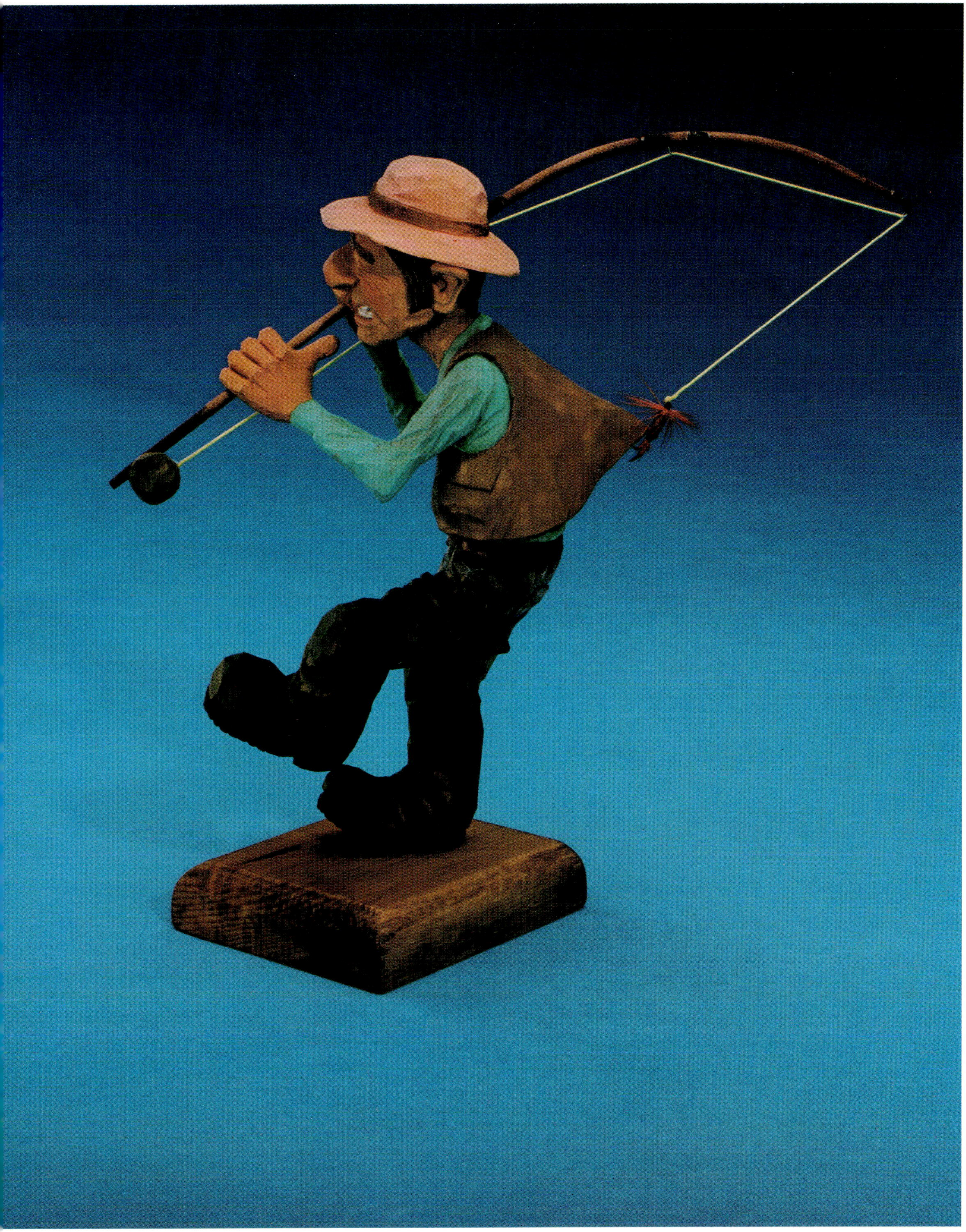

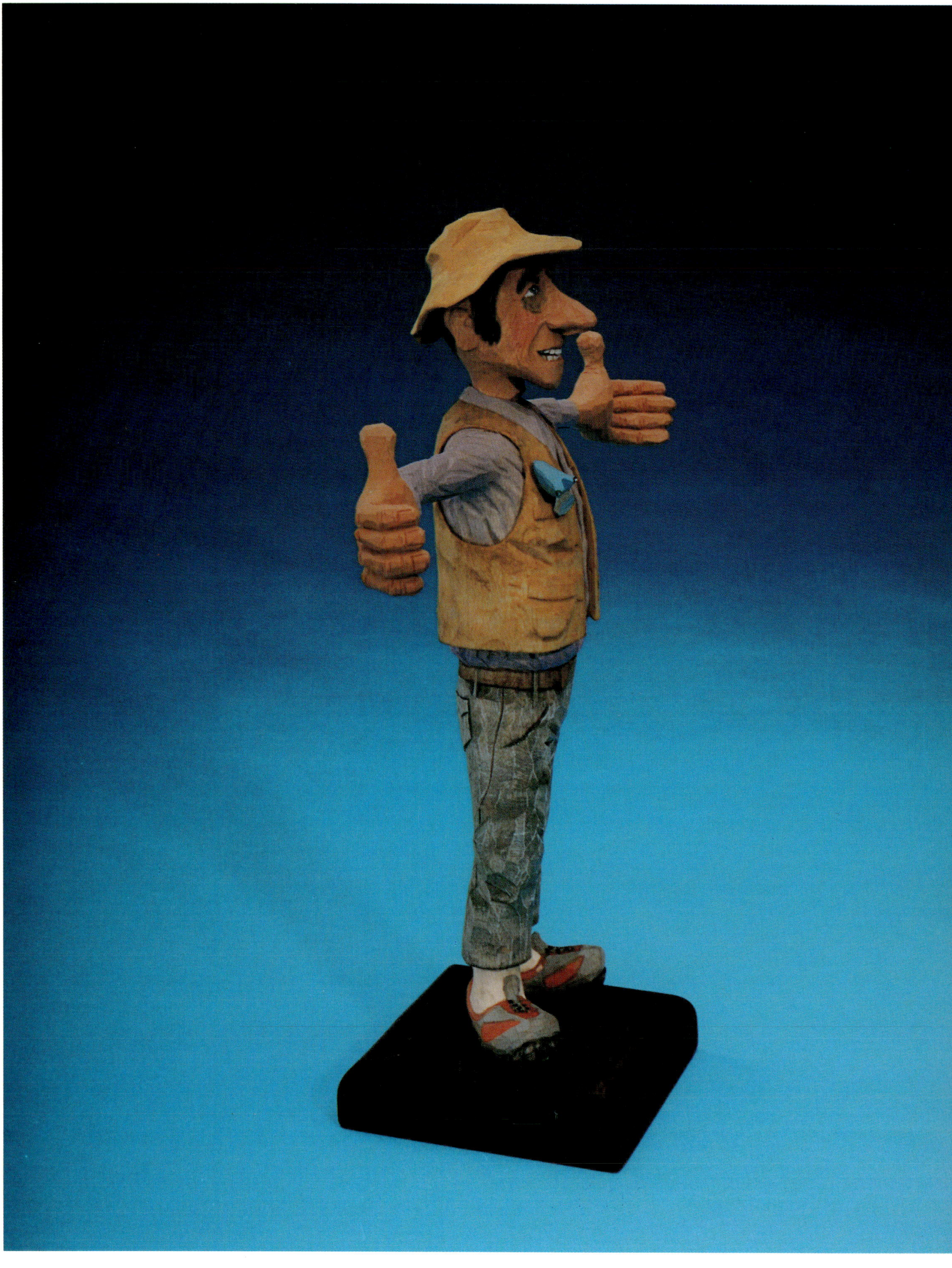

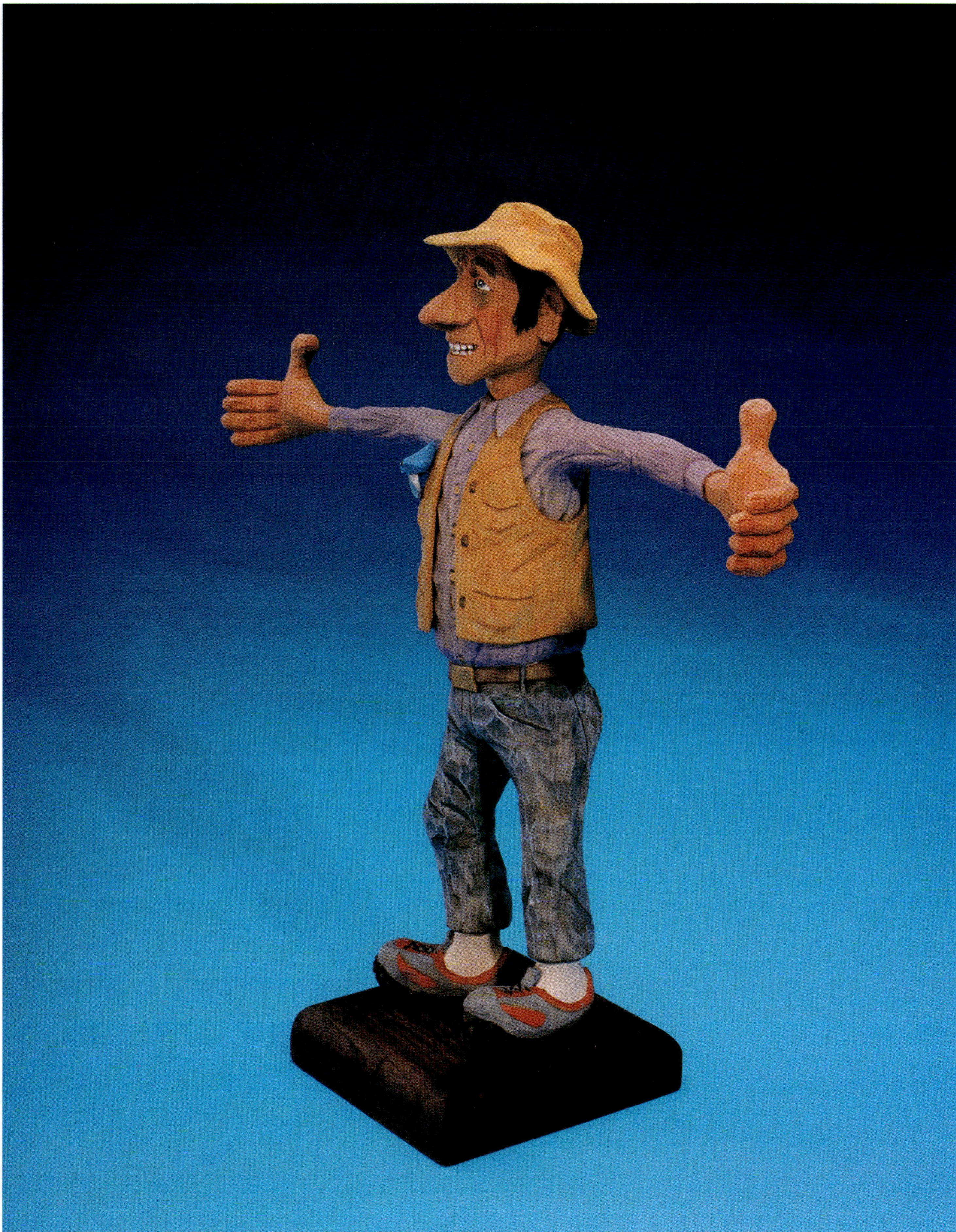

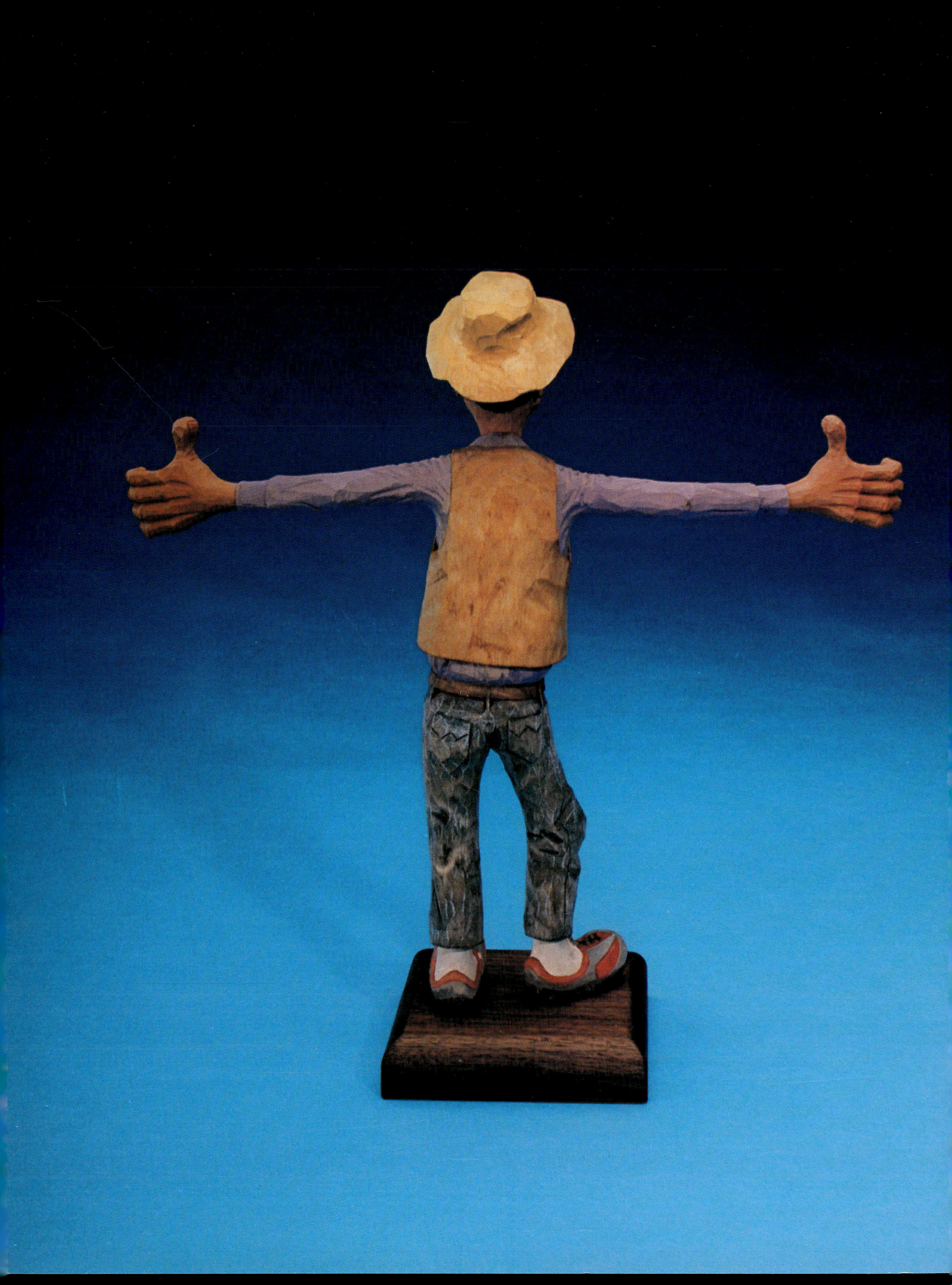